NO

ONE'S

WITNESS

Black Outdoors Innovations in the Poetics of Study

A SERIES EDITED BY J. KAMERON CARTER AND SARAH JANE CERVENAK

RACHEL ZOLF

NO ONE'S WITNESS

A MONSTROUS POETICS

DUKE UNIVERSITY PRESS / *Durham and London* / 2021

Designed by: Matthew Tauch
Typeset in Portrait Text by Copperline Book Services

Library of Congress Cataloging-in-Publication Data
Names: Zolf, Rachel, [date] author.
Title: No one's witness : a monstrous poetics / Rachel Zolf.
Other titles: Black outdoors.
Description: Durham : Duke University Press, 2021. | Series: Black
outdoors | Includes bibliographical references and index.
Identifiers: LCCN 2020046228 (print) | LCCN 2020046229 (ebook)
ISBN 9781478013334 (hardcover)
ISBN 9781478014249 (paperback)
ISBN 9781478021551 (ebook)
Subjects: LCSH: Celan, Paul—Criticism and
interpretation. | German literature—Jewish authors—History
and criticism. | German literature—20th century—History and crit-
icism. | Holocaust, Jewish (1939–1945), in literature. |
Psychic trauma in literature. | Poetics.
Classification: LCC PT2605.E4 Z978 2021 (print) |
LCC PT2605.E4 (ebook) | DDC 811/.54—dc23
LC record available at https://lccn.loc.gov/2020046228
LC ebook record available at https://lccn.loc.gov/2020046229

Cover art: James Allister Sprang, *Concrete Color Arrangement #12*,
2017. Archival Ink Print. Courtesy of the artist.

CONTENTS

ACKNOWLEDGMENTS

I would first like to thank Fred Moten, brilliant thinker and poet, for his crucial writing and friendship, for generously entering a conversation with me, and for helping me push past the third to a fleshly something (no-thing) more. My deep gratitude also to Judith Butler for her steadfast support for my work as a poet and thinker, for helping me trust that I could be both at the same time, and for her work as a guiding force.

Tremendous thanks to Elena Basile for reading several drafts and thinking with me as this book changed course and became something (no-thing) new. Many thanks to the following people for conversations over the years that have deepened this work: Emily Abendroth, Emily Beall, Margaret Christakos, Moyra Davey, Sarah Dowling, Laura Elrick, Andrea Geyer, Che Gossett, Sharon Hayes, Jeff T. Johnson, Eunsong Kim, Gregory Laynor, Robert Majzels, Airea D. Matthews, Laura Meyers, Marcia Oliver, M. NourbeSe Philip, Heike Raschl, Ariel Resnikoff, Lytle Shaw, Cheryl Sourkes, James Allister Sprang, Emma Stapely, Fenn Stewart, and Divya Victor. My gratitude to Glenn Ligon, Dread Scott, Sharon Hayes, Richard L. Copley, Laura Elrick, Bracha L. Ettinger, James Allister Sprang, and Bhanu Kapil for giving me access to images for this book, to Stephen Motika for image assistance, and to Gregg Bordowitz for helping with contacts. An earlier version of the study in chapter 6 appears in different form in *A Forest on Many Stems: Essays on the Poet's Novel* (Nightboat Books, 2021). Finally, thanks to J. Kameron Carter, Sarah Cervenak, and Ken Wissoker for believing in this queer book, to the anonymous readers for their feedback, and to Annie Lubinsky and the rest of the hardworking Duke staff for shepherding the book through the press. Thanks also to Josh Rutner for the indexing.

No One's Witness was written over a number of years in which I went through numerous challenging life experiences compressed into too short a period of time: difficult deaths of all my immediate family members and one friend, relationship breakups, multiple moves across a border, immigration issues, graduate school, a new job, a new relationship, and, most recently, a new baby. I am so grateful to my love Julia Bloch for bearing witness with me through much of this—and for assiduously commenting on drafts and copyediting the monster! Most of all thanks to you and Rafa and all our queer kith and kin for creating a new family with me.

Writing these acknowledgments in the midst of the COVID-19 pandemic, I wonder if the book would have been different if written during or after this particular end of the world. Perhaps, but the swarm, field, plenum, chorus persists, insists, even if the No Ones touch not touching. The book lives in now-time, and as a friend wisely said when Julia and I finally decided to let the other creature in our family, the one-eyed semiferal feline (Heavy) Meadow, roam outside every day, it's a profound experience just letting go.

No One's Witness is dedicated to Akilah Oliver (1961–2011), luminous poet and thinker and No One and friend.

OPENING

What if, instead of The Ordered World, we could imagine The World as a Plenum, an infinite composition in which each existant's singularity is contingent upon its becoming one possible expression of all the other existants, with which it is entangled beyond space and time.

DENISE FERREIRA DA SILVA

Can this being together in homelessness, this interplay of the refusal of what has been refused, this undercommon appositionality, be a place from which emerges neither self-consciousness nor knowledge of the other but an improvisation that proceeds from somewhere on the other side of an unasked question?

STEFANO HARNEY AND FRED MOTEN

are there greeters there [are you one] when we former ghosts arrive

AKILAH OLIVER

Could it be that language happened?

M. NOURBESE PHILIP

The flesh gives empathy.

HORTENSE SPILLERS

Niemand / zeugt für den / Zeugen.[1] "These three lines resist even the best translation."[2] In English, does the first line/word translate as a (non)figure named "No one" or "Noone" or "Nobody"—or no one at all? In the French translation of *Niemand*, is *Personne* a person? Does this pronoun *Niemand* perform an action, *zeugt*, such that it "witnesses" something or someone with its very own eyes, or does it "bear witness" to or for something beyond normative knowledge—something encompassed in the noun *Zeugen*/witness? Or does (or should) the pronoun *Niemand* perform no such action at all? Or is it neither one nor the other, *ne-utre*, neutral? And what is the weight of the preposition *für*/for or the article *den*/the? A panoply of inflections accompanies each translation choice, long before interpretation confronts the poem. The poem resists, and a messy resistancy is necessary to approaching the poem.[3] When the interpreters arrive, the poem prefers not to.

....

STUDY · A class is studying Herman Melville's story *Bartleby, the Scrivener*, and students are bewildered by Bartleby's refusal to move, keep copying, conform. They feel frustrated, can't grasp Bartleby's preferred (in)actions.[4] The professor (a writer) asks everyone to stand and stay silent beside their chairs. A number of minutes go by. The spaces between bodies begin to palpate the room. More time passes and the shuffling settles. After a few more breaths, the teacher asks, "What are you doing?" and a student responds, "I think we're writing."

....

Maurice Blanchot makes a claim for a certain kind of activated patience: "To write: to refuse to write—to write by way of this refusal."[5] Fred Moten makes a claim for blackness as "a theater of the refusal of what has been refused."[6] Not dissimilar to Bartleby's refusal that enacts what it refuses (a waiting that is a writing), Romanian Jewish poet and Nazi holocaust survivor Paul Celan's poem "Aschenglorie" (Ashglory)— the poem that ends with *Niemand / zeugt für den / Zeugen*—prefers not to clarify whether no one *can* or *should* (or conversely whether a generic one *can't* or *shouldn't*) bear witness for the witness, or whether an aporetic (non)figure called Noone or Nobody (or even my own variation, No One) is in the process of doing just that (i.e., witnessing).[7] This paradox enacts and indexes the limits not only of poetic interpretation but of witnessing itself. Like the slippery theological-political terms "neighbor" or "sovereign" or "friend" or "host" or, more abstractly, "justice" or "democracy" or "responsibility" or "forgiveness," the term "witness," as noun or verb, refuses to sit still and yield a "proper" (*propre*, French, "clean," an anagram of Celan) meaning.[8] "Witness" operates under a contradictory signification, whether we are discussing its juridical definition of giving testimony in a court of law or its theological definition of testifying spiritually/bearing witness to something beyond knowledge and meaning.[9] Indeed, thought reaches a limit in trying to grasp the conceptual contours of witnessing, but it is a *necessary* limit, a limit that can *perhaps* become a threshold, the mirror a window, if one prefers projective metaphors. Threshold like poetry and its fraught relation to philosophy, wherein perhaps *poesis* (making, generating— an upending force that *zeugt* also contains) and poetics can push beyond the tired tropes of Aristotle, Heidegger, Hölderlin, and the *New York Times*.[10] Threshold like Blanchot on Bartleby:

> This is abnegation understood as the abandonment of the self, a re-linquishment of identity, refusal which does not cleave to refusal but opens to failure, to the loss of being, to thought....We have fallen out of being, outside where, immobile, proceeding with a slow and even step, destroyed men come and go.[11]

Perhaps Niemand/No One is akin to one of these destroyed lives, not simply a Bartleby or a zombie but a new form of life both immobile and proceeding with a slow and even step, a new "'genre' of the human," to apply Sylvia Wynter's terminology, outside the shopworn white-western-imperialist scope of humanist Man.[12] Or if we set aside the human and its disastrous violences, perhaps No One is simply life. Perhaps the infamous *Muselmann* ("Muslim"), the "living dead" figure of the Nazi camps, is a No One, a destroyed yet still living life, a life without the decision-making capacity of Bartleby because "'I'd prefer not to' is simply not an option" for people in states of extreme subjection, as Alexander Weheliye argues: people enduring the Nazi camps or plantation slavery and its afterlives, for example.[13] Fully self-present and self-possessed agency and subjectivity was—and in many ways still is—impossible. For Frank Wilderson, "if, when caught between the pincers of the imperative to meditate on Black dispossession and Black political agency, we do not dissemble, but instead allow our minds to reflect on the murderous ontology of chattel slavery's gratuitous violence—seven hundred years ago, five hundred years ago, two hundred years ago, last year, and today, then maybe, just maybe, we will be able to think Blackness and agency together in an ethical manner."[14] For Moten, blackness encompasses nonnormative lives who refuse refused subjectivity and individuation, who "prefer not to, in stuttered, melismatic, gestural withdrawal from that subjectivity which is not itself, which is not one, which only shows up as thwarted desire for itself, as the lurid autocathectic lure of an airy fiend that walks beside you in a storefront window."[15] Perhaps No One lives in that gestural withdrawal.

There is an activated waiting that is not *about* the ontological subject, not projecting from the person as central site of knowledge and speech, but rather encompassing a paraontological form of being "that is neither for itself nor for the other."[16] *Paraontological* is Nahum

Dimitri Chandler's term that Moten has called an "undercommon disruption of ontology."[17] Moten writes that paraontology "derived from [Chandler's] engagement with [W. E. B.] Du Bois's long anticipation of [Frantz] Fanon's concern with the deformative or transformative pressure blackness puts on philosophical concepts, categories, and methods."[18] Para- as protecting against, warding off, but also queerly alongside, prior to, and beyond ontology. Blackness as "the anoriginal displacement of ontology...ontology's anti- and antefoundation, ontology's underground, the irreparable disturbance of ontology's time and space."[19] Perhaps the person has been destroyed and/or never allowed to exist, and there is only no-thing or no-body or No One, a monster constitutively composed of multiple parts; not an individuated one but an entangled social (non)figure who (non)performatively "consent[s] not to be a single being," a phrase Moten borrows and shifts from Édouard Glissant.[20] As Denise Ferreira da Silva claims, expanding on concepts from particle physics, "when the social reflects The Entangled World, sociality becomes neither the cause nor the effect of relations involving separate existants, but the uncertain condition under which everything that exists is a singular expression of each and every actual-virtual other existant."[21] For Moten, "I who have nothing, I who am no one, I am who am not one" is also a "surreal presence—not in between some things and nothing is the held fleshliness of the collective head."[22] Perhaps No One(s) bear(s) witness to Ferreira da Silva's "difference without separability."[23]

My aim in this book is to enact a knowledge assemblage that brings into apposition (nonhierarchically, not as a mode of comparison or analogy but as a contiguous and interconnected constellation—drawing on Glissant's torquing of Gilles Deleuze and Félix Guattari's enmeshed network, the rhizome, into his concept of Relation) concepts and methodologies from black studies (and black study), twentieth-century European philosophy, queer theory, and experimental poetics.[24] While I will refer to trauma studies as a well-trod stage for examining the process of witnessing, its white, Eurocentric, Shoah-as-singular-event frame is insufficient to encompass an abyssal ongoing trauma such as racial slavery and its afterlives that, to torque Wilderson slightly, is "a condition of [para]ontology and not just...an event of experience"; or, as Moten says, more "durational field rather than event," an "unremitting non-remittance."[25] Much as (overwhelmingly white and Eurocentric) Celan scholars may disagree, it is impossible to confront Celan's poetry, and the Nazi holocaust in general, without confronting trans-atlantic slavery and its afterlives amid ongoing colonialism. Black studies specifically, with its over-two-hundred-year examination of race, history, society, culture, ontology, and ideas of witnessing, and with its rich internal differentiation, charts a field of thought that perhaps makes it possible to start understanding these irreducible, incalculable three lines by Celan—*Niemand / zeugt für den / Zeugen*—as an index of the im/possibility of witnessing and witnessing witnessing.

The No One who keeps emerging through its dis/appearance in this book eschews individuation while always already becoming within differential entanglement. I am seeking to activate a No One who/that is paraontological and hauntologically informed by the no-thingness that has been historically ascribed to blackness and that blackness enacts within, apposite to, and beyond the No One. No One is a slippery concept that, particularly in the context of Celan's work, could encompass God and the poet and the reader and the poem—though Moten might argue that those No Ones can be black things too. No One could be a theological-political limit concept, but it is more and less than that. No One is an unhomed site to think about no-things that refuse received notions of subjectivity and objectivity, oneness, twoness, and thingli-ness. Odradek has no fixed abode. But let's not get ahead of ourselves. "Monsters cannot be announced. One cannot say: 'Here are our monsters,' without immediately turning the monsters into pets."[26]

Jacques Derrida was what Friedrich Nietzsche might call a "new style of philosopher...[a] philosopher of the dangerous Perhaps...arriving on the scene."[27] Indeed, Derrida borrowed Nietzsche's concept of "the dangerous Perhaps" and morphed it to encompass a messianic justice to-come (*à-venir*) as im/possible (non)event of the *avenir* (future), or what he calls "messianic hope" that is "messianic without messian-ism."[28] Derrida writes of "those 'perhapses' which have for decades explicitly marked the privileged modality, messianic in this instance, of the statements that matter the most to me."[29] He speaks of the "necessity or ineluctability of this 'perhaps'" and "what is going to come, *perhaps*, is not only this or that; it is at last the thought of the *perhaps*, the *perhaps* itself....the thought of the 'perhaps' perhaps engages the only possible thought of the event."[30] And, at the center of one of his key essays:

Justice remains *to come*, it remains *by coming* [*la justice reste à venir*], it *has*
to come [*elle a à venir*], it *is* to-come, the to-come [*elle est à-venir*], it deploys the very dimension of events irreducibly to come. It will always
have it, this à-venir, and will always have had it. *Perhaps* this is why justice, insofar as it is not only a juridical or political concept, opens up
to the *avenir* the transformation, the recasting or refounding [*la refon-
dation*] of law and politics.

"Perhaps"—one must [*il faut*] always say *perhaps* for justice.[31]

No One's Witness: A Monstrous Poetics draws on concepts from European
philosophy such as Derrida's messianic perhaps (*peut-être*, maybe, could
be, by chance) and the to-come, and Deleuze and Guattari's notions of
becoming and virtuality, but is most influenced by how these concepts
converge and resonate with black studies theorizing on blackness as a
radical and excessive paraontological social force. Moten's concepts of
blackness as absolute no-thingness and consent not to be a single being;
Ferreira da Silva's concepts of no-bodies, the plenum, and difference
without separability; and Hortense Spillers's concept of the flesh (and
its monstrosity) ground my thinking in this book. Weheliye's theorizing on Spillers's flesh and Wynter's genres of the human against Man is
also important to my thinking as Weheliye draws the Muselmann into
the field of the flesh in apposition to black flesh under extreme subjection while providing a vital critique of Giorgio Agamben's biopolitical
claims centered around the Muselmann as the "absolute biopolitical
substance" and "complete witness" of the Nazi camps, "who by definition cannot bear witness."[32] In *No One's Witness*, the Muselmann as
No One does bear witness, in and through the monstrous, incalculable
flesh. Saidiya Hartman's theorizing on and enactment of choral and
fleshly empathy and witnessing are also significant for my argument
for No One's im/possible speech, as is Jared Sexton's theorizing on abolition as a movement of movements toward unsovereign landless, self-
less existence.

Radical black theory as the critique of western "civilization" and
black feminist theory in particular, with its critique of the regimes of
Man, the human, and the self and, as Spillers writes, its insurgently
"*claiming* the monstrosity" of "unprotected...female flesh 'ungendered'"
as "a primary narrative" and "a praxis and a theory, a text for living and
for dying, and a method for reading both through their diverse mediations," are crucial apposite interlocutors to my theorizing of No One's

monstrous witness.[33] For Moten, "blackness as a kind of aesthetic and social force is not determined and structured by what it is people have been calling the black/white binary. Blackness is this other (no-)thing" that "is not the property of black people. Everybody has the right and an option to claim blackness."[34] Blackness is a monstrous social force, with the Latin roots of monstrosity from *monstrum*, portent, prodigy, atrocity, and marvel, and *monere*, to warn, with a link to *monstrare*, to point and show, and a Proto-Indo-European root, *men-*, to think with. Moten and Stefano Harney's call for an undercommon sociality and Laura Harris's study of the "aesthetic sociality of blackness" and its monstrous "motley crew," an "interclass and interracial and queer collaboration and...disruption and reconfiguration of gender structures....a different way of being and belonging together, of acting and creating in concert, for themselves but also for others: not citizenship but a kind of critical noncitizenship, a free and motley association that would materialize in dissident, disruptive work and works, the undocuments of the undocumented," ground the disruptive, ensemblic, monstrous assemblage that constitutes this book.[35]

The etymological roots of witnessing and testimony contain not only a masculinist *testes* but also *terstis*, the one who is present as a third. Perhaps No One, in its witnessing for the witness, occupies a gender-neutral third (or more) grammatical "person" (who is not a person) not caught up in the specularity of the I-you binary. Something happens, some-thing is *demonstrated*, when the heterogeneous political (or social, Moten would say) third or more interrupts not only the individual but the closed space of Emmanuel Levinas's transcendental ethical two (me and the other, but also reader-writer, reader-text, writer-text, etc.). Misappropriating Jacques Lacan in kindergarten, "It is only because we count *three* that we can manage to count *two*."[36] Yet, to be clear, when "we" invoke the three we are not invoking third-way neoliberal politics, the synthesis, or an Oedipal daddy-mommy-me triad. Indeed, it may be impossible to calculate No One and its relation to first, second, or third "persons" at all. Moten again: "To invoke the more (or less) incalculable is to recognize how life-in-danger takes certain conceptual apparatuses over the limit, in unnatural defiance of their rule, placing *them* in danger, such that the difference between internal and external imposition, or that between major and minor struggle, fails properly to signify."[37] No One is numerous and innumerable, improperly invoking queer forms of life that swerve toward incalculable speech. As Derrida suggests, "justice [to come] is incalculable, it demands that one calculate with the incalculable."[38]

A dangerous perhaps measures the span of such thresholds and strange turns. As do certain forms of literature and art, particularly the Deleuzian and Guattarian "minor" ones that in their "collective assemblages of enunciation," in their monstrously political language gestures, explode dominant forms from within.[39] For Celan, a thinker of a dangerous perhaps and a minor writer who takes language over its limit, breaking the hold of the German language on his own and his era's wounded consciousness:

> Poetry is perhaps this: an *Atemwende*, a turning of our breath. Who knows, perhaps poetry goes its way—the way of art—for the sake of just such a turn? And since the strange, the abyss *and* Medusa's head, the abyss *and* the automaton, all seem to lie in the same direction—it is perhaps this turn, this *Atemwende*, which can sort out the strange from the strange? It is perhaps here, in this one brief moment, that Medusa's head shrivels and the automatons run down? Perhaps, along with the I, estranged and freed *here, in this manner*, some other thing is also set free?
>
> Perhaps after this, the poem can be itself...can in this now art-less, art-free manner go other ways, including the ways of art, time and again?
>
> Perhaps.[40]

The breathturn (*Atemwende*) is an untranslatable caesura, an abyssal event, a dangerous perhaps wherein the poem becomes not simply an author's vocable breath—the poem breathes—but its own queered materiality, its line of escape from Medusa's (also known as the Gorgon's) obliterative gaze that turns the bearer to stone. A becoming otherwise, a becoming No One, a becoming monstrous, pointing and showing something terrible and potentially miraculous. To draw on Spillers's crucial essay "Mama's Baby, Papa's Maybe: An American Grammar Book" and her distinction between the black body and the ethereal, elusive flesh, perhaps here in this book the last three lines of the poem "Aschenglorie" could be made flesh so that a grammar something like Weheliye's *habeas viscus* ("you shall have the flesh") could let *some other thing* be *set free*. Spillers's "hieroglyphics of the flesh" and Weheliye's habeas viscus, "the differently signified flesh," inscribing lines of flight from the bounds of bare life and biopolitical discourse, the thingly flesh "embod[ying] both more and less, but above all something other, than it does in the world of Man."[41] This book embodying No One's witness, a language No One speaks, a monstrous poetics, (un)making and sur-viving word and world.

Niemand / zeugt für den / Zeugen. What follows is an attempt to turn and churn Celan's three lines, this performative gesture, into thought— on the ethicopolitical, paraontoepistemic, and affective limits of the subject and witnessing and the subject of witnessing; and how the time of the now (Walter Benjamin's messianic *Jetztzeit*, through which past memories of suffering flash up and reorient the present and future) attends the time to come, perhaps even in a poem or a work of art.[42] "One cannot write without bearing witness to the abyss of time in its coming," writes Jean-François Lyotard.[43] While, for Celan, "the strange, the abyss *and* Medusa's head, the abyss *and* the automaton, all seem to lie in the same direction," and the breathturn is a Jetztzeit-like caesura that perhaps effects change and sets some-traumatic-thing free, for Glissant the sea, the Middle Passage, is the "womb abyss" from which time begins and accumulates, an abyss where "memory of the past weaves itself back *into* the abyss without seeking retrieval or reactivation," as Glissant scholar John E. Drabinski puts it.[44] These two concepts of abyss converge with Harriet Jacobs's concept of the perilous abyss that an enslaved girl is entrapped within, wherein a self-possessed decision is not just impossible but unthinkable.[45] Travailing syllable by syllable through three abyssal lines of poetry by Celan, *No One's Witness* attempts to sort out a poetics of the strange, the strange, and the monstrous apposite to but also swerving from Celan. Perhaps via errant detour this poetics can approach a space of dangerous thought.

In theorizing this dangerous perhaps of No One's speech, I am not interested in engaging in an exhaustive discourse analysis of witnessing per se, nor in dwelling in the well-trod terrain of the "poetry of witness."[46] As Nathaniel Mackey, writing about his book *Eroding Witness*, claims, "If somebody were to say to you that poetry is an act of witnessing, that would conjure some pretty definite images, pretty reassuring and familiar images of what the function of poetry is. But for someone to say that the function of poetry is to simultaneously witness and erode its witness, to witness and erode its witnessing...announces a different vocation for poetry, a trajectory for the poem that differs from that more common understanding."[47] No One performs and enacts this erosion, this eating away at witnessing and the witness—and the subject and the self, the one, Man, and the human.

No One's Witness also counters the knee-jerk association of witnessing with the Nazi holocaust, given the overwhelming Eurocentric emphasis in trauma studies on that particular event as exceptional. In *Discourse on Colonialism*, Aimé Césaire obliterates that notion of exceptionality:

> And then one fine day the bourgeoisie is awakened by a terrific boomerang effect: the gestapos are busy, the prisons fill up, the torturers standing around the racks invent, refine, discuss.
>
> People are surprised, they become indignant. They say: "How strange! But never mind—it's Nazism, it will pass!" And they wait, and they hope; and they hide the truth from themselves, that it is barbarism, the supreme barbarism, the crowning barbarism that sums up all the daily barbarisms; that it is Nazism, yes, but that before they were its victims, they were its accomplices; that they tolerated that Nazism before it was inflicted on them, that they absolved it, shut their eyes to it, legitimized it, because, until then, it had been applied only to non-European peoples; that they have cultivated that Nazism, that they are responsible for it, and that before engulfing the whole edifice of Western, Christian civilization in its reddened waters, it oozes, seeps, and trickles from every crack.[48]

While writing this book in a time and place (the United States) where waters always already ooze red, and Nazism, internalized and externalized, spills over, I am interested in certain usages of the witness as a figure and concept, particularly Agamben's yoking of the witness with the Muselmann, the "'walking corpse' par excellence" inmate of the Nazi death camps who, in Agamben's formulation, is always already on the way to death without any spark of life to dwell in or on.[49] I am interested in how Agamben can publish a whole study on the Muselmann as a quintessential *homo sacer* figure (a sacred man, i.e., a disposable human representing bare, mere life in today's biopolitical context—in Roman law a person so debased he "*may be killed and yet not sacrificed*") and "complete witness" (i.e., already dead nonwitness) without examining the racialized nature of the term Muselmann (German for "Muslim," now considered a racial slur) that Weheliye and others point to, and that term's reverberations with real people, not just in the Nazi camps but in now-time.[50] People such as a Muslim suicide bomber, who after successfully completing their political act is deemed a *shahīd*, a martyr or *witness* to the truth. Or four unnamed Muslim boys blown up by the Israeli Defense Forces while they play soccer and hide-and-seek on a Gaza beach—perhaps they are also *homines sacri*.[51] But these people are also much more than that designation, as are the *Muselmänner* of the Nazi camps, whom Agamben emphasizes "no one wants to see," while, as will become evident in this book, the Muselmänner may be No Ones who *want* to see and to speak and to witness, however indecipherable their looking and sounding.[52] Whether they are kicking the ball or hunting for food or falling out of line and getting beaten with a stick, the Muselmann/Muslim is a life engaging in forms of fugitivity and dreaming of alternate futures, not just an always already dead and silent figure ready to be donned, dissected, and/or disavowed.

When it comes to re-figuring the constitutive and operational protocols that racialize Agamben's homo sacer and its unfreedoms, Hartman's theorizing on the "spectral and spectacular character of [black] suffering" is a crucial touchstone.[53] In the opening of *Scenes of Subjection: Terror, Slavery, and Self-Making in Nineteenth-Century America*, Hartman decides not to reproduce the primal scene of Frederick Douglass witnessing his Aunt Hester being brutally beaten by Captain Anthony. Hartman's reasoning resonates today as video footage of black lives being murdered by police circulates widely on social media:

> What interests me are the ways we are called upon to participate in such scenes. Are we witnesses who confirm the truth of what happened in the face of the world-destroying capacities of pain, the distortions of torture, the sheer unrepresentability of terror, and the repression of the dominant accounts? Or are we voyeurs fascinated with and repelled by exhibitions of terror and sufferance? What does the exposure of the violated body yield? Proof of black sentience or the inhumanity of the "peculiar institution"? Or does the pain of the other merely provide us with the opportunity for self-reflection? At issue here is *the precariousness of empathy and the uncertain line between witness and spectator.* Only more obscene than the brutality unleashed at the whipping post is the demand that this suffering be materialized and evidenced by the display of the tortured body for endless recitations of the ghastly and the terrible. In light of this, how does one give expression to these outrages without exacerbating the indifference to suffering

that is the consequence of the benumbing spectacle or contend with the narcissistic identification that obliterates the other or the prurience that too often is the response to such displays?[54]

These are essential questions to ask in the age of social media and continuous "trauma porn," when too often viewers are complicit (folded together) with the structures that enable these scenes to proliferate. What, for example, is the role and responsibility of the white viewers of Philando Castile's "hypervisible" murder by police on Facebook Live "in real time" on July 2, 2016?[55] Are they witnesses to the witnesses of the murder, Castile's girlfriend Diamond Lavish Reynolds and her daughter Dae'Anna, or are they some other sadistic monstrosity? Hartman asks, "Is the act of 'witnessing' a kind of looking no less entangled with the wielding of power and the extraction of enjoyment?"[56] Douglass describes his seven-year-old self, hiding in a closet and looking helplessly through the slats at his aunt being brutalized before him, as "a witness and a participant."[57] Douglass's witnessing, and black witnessing in general, occurs in a space of collective experience and traumatic memory far different from that of the white reader/viewer, as Elizabeth Alexander notes.[58] But in telling this story in his memoir, Douglass, as Christina Sharpe claims, "positions his white readers to reckon with what he knows about the all-encompassing and routinized violence in slavery, positions them to see that they are witness to and participant in brutal scenes of conception and transformation."[59] Encountering the "monstrous intimacies" (Sharpe's term) of transatlantic slavery and its afterlives demands that white viewers/readers look directly at Medusa's obliterative head and listen to what is said and unsaid in the monstrous duration, not as voyeurs or spectators but as participants in an ongoing disaster.

To avoid the kinds of violent appropriations that can attend "the precariousness of empathy" means performing witness as a literally self-less praxis. Moten calls for a new modality of empathy, an "empathy of no-bodies, an empathy of the flesh, an empathy against the metaphysics of Individuation, which is that which comprises and compromises witness. I believe a poetics of witness seeks to undo that compromise but can't. But is there a poetics of fleshly empathy, of entanglement, of absolute no-thingness, of 'difference without separation,' as Denise [Ferreira da Silva] would put it? For me, that's what a black poetics would enact."[60] In this book I am attempting, through No One, to travail alongside the black poetics of Moten, Spillers, Ferreira da Silva, and Hartman—and of M. NourbeSe Philip, Claudia Rankine, Glenn Ligon, Akilah Oliver, and others—to enact a monstrous poetics of fleshly empathy, an empathy of unselfsovereign no-bodies, an undercommon entanglement in and through the flesh, while No One(s) bear(s) witness for the witness(es).

As part of my practice of writing this book, I have examined the undersides of certain philosophical concepts whose construction or political effects and affects are generally accepted and unquestioned. For example, Blanchot's "neutral" is a rich theoretical concept (he calls it "a word *too many*") that could apply to No One as excessive third-or-more-person witness, and to certain kinds of writing as a potential space for witnessing at a remove.[61] The neutral is also a term that must be deconstructed for its political limits—for example, another term for the neutral that is deployed, however unconsciously, by Jean-Paul Sartre and Roland Barthes is "white writing"—and not just because Blanchot's politics had its limits.[62] Instead of Barthes's *Writing Degree Zero* as exemplifying the neutral, perhaps a more fruitful concept to ponder is Spillers's excessive flesh as "zero degree of social conceptualization," always already on a line of flight (a flight Deleuze borrowed/stole from George Jackson) from physical and conceptual capture.[63] "What could such flesh do?" ask Harney and Moten—and this book suggests some such actions in the flesh.[64]

A linked example is the concept of the impersonal: while I am attracted to Deleuze and Guattari's comprehensive destruction of the majoritarian notion of Man in favor of the preindividual impersonal event, I question if all being-things must be abstracted along with Man when racial capitalist colonial power structures continue to oppress certain marked lives more than others, employing racializing techniques that, as Weheliye claims, "discipline humanity into full humans, not-quite-humans and nonhumans."[65] Moten's theorizing of no-thing and Ferreira da Silva's theorizing of "entangled particles (that is, every existing particle) [that] exist with each other, without space-time" in "difference without separability" offer important new ways of thinking virtuality and nonlocality.[66] As Moten writes, "The interplay of physics and blackness is precisely at this intersection—this mutual sexual cut—of the theory of nothing and the theory of everything. And who are the theorists of everything and nothing, everywhere and nowhere? Refugees, flightlings, black things, whose dissident passage through understanding is often taken for a kind of lawless freedom."[67] No One is a theorist of nothing and everything, of what Celan deems "the eternalized Nowhere, here, / in the memory of the over- / loud bells in—where only?"[68]

The thrust of this book, which makes its own dissident passage through understanding, is not to exhaustively propose one argument but to enact a monstrous assemblage composed of heterogeneous strands of thinking in response to questions such as: What happens when the incalculable political (or social) three or more or Moten's "more + less than one" or some combination thereof interrupts the ethical one or two—what precisely happens when No One *does* bear witness for the witness?[69] How does the human's supposedly constitutive formation in relation signify beyond the Levinasian face-to-face hostage-taking/caress of transcendental me and transcendental you as other? The neighbor/witness, the unavoidably immanent other other or "third party," always already interrupts "our" ecstatic embrace, making "us" beside ourselves (*ek-stasis*, Greek, "standing outside oneself") with confusion and vulnerability and potential radical openness.[70] But the neighbor you love to hate across the always already white picket fence is understood as neighbor only insofar as they are deemed a some-thing, a some-body. What about forms of nothing, forms of not standing but collectively falling? Moten and Harney: "We fall so we can fall again, which is what ascension really means to us. To fall is to lose one's place, to lose the place that makes one, to relinquish the locus of being, which is to say of being single. This radical homelessness—its kinetic indigeneity, its irreducible queerness—is the essence of blackness."[71] This "sharing of a life in homelessness" is resonant with the non-Zionist secular Jewish messianic thought and writing practices of Derrida, Benjamin, Franz Kafka, and Celan that I draw on throughout this book.[72] Jared Sexton writes about abolition as "the interminable radicalization of every radical movement," and with this radicalization comes an unsovereign unhoming: "No ground for identity, no ground to stand (on). Everyone has a claim to everything until no one has a claim to anything. No claim....The flesh of the earth demands it: the landless inhabitation of selfless existence."[73] What follows and folds and falls and fails and fleshes is No One making a claim to a theorizing without a claim, No One as an im/possible, anoriginal, paraontological, emergent form of life queering normative ways of thinking life, the subject, witnessing, and form itself. This gesture toward the emergent is not a modernist thrust into the prophetic wilderness; it is a future anterior push at the now, a dangerous perhaps.[74]

A NOTE ON FORM   In this scenography, nothing comes on the scene punctually. Nothing comes on the scene on its own terms; which is to say, it comes on the scene on other terms. Distinctions move laterally or obversely vibrating through chains and networks of associations. It is in this lateral, or obverse, movement that we can describe the formation of form. Everything in this paragraph moves by indirection. Nothing settles down. Form would be deflection as indirection; for each movement is inflected back into itself, doubled and redoubled by the differences that organize its formation. The prose itself, by its syntax and the *confusions* of its meanings, remain not only the site of a question, but the very movement or form of a question.

NAHUM DIMITRI CHANDLER

I am a poet, and with this book I am presenting *un essai*, an attempt, a try, a trial that is exposed to its own failure, like all language acts. This essay comes from a lineage of poetics writing, *makings* in form and theorizing, enactments of literary, political, and philosophical argument through experimental and improvisatory language forms rather than via expository persuasive prose. The poetic is not unlike blackness as a social and aesthetic force that upends received categories and concepts and ways of being. It is no wonder that Aristotle tried in vain to contain the poetic within his taxonomic organon and Plato banished poets from his utopian Republic. The long history of poetics writing in western literature includes works from a vast range of poet-thinkers, from Philip Sidney, Alexander Pope, and William Wordsworth to Gertrude Stein, Charles Olson, Amiri Baraka, and Moten, Glissant, Césaire, and Celan.[75] The works of poetics by these writers and many more are deeply scholarly while operating outside of, and in many cases rejecting, the accumulative rigidity of normative scholarly apparatuses, whether from the Renaissance, the Romantic era, or now. In these works, the distinctions among poetry, criticism, and theory blur to such a degree that any taxonomic desire becomes fruitless and inconsequential. This book aims to make a contribution to this great poetics—or, as poet-thinker Joan Retallack would say, *poethics*—tradition. For Retallack, "a poetics can take you only so far without an *h*. If you're to embrace complex life on earth, if you can no longer pretend that all things are fundamentally simple or elegant, a poetics thickened by an *h* launches an exploration of art's significance *as*, not just *about*, a form of living in the real world. That *as* is not a simile; it's an ethos. Hence the *h*. What I'm working on is quite explicitly a poethics of a complex realism."[76] As I will elaborate, Ferreira da Silva has drawn on Retallack's term to theorize a black feminist poethics of complex realism that is important to how I am thinking about No One's monstrous witness, No One as a poethical (non)figure or (non)image of poethical thought, No One enacting a fleshly poetics of entanglement alongside Moten's notion of black poetics mentioned above.[77] With this book I am working through in prose a wide range of thinking and research about witnessing, writing, and the social that I have demonstrated in my poetry for over twenty-five years—and that black study has helped me work through to a new place. Indeed, this experiment, this performance, this try, *is* a poem generated from reading, one that generates its own form in the process of its (un)folding. Like many experimental poems and theoretical texts that enact their ideas through form, *No One's Witness: A Monstrous Poetics* teaches you how to read it as it spirals along, and I hope this book will be read with a consciousness that what remains unsaid is an incitement to readers to generate more.

As the table of contents demonstrates, each chapter of this book begins from a word from the English translation of the last three lines of Celan's poem "Aschenglorie" (Ashglory): *Niemand / zeugt für den / Zeugen*; "No one / bears witness for the / witness" (one possible translation). There are chapters for "No," for "one," for "bears," "witness," and so on—along with chapters on the caesura between "No" and "one" and on the (non)figure of the No One. Across each chapter, I imagine whether an incalculable, irreducible No One can perhaps enact an improvisation of an im/possibility of bearing witness. Against the manifest interpretation of the three Celan lines that no one can or should bear witness for the witness, a manifold No One's fleshly speech im/possibly performs just that. No One as never one, never the space and speech of the sovereign self-possessed individual, No One as some no-thing altogether different and diffuse, plural and perverted, monstrously generative. *Niemand / zeugt für den / Zeugen*. The heterogeneous monster that is this book articulates by way of a set of interlocking *essais* that spiral out from each word/chapter. Together they enact a call to an undercommon social poesis, with monstrosity's etymological roots bearing a pointing, a showing, an overexposure even, a demonstration of some-thing deviant, excessive, uncontainable, and possibly miraculous—an out form of collective becoming otherwise in another world always already here and to come, dancing.[78]

All chapters include "studies" of cultural concepts and products, primarily drawn from literature and art, that ground their arguments. These forays into literature and art are not meant as explicatory close readings. On the contrary, they seek to highlight how the creative works of M. NourbeSe Philip, Glenn Ligon, Sharon Hayes, Dread Scott, Bhanu Kapil, Akilah Oliver, Saidiya Hartman, Juliana Spahr, and others performatively index and draw toward the philosophical concepts and political questions in the book. But I am not forgoing close reading altogether—the whole book is indeed a hyperclose, granular reading of three lines from a poem by Paul Celan.

The form or style of writing in this book is fragmentary, associative, accretive, and recursive—a lesbian spiral or Möbius strip or another allegorical image that isn't linear or dialectic, that allows for future anterior spaces of radical secular messianic hope.[79] Actively waiting (i.e., acting) for a world that will perhaps have come or perhaps never come, but still an event worth attending—and making every day. One wag famously suggested that "philosophy ought really to be written only as a *poetic composition*," and my thinking and formal process constructing this book could be interpreted as enacting that directive.[80] The bringing together, and sometimes clash, of disparate voices that occurs here on these pages is deliberate. I consider myself a cocreator rather than a solo author; I am engaged in an ensemblic practice, a choral architecture, a social poetics (an out kind of social ecology, even) of the incalculable more + less than one + three or more. My compositional methods in theoretical prose and poetry are very similar, methods that include a perhaps embarrassing attachment to a kind of montage shock effect or Benjaminian citational assemblage leaping out and relieving the reader of their convictions. Benjamin described his *Arcades Project* in this way: "Method of this project: literary montage. I needn't *say* anything. Merely show. I shall purloin no valuables, appropriate no ingenious formulations. But the rags, the refuse—these I will not inventory but allow, in the only way possible, to come into their own: by making use of them."[81] I am not following Benjamin's method exactly, but embedded in all my writing is a similar emphasis on showing over saying. As is the constellatory interpenetration of reading, gleaning, and making use, as well as the possibilities of montage or assemblage for pushing readerly thinking and affect.

Celan's last poem before he committed suicide in the Seine in 1970 includes the line "du liest," which translates as both "you read" and "you glean."[82] My writing practice consists of reading and gleaning and assembling the refuse, the refused, refusal. Assemblage has always appealed to me as a concept and a praxis that pushes beyond the two-dimensional page (or the limits of the montage film cut and basic collage forms) into new configurations of space, time, and thought. Ferreira da Silva's black feminist "raw materialist" and "at least four dimensional... poethical...compositional...or fractal thinking" is an important apposite method for how a constellatory assemblage can form.[83] I create multi-dimensional assemblages that are "contradictory and mobile," as Benjamin might say; that openly "evade rest," as Glissant's work enacts; and that employ Deleuzian "irrational cuts."[84] My writing attempts to generate "mad" (or ungovernable) affects in the reader, and Benjamin's "craziest mosaic technique you can imagine" is an aid to that process.[85] As Shoshana Felman suggests, "The more a text is 'mad'—the more, in other words, it resists interpretation—the more the specific modes of its resistance to reading constitute its 'subject.'"[86] I imagine disavowed "sticky" affects being drawn to the surface of readerly bodies through the reading process, circulating and sticking to other readerly bodies and perhaps doing something, kind of like montage shock affects. As Sara Ahmed writes in *The Cultural Politics of Emotion*: "Stickiness...is about what objects do to other objects—it involves a transference of affect— but it is a relation of 'doing' in which there is not a distinction between passive or active, even though the stickiness of one object might come before the stickiness of the other, such that the other seems to cling to it."[87] I want readers to cling to one another and make something social happen.

To borrow from Nahum Dimitri Chandler, "I have attempted to carry out a certain practice of intervention in discourse, to enact a certain politics of theoretical discourse."[88] In the epigraph that opens this "Note on Form," Chandler is referring to his im/possible effort "to read with Du Bois; writing," and the paragraph can describe both Du Bois's writing in the opening of *The Souls of Black Folk* and Chandler's *own writ-*

ing with and through Du Bois, using form, association, and constant uncontainable movement to ask unaskable questions.[89] In the scenography that is *No One's Witness*, I am attempting some-thing apposite in form as I dwell with the no-thing that comes on the scene on its own terms. Something happens when Moten's and Blanchot's words and my words are placed side by side, some-thing dangerous, perhaps—and some-thing monstrously social. Something similar happens when Moten's and Wilderson's words are placed side by side in apposition. The uneasiness of a distinction or opposition between Afro-Pessimism and so-called Black Optimism (Moten would say Black Ops) is brought to bear in this formal montagic juxtaposition. When concepts by these important thinkers hold space together in the same paragraph, on the same page, their seemingly rigid differences soften and their overlapping resonances emerge; they gather together, in and as dehiscence.[90] I perform these kinds of monstrous citational assemblages throughout this text as a form of readerly and writerly witnessing and cohabitation.

My use of "ensemble" to describe the cocreative practices of writing and reading is influenced by Moten's beautiful elongation of that musical term to write against individuation and toward, within, and through difference across his body of work. Poststructuralist notions of the death of the author and the birth of the reader as coproducer of meaning that have been taken up by experimental poets for over half a century are also embedded in my psyche and practice, as they are in those of many of the thinkers and artists I cite and study. Sometimes I elaborate on the appositional juxtapositions of my assemblages, and sometimes I leave them to resonate. And as in my poetry books, I and you and we dwell here in difficult affective content and questions of the ethics of representation. The formal and content decisions I make in assembling my ideas and sentences, the cuts and tears of decision, are necessarily partial. They are deeply thought through and made toward generating complex forms of thinking, feeling, and acting. Borrowing from Derrida on his experimental text *Glas*, I aim to create a text that "produces a language of its own, in itself, which while continuing to work through tradition emerges at a given moment as a *monster*, a monstrous mutation without tradition or normative precedent."[91] No One's witness: a monstrous poetics, a language No One speaks, a dangerous perhaps. I am a white-skinned, middle-class, secular Jewish, gender-queer, dyke poet and thinker and educator and lover and abuse survivor and alto sax player and friend and settler and other positionalities

as well. I and we are here (like and unlike Abraham) desiring to abolish
the white self-same self. There is a poem, and there is *un essai*, a radical try, poethical wager. A travailer is made.[92] Do these words matter
when forty-nine Latinx and black, queer and trans people are massa-
cred in Orlando while they dance?[93] There is the so-called constative
and the so-called performative. There is testimony, and there are four
chimneys blown beyond knowledge to deformed freedom.[94] There is
author, vendor, rhetor as witness, survivor, balls. There is a monster
in the neighbor's face. That alien traumatic kernel of *Das Ding* in the
Nebenmensch adjoins and hystericizes me as the both/and that exceeds
and opens thought.[95] Yes and no are unsplit neighbors housed in abra-
sive proximity in the noem.[96] Nothing settles down.[97] There is a thinking encrypted in silence and a thinking encrusted in noise. There is
a listening to what is unsayable. There is blur when we try to see one
thing.[98] There is a reach, a touch, an impress. There is a limit and a
limit and a limit and, peut-être, a threshold, break. Nothing for [N]o
[O]ne.[99] As the impure products of Amerika go crazy, there is *un éveil*,
a queerly errant arousal.[100] There is a veil, im/movable.[101] Everything
in this paragraph moves by indirection. No One arrives to witness and
adjust. There is an experience that cannot be translated. No One(s)
drive(s) the car to Orlando. There is an experience that cannot be undone. I is undone. There is a time that could have been then and a time
that will have been now and a time always already to come. These co-
incide. Nothing comes on the scene punctually. Another city gathers,
dancing.[102] Language is flesh, flesh language. You are what we gain from
this disorientation.[103]

1

No

No one
bears witness for the
witness.

PAUL CELAN

Refusal ("No") precedes the body, the person, the "one." Refusal of easy capture, of productive outlay, of consumable meaning. And refusal of the self-same one itself. Bartleby refuses, the poem refuses, and Moten enacts "a theater of refusal, a theater of refuse, a theater of refuse, a theater of the refused, a theater of the refusal of what has been refused, a theater of the left over, a theater of the left behind, a theater of the left, a theater of the (out and) gone."[1] *Apophasis* (Greek, "to say no") is a rhetorical device in which the speaker or writer "asserts or emphasizes something by pointedly seeming to pass over, ignore, or deny it."[2] The device tends to be used ironically, but doesn't have to be, as in John Milton's line: "No light, but rather darkness visible," which conjures light far more than it conjures darkness.[3] Or in Blanchot: "Such is the disaster: the night lacking darkness, but brightened by no light."[4] Or, jumping ahead a syllable in Celan's poem, "No one" says no to the one while conjuring not just one, but more and less than one. According to Felman, "Radical negativity (or 'saying no') belongs neither to *negation*, nor to *opposition*, nor to *correction* ('normalization'), nor to *contradiction* (of positive and negative, normal and abnormal, 'serious' and 'unserious,' 'clarity' and 'obscurity')—it belongs precisely to *scandal*: to the scandal of [these terms'] nonopposition."[5] There is also an apposition or "paraontological interplay" among blackness, no-thingness, and thingness, "an aesthetic sociality" that Moten, Ferreira da Silva, and others explore: "Is it possible to desire the something-other-than-transcendental subjectivity that is called nothing? What if blackness is the name that has been given to the social field and social life of an illicit alternative capacity to desire?" writes Moten. "Nothing is not absence. Blackness is more and less than one in nothing."[6] Negativity as fugitive, nothingness fully inhabited, no-where as no place, utopic, "not there...where we remain, in motion."[7] No One as an aesthetic sociality, "another way of being in the world," entangled in difference, dancing and refusing the one and transcendence; a scandal of the imagination, perhaps.[8]

Indeed, negation is never as it seems or seams in Celan. His poems strive to "keep yes and no unsplit," and perhaps this is why one of his translators, Pierre Joris, first chose to translate Niemand in "Aschenglorie" using the neologism "Noone."[9] At first I thought the joined seam of letters was a typographical error, but then I thought again. In the French translation of Niemand, *Personne* means both person and not-person, nobody. Yes and no unsplit. Like the suffocating suture of "Noone," an indeterminate (non)figure, unsplit as Niemand is also unsplit, so perhaps closest to the German, yet dehiscent. Uncontainable, incalculable, like Blanchot's *le pas au-delà*, a step (pas) beyond (au-delà) that is also not—*pas*—beyond.[10] Or the neologism "noem," which some English translators use to denote Celan's use of *Gedicht/Genicht* in a poem entitled "Eroded."[11] A noem is a no-poem, a poem eroding its witness. A noem gestures toward no-thing, as in another Celan poem the neologism *Tiefimschnee* (Deepinsnow) disintegrates to *Iefimnee* (Eepinno), then *I—i—e* (I—i—o), the last line eroded to just vowels, letters that in a language such as Hebrew would not appear at all.[12] Not unlike the wipe across the forehead of the "discursive monster" known as the golem that turns "emeth" (Hebrew for truth, testimony) minus its "e" (Hebrew aleph) to "meth," death, ash, obliterated clay.[13] Noem also calls up and contains both *noesis* and *noema*, the thought-word/subject and thought-object, what the sound stands for; noema in particular denoting in rhetoric "a figure of speech whereby something stated obscurely is nevertheless intended to be understood or worked out," which brings to mind Glissant's "right to obscurity" that I will explore in this book; and noem draws us to the related *nous*: mind, intellect, which in French transforms into the slippery collective *we*.[14] "Our homelessness. Our selflessness. None of which can be ours," claim Harney and Moten.[15] Perhaps the noem is a kind of absolute nothingness in the sense Japanese philosopher Nishida Kitarō conceives and Moten activates. Kitarō's third *basho* is a field of absolute nothingness that is a process, not a thing, neither subject nor object of itself, that is, not relative; something like Mu, the absolute nothingness that Moten hears in the improvisatory ensemble of Don Cherry, Ed Blackwell, Mackey, Wilderson, and Fanon, a field of absolute nothingness that is incomparable and incalculable and constitutes blackness.[16]

It is also true that the "nie" of Niemand means "never" in German. Niemand is not just "not-one" but "never-one" or even my mistranslated torque, Never Man, another genre of life that doesn't exist in comparison to Man but in deferred apposition. Time exposes itself right away, just not in translation. Derrida's secular "messianism without content" comes to mind, the never-one, whom some await without any real call to hang on to.[17] And another Never Man comes to nous, proceeding with an uneven, immobile step beyond and not beyond the thresholds of life and death, the Muselmann of the Nazi camps, whom Agamben deconstructs as a concept and figure but avoids dealing with as a Muslim; and whom Weheliye includes in the "racializing assemblages" of the flesh of the disaster that is always already now-time.[18] Meanwhile, a "generative and general swarm" of Never Men refuse the refusal of black thingliness as "the social life of no-things bumps and thuds and grunts in plain song."[19]

....

STUDY · September 9, 2009: A black man walks down 125th Street in Harlem in an anachronistic 1960s suit and hat carrying a white placard protest sign that states in bold black printing, "I AM <u>NOT</u> A MAN." The man is an artist, Dread Scott, who makes "Revolutionary art—to propel history forward" and whose chosen professional name echoes with one Benjaminian "slight adjustment" that of Dred Scott, an enslaved African man who sued the US Supreme Court for his and his family's freedom in 1857.[20] Dred Scott lost because he did not possess "standing" as an American "citizen" or "person" or "human" under the law and was considered rather the property of his owner, "so far inferior that they had no rights which the white man was bound to respect," as Chief Justice Roger Taney's decisive cut of a decision stated.[21] The sign Dread Scott holds in 2009 references an iconic civil rights–era sign held by 1,300 black sanitation workers on strike in Memphis in 1968, with one slight adjustment: the 1968 sign stated, "I <u>AM</u> A MAN." The workers had adapted that slogan from the first sentence of Ralph Ellison's famous novel: "I am an invisible man."[22] By removing "invisible," the workers declared their enduring visible presence. In late March 1968,

Martin Luther King Jr. traveled to Memphis to support the workers in their strike for wages equal to their white counterparts' and against unsafe working conditions that had led to the deaths of coworkers. On April 4, the day after King addressed the sanitation workers in Memphis, he was assassinated as he stood on the balcony of his room at the Lorraine Motel. As Scott walks along 125th Street for precisely one hour holding his sign and its inverted message, sometimes his hands are in the air, sometimes his pockets are turned out, and sometimes his pants are down at his ankles so that he must shuffle awkwardly and fall—all gestures that black men must make on the street every day as they are summarily stopped and frisked and violated by police for "walking while black."[23] As Scott stumbles along, one passerby attempts to reassure him with "Look brother, you ARE a man, and don't you forget it"; another, Scott commented, "took it as a gender thing," saying, "Yeah, you look like a sissy to me." Scott laughs as he recalls the sissy remark in an interview, perhaps because interpreting the sign as a critique of gender norms is an obvious first, merely surface, layer (and presumably not because he considers it laughable to be a sissy).[24] Although it is interesting to think of Scott's performance as a kind of insurgent ungendering, alongside Spillers's exhortation to claim the monstrosity of ungendered female flesh. Scott's performance and voiceless speech act (itself a kind of nonperformative performance) could also be interpreted as saying something along the basic lines of "I am not a man because the world I live in doesn't recognize me as a man, doesn't consider me to be a human with all the rights that attend that basic state; I am deemed a Nobody."[25] Or, swerving away from the politics of recognition and its tendency, as Hartman notes, to "tether, bind, and oppress," one could interpret Scott's gesture along the lines of a monstrous combination of Wynter's, Wilderson's, and Harney and Moten's theorizing:[26] "I am not a Man because I refuse to be a Man; if 'the position of the Black is...a paradigmatic impossibility in the Western Hemisphere, indeed, in the world, in other words, if a Black is the very antithesis of a Human subject,' then I refuse to take the colonial-genocidal phallus of Western

FIGURE 1.1 Richard L. Copley, photograph of striking sanitation department workers, April 1968, Memphis, Tennessee. © Richard L. Copley. Courtesy of the artist.

FIGURE 1.2 Dread Scott, performance still from *I Am Not a Man*, New York, 2009. © Dread Scott. Courtesy of the artist.

FIGURE 1.3 Sharon Hayes, detail from
In the Near Future, 2009. Courtesy of Sharon
Hayes and Tanya Leighton Gallery.

Renaissance and Enlightenment Man as my nomos and logos.[27] 'Fuck a home in this world.'[28] No."

November 6, 2005: A white woman stands in front of St. Patrick's Cathedral in midtown Manhattan for exactly one hour wearing nondescript contemporary clothing and carrying a white placard protest sign that states in bold black painted strokes, "I AM A MAN." The woman is an artist named Sharon Hayes, who could also be called a lesbian or queer person or even sissy in a certain parlance. The tourists and other folks passing by may or may not know these identifying factors about the person on the street with the placard, or that the sign she carries references the Memphis sanitation strike of 1968 and photos of the strike that have since circulated widely. The passersby also may or may not know that St. Patrick's Cathedral was the site of the massive Stop the Church protest by ACT UP in 1989, aimed directly at Cardinal John O'Connor and the Roman Catholic Church's stance against AIDS education, condom distribution, and abortion. The action was in line with ACT UP's practices of identifying key New York City players who were fanning the flames of the health crisis through their words, policies, or actions. Hayes's one-hour action that day was part of a larger multiyear project called *In the Near Future*, in which she brought iconic signs into relation with iconic sites of protest, but the sign and the site deliberately didn't match. They were anachronistic, "errors in time," or perhaps they were errors in now-time (Benjamin's Jetztzeit), future anterior errors wherein past and future trauma and possibility shoot through the now and reorient it and us.[29] In each of the actions performed from 2005 to 2008, Hayes was examining "how the speech act of protest makes meaning" through the "triangular relationship between the words on the sign, the body that holds the sign, and the time and place in which the sign is held."[30] I would push that triangular relationship into a different shape to include the viewers of the actions, some of whom were invited to document the actions, and whose photos became part of an installation element of *In the Near Future* in which still other viewers pushed the shape even more. Through a multiplication of authorship, the individual re-action of protesting becomes a

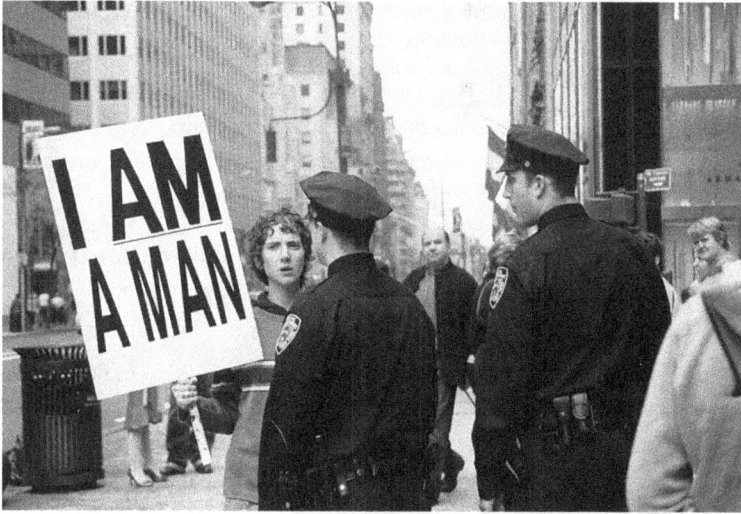

collective act of renarration and witnessing, a collective assemblage of enunciation.

In discussing *In the Near Future*, Hayes uses the word "action" instead of "performance" and the word "demonstrator" instead of "activist." Demonstration has an obvious link to protest, but also to Brechtian epic theater, in which, as Hayes states, "actors are replaced by demonstrators...[who] propose that the event has taken place; what you are watching is a repeat. To think through my actions in *In the Near Future* as a certain kind of demonstration that asks for a form of critical viewership is helpful."[31] Hayes makes an attempt to, as Moten says of his own work, "demonstrate demonstration itself."[32] Her work doesn't just mimetically reproduce protest as directed toward the state; instead, *In the Near Future* affectively "show[s] us to us," demonstrating how people gather in the undercommons with love toward one another rather than in desire for state recognition.[33] *Protest* is etymologically linked to "testimony," and in testimonial terms, *demonstration* is also a monstration (or in Hayes's case a remonstration), a showing that gives evidence as proof. A common translation for "habeas corpus" is "show me the body," which is a slight mistranslation from the more literal "you shall have the body." From there perhaps "you shall have the flesh," Weheliye's habeas viscus, "show me the flesh," which always already slips from grasp. A demonstrator also holds proof of a monster (and demon) inside it, lodged in its Latin root *monstrum*, a deviant, unorthodox excess that can't be contained; and from its verb root *monstrare*, "to show" (and not just an art show), "to reveal," holding its potential for miraculous revelation. Derrida inimitably teases out the daimon and its further relation to the undecidable:

> Monsters are living beings. The monster is also that which appears for the first time and, consequently, is not yet recognized. A monster is a species for which we do not yet have a name, which does not mean that the species is abnormal, namely, the composition or hybridization of already known species. Simply, it *shows* itself [*elle se* montre]—that is what the word monster means—it shows itself in something that is not yet shown and that therefore looks like a hallucination, it strikes the eye, it frightens precisely because no anticipation had prepared one to identify this figure.[34]

According to Derrida scholar Anais Spitzer, "a monstrum...is a message that comes from afar, improperly entering into the regulated order as an undomesticated stranger. Monsters disclose disclosure."[35] A monstrum is a sign or portent or miracle, an excessive message from future anteriority. Benjamin writes of the monster as *Unmensch* or UnMan in an essay on Karl Kraus in which Paul Klee's *Angelus Novus* is not the melancholic figure of history/futurity whom Benjamin later crystallizes, but rather a predatory cannibal angel equipped with nasty claws. The Unmensch (and perhaps we could also call on Immanuel Kant's *Unding* as negative nothing, impossible monster) is both a demonic brute who could also be considered a kind of homo sacer figure and a creature who has *sur-vived* (over/beyond life, to live on) humanity and its biopolitically destructive speech acts: "The monster stands among us as a messenger of a more real humanism. He is the conqueror of the empty phrase."[36] One could say the Unmensch or No One occupies "demonic ground," which is Wynter's term for a "vantage point outside the space-time orientation of the humuncular observer," or what Moten might call a "refusal of standpoint," a standpoint "from no standpoint because this is what it would truly mean to remain in the hold of the ship."[37] "No ground for identity, no ground to stand (on)," exhorts Sexton.[38] For Wynter, the "'demonic model' [lies] outside the 'consolidated field' of our present mode of being/feeling/knowing, as well as of the multiple discourses, their regulatory systems of meaning and interpretative 'readings,' through which alone these modes, as varying expressions of human 'life,' including ours, can effect their respective autopoesis *as such* specific modes of being."[39] Katherine McKittrick, in her discussion of Wynter's demonic ground, draws on not only the demonic spirit's possession of the human being but the demonic's connotations in mathematics, physics, and computer science as "a working system that cannot have a determined, or knowable, outcome. The demonic, then, is a non-deterministic schema; it is a process that is hinged on uncertainty and non-linearity because the organizing principle cannot predict the future."[40] For Weheliye, Wynter's demonic ground represents "perspectives that reside in the liminal precincts of the current governing configurations of the human as Man in order to abolish this figuration and create other forms of life."[41] Because for all of Benjamin's Marxist humanism and historical materialist dreaming, Césaire is correct to claim that "the West has never been further from being able to live a true humanism—a humanism made to the measure of the world."[42] One could perhaps argue that the demonic is in conversation with de-monstration, which Derrida posits "makes its proof without showing [*montrer*], without offering any conclusion as evidence, without giving anything to carry away, without any available thesis. It proves according to another mode, but by marching to its *pas de démonstration*. It transforms, it transforms itself in its process rather than advancing the signifiable object of a discourse. It tends to fold into itself everything that it makes explicit, to bend it all to itself."[43] A theorizing with-out a claim, from no standpoint, trans-forming within the fold, or perhaps, as Sexton claims, an abolitionist "politics without a claim...preventing any order of determination from taking root."[44] No One bears witness to demonic de(-)monstration.

An artist friend of Hayes's living in Berlin watches online images of a protest in Ferguson, Missouri, in 2014, after the fatal shooting of black teenager Michael Brown by white police officer Darren Wilson, and notices someone in the crowd carrying a sign with the words "I AM A MAN" on it. The artist writes to Hayes saying that they saw the sign "and thought of your work."[45] The demonstration fails in this moment, an error in now-time, the speech act of protest producing skewed, monstrous, queered signification. In his testimony before a grand jury, Wilson claimed that Brown came at him with "the most intense, aggressive face. The only way I can describe it, it looks like a demon." Wilson "saw... that face coming at me" and fired twelve bullets into Brown's body.[46] This face-to-face encounter exposes the flaws in Levinasian ethics:

FIGURE 1.4 Airport workers on strike picket, Thursday, April 2, 2015, at Philadelphia International Airport. Associated Press/ Matt Rourke.

this monstrous "it" whom Wilson conjures from a monstrous distortion of Brown as a person can't occupy any of Levinas's ethical figures of self, other, or third; nor can it occupy Blanchot's third-person "neutral" stance or even Deleuze's fourth-person singular "it." This (non)figure may be No One made flesh, habeas viscus, not a form or a self "that he cannot have and cannot be," but, as Moten posits, an impossible to numerate or calculate fleshly nonstandpoint through which "we might begin to think the radical informality of we, the nothing, the blackness that is before, and deep, in the break, not in between. The world and the face are failed project, harsh projection."[47] Brown's demonic face as "it" cannot speak or bear witness to himself and his own desubjectification. As Bryan Wagner notes, "Because blackness is supernumerary, it is impossible to speak as black without putting yourself into tension with the condition that you would claim. Speaking as black can mitigate your condition, or make you into an exception or a credit to your condition, but it cannot allow you to represent your condition, as speaking is enough to make you unrepresentative."[48] Perhaps this daimonic (non) figure replete with knowledge, this supernumerary black "it," is saying, by not/un/de-saying, "I claim monstrosity; I am an incalculable language that No One speaks."[49] And it may be no coincidence that Dred Scott is buried just a few miles from Ferguson.

The keen art-critical interest in Hayes's action, which is one of twenty-six actions that make up her larger project, could be partly due to the fact that one of the documentation photos of *In the Near Future* that has circulated widely in art circles and beyond shows two cops talking to Hayes while she holds the "I AM A MAN" sign—alas, it is a catchy image. This photo even shows up as a remonstration (in the sense of both a repeat showing and a reproach or critique) on the cover of a scholarly book called *Feeling Women's Liberation*.[50] Hayes's reciting of the sign has been interpreted as a statement on gender, even as a transgender activist statement, even though Hayes is not transgender and never intended any of the signs to refer to her indexical "I" at all.[51] Perhaps it is the indirect directness of this sign that rankles, in the way that the anachronistic qualities of Hayes's other signs in that

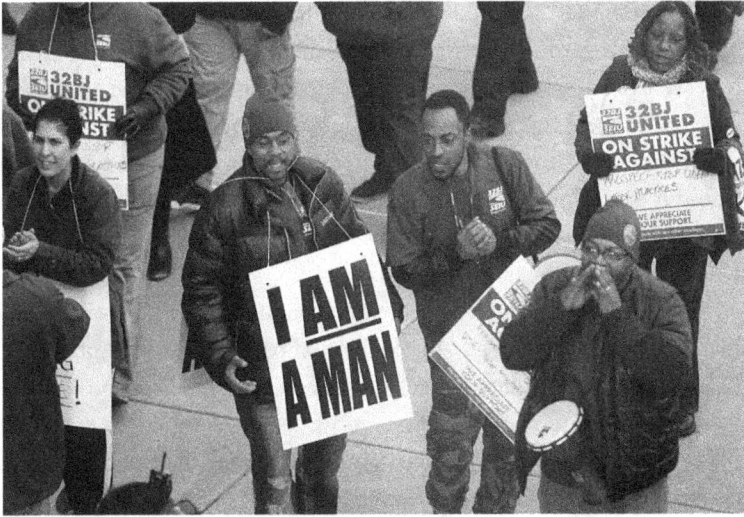

project, such as "Ratify the ERA Now" or "Who Approved the War in Vietnam?," are more directly indirect. But it is interesting that Hayes's use of the discursive monster "I AM A MAN" has never been probed by art critics in terms of the racial problematics of cultural appropriation. One could even make an argument that Dread Scott's 2009 performance is a direct or indirect critique of Hayes's 2005 performance, Scott producing his own inverted, perverted discursive monster, sign, portent—though as far as I know, Scott himself never makes mention of this connection.

Travailing the interpretive route regarding Hayes's sign, one could perhaps translate it as saying something like "I am a man not just because Simone de Beauvoir and Jacques Lacan tell me woman—and by extension lesbian—doesn't exist, but also because I am white and complicit with liberal Enlightenment humanist white supremacy; I am considered human, while many other groups of people are considered nonhuman or not quite human at all; and I can easily speak and give an account of myself while other people cannot." But, alas, it may be better in this case not to speak at all, to let this particular sign recirculate within a more "proper" cultural context, such as in a 2015 strike by Philadelphia airport workers for higher wages (see figure 1.4). Or Harney and Moten would argue against Hegelian protest and petitioning and "the demand for recognition that actually constitutes business as usual" altogether: "Rather than dissipate our preoccupation with how we live and breathe, we need to defend our ways in our persistent practice of them. It's not about taking the streets; it's about how, and about what, we should take to the streets. What would it be and what would it mean for us jurisgeneratively to take to the streets, to live in the streets, to gather together another city right here, right now?"[52] No One(s) drive(s) the car to here and now.

1988: Twenty years after the Memphis sanitation strike, artist Glenn Ligon, who is black and gay, makes his first painting using re-presented language: *Untitled (I Am a Man)*. Shiny black enamel letters on a bright white background transmute the iconic protest sign with a couple of slight adjustments: the sentence falls on three lines instead of two, and the body holding the sign is no longer visible. Though the body and the flesh, in Spillers's terms, still persist, insist, through the black "Man" alone on its line surrounded by whiteness, a Man who, in conceptual-art parlance, could stand in for the human form common to (white, cis, straight, western, Enlightenment) figurative painting—or a (non)figure who monstrates another genre of life, a future anterior black queer man. The next year, 1989, another *Untitled* painting on paper by Ligon reappropriates the language "Am I Not a Man and a Brother?" that eighteenth- and nineteenth-century organizations such as the British Society for Effecting the Abolition of the Slave Trade circulated on woodcuts, reliefs, coins, and other forms showing images of supplicating enslaved black people. Here Ligon reworks the maroon-fleshy ground of his paper to such a point that the "I" and other letters of the appropriated phrase disintegrate and "AM NOT MAN AND ROTHER" rises to the painting's "scabrous," perhaps even rott(h)ing or ro*thing* flesh/ surface.[53] From the impure (non)figures of Gothic horror to the zombie's rotting flesh to the suicide bomber as "monster-terrorist-fag" caught within a necropolitical ballistic embrace of victim and witness, monsters are always already queered beings (or "deformed" subjects,

FIGURE 1.5 Glenn Ligon, *Untitled (I Am a Man)*, 1988. Oil and enamel on canvas, 40 × 25 in. (101.6 × 63.5 cm). Collection of National Gallery of Art, Washington, D.C. Photographer credit: Ronald Amstutz. © Glenn Ligon. Courtesy of the artist, Hauser & Wirth, New York, Regen Projects, Los Angeles, Thomas Dane Gallery, London, and Chantal Crousel, Paris.

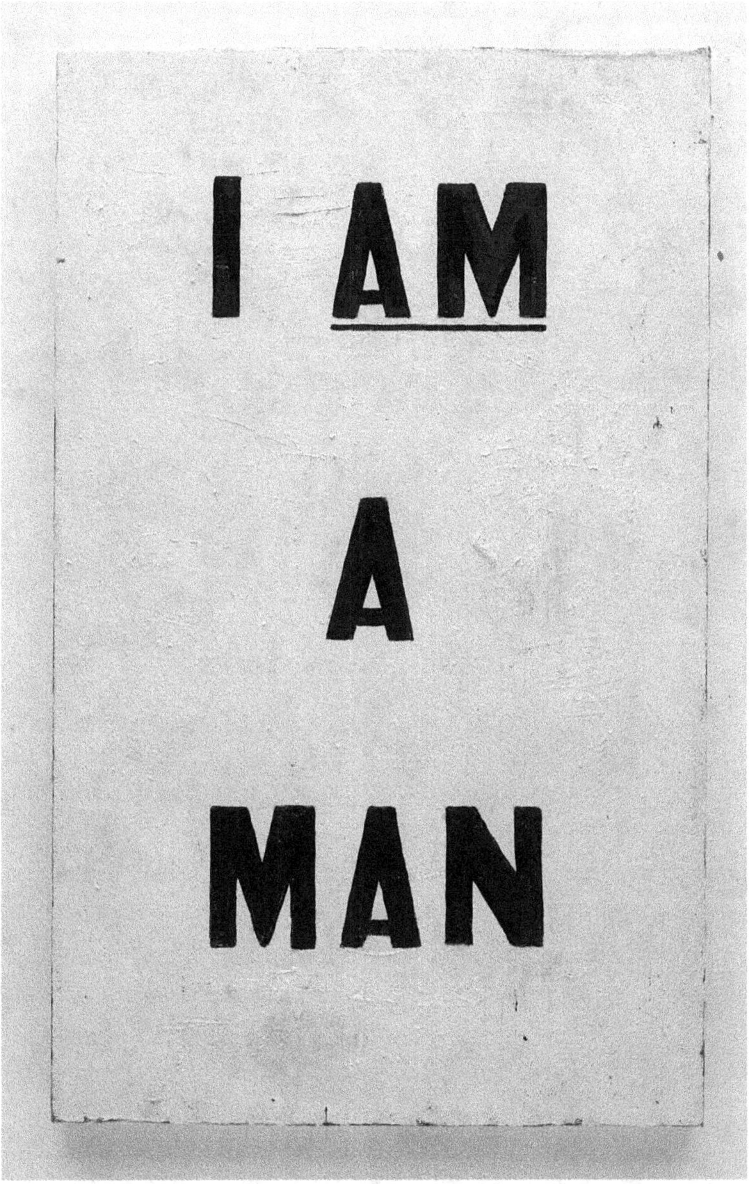
I AM
A
MAN

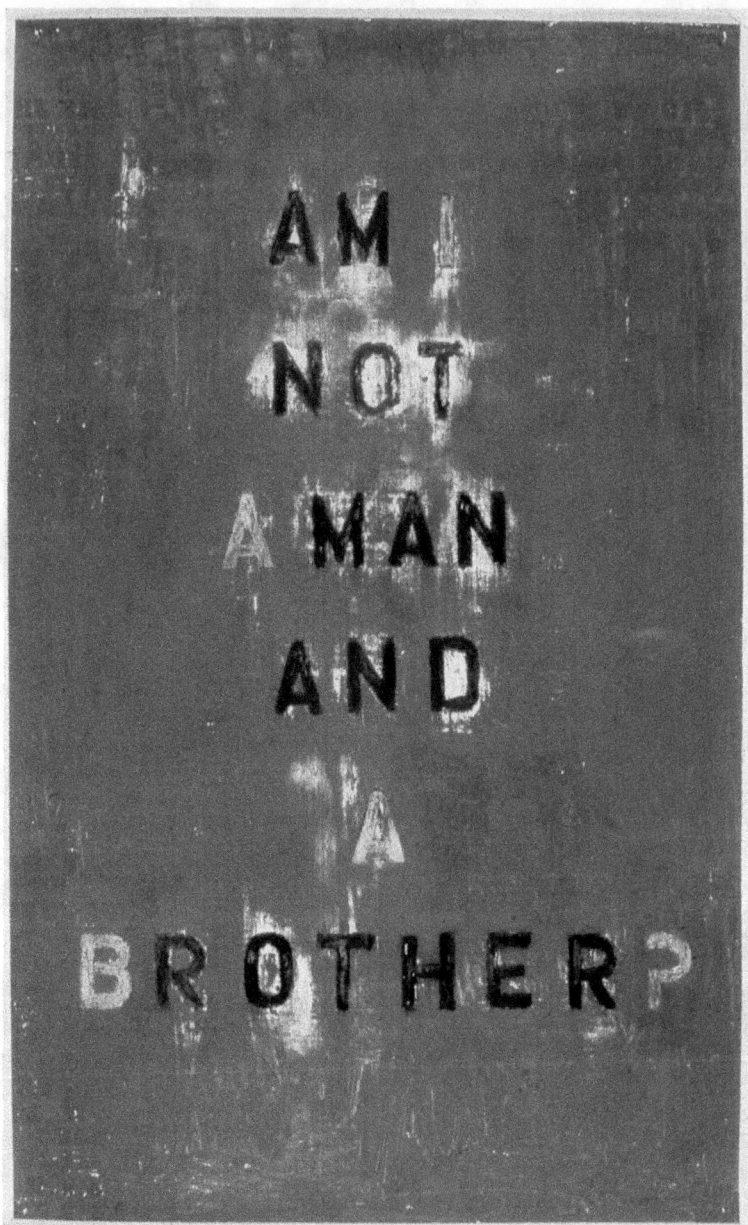

FIGURE 1.6 Glenn Ligon, *Untitled (Am I Not a Man and a Brother)*, 1989. Oil on paper, 48 × 30 in. (121.9 × 76.2 cm). © Glenn Ligon. Courtesy of the artist, Hauser & Wirth, New York, Regen Projects, Los Angeles, Thomas Dane Gallery, London, and Chantal Crousel, Paris.

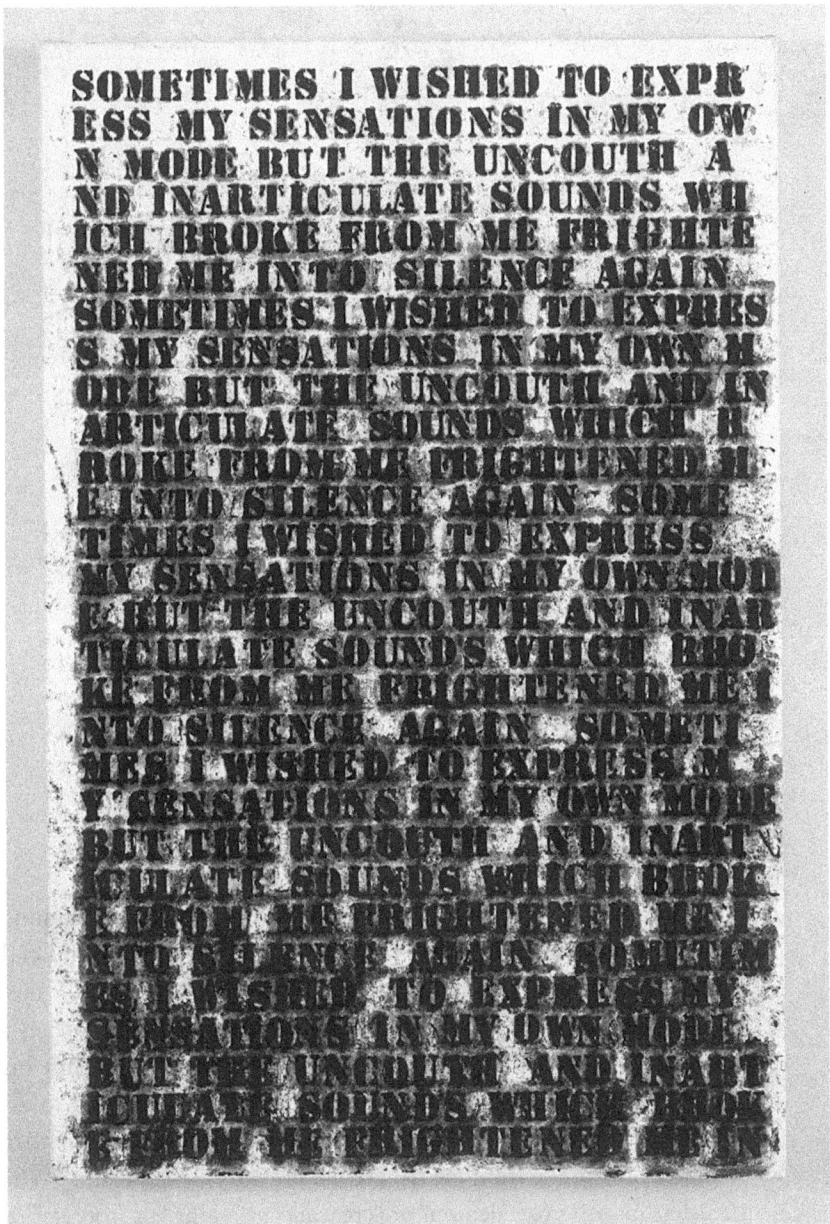

FIGURE 1.7 Glenn Ligon, *Study for Frankenstein #1 (Study #2)*, 1992. Oil stick and gesso on canvas, 30.5 × 20 in. (77.47 × 50.8 cm). © Glenn Ligon. Courtesy of the artist, Hauser & Wirth, New York, Regen Projects, Los Angeles, Thomas Dane Gallery, London, and Chantal Crousel, Paris.

Moten might say, black ~~subjects~~/no-things) on the way to claiming their own sissy monstrosities—or what Jack Halberstam would call their "wildness" and "aesthetic rupture."[54] Indeed, in 1992 Ligon makes three text-based "study" paintings from a sentence in Mary Shelley's *Frankenstein* in which the monster expresses his confusion about his newly formed body and sensory feelings: "Sometimes I wished to express my sensations in my own mode, but the uncouth and inarticulate sounds which broke from me frightened me into silence again."[55] The nameless monster (or "demon" or "creature" or "thing" or "spectre" or "being," as Victor Frankenstein calls him) has just awakened alone in the woods after fleeing the lab where he was constructed, and he has no access to standard language at this point in the book. And yet the repetition of the stenciled black oil-stick sentence multiple times in each of the three paintings—each painting with different line and word breaks, and each becoming increasingly abstracted and unreadable as the sen-

FIGURE 1.8 Anonymous, *Am I Not a Man and a Brother?*, 1837. Woodcut on woven paper, 10.5 ×9 in. (26.7 × 22.8 cm). Image courtesy of the Library of Congress Rare Books and Special Collections Division, Washington, D.C.

tence proliferates and erodes, black smudges scabbing the white paper in Ligon's signature style at that time—has a performative effect on the appropriated language content (in a slightly different mode from how "I AM A MAN" is also a performative). The series of paintings—*Study for Frankenstein #1, Study for Frankenstein #1 (Study #1)*, and *Study for Frankenstein #1 (Study #2)*—expresses by not expressing, performs by not performing, breaking its own uncouth and inarticulate mode of speech out of the not-so-silent visual field again and again, in a wild aesthetic rupture not dissimilar to how No One bears witness for the witness No / One bears / witness /for\ the witness N/o On/es be/ar w/it\ne$s f/or t/he whit\n|e|s|&is.

In 2000, twelve years after Ligon paints *Untitled (I Am a Man)*, he produces a diptych entitled *Condition Report*. The left panel is a reduced-size print of the *Untitled (I Am a Man)* painting, and the right panel is another print of the painting with handwritten annotations by a painting conservator that point to (*monstrare*) the scratches and marks and imperfections that have degraded the painting—and perhaps by inference its subject matter and even its market value. In two interviews Ligon points to the processes of history and bodily mattering that surface in *Condition Report*: "It was about detailing not only the physical aging of the painting over time—all the cracks and paint loss and all of that—but also changing ideas about masculinity, changing ideas about the relationship we have to the Civil Rights Movement."[56] A "hieroglyphics of the flesh" of the painting, its subject and its subject matter made visible, marked, strange, showing the nicks and gashes in Man.[57] Ligon again:

> I think there's a distance between the origins of the sign and me as an artist in the late 80s making a painting of that sign. And one of the ways that the distance between one historical moment and another is measured in the painting is by its cracks, the fact that the painting is aging, the fact that the painting is falling apart, which is, for me,

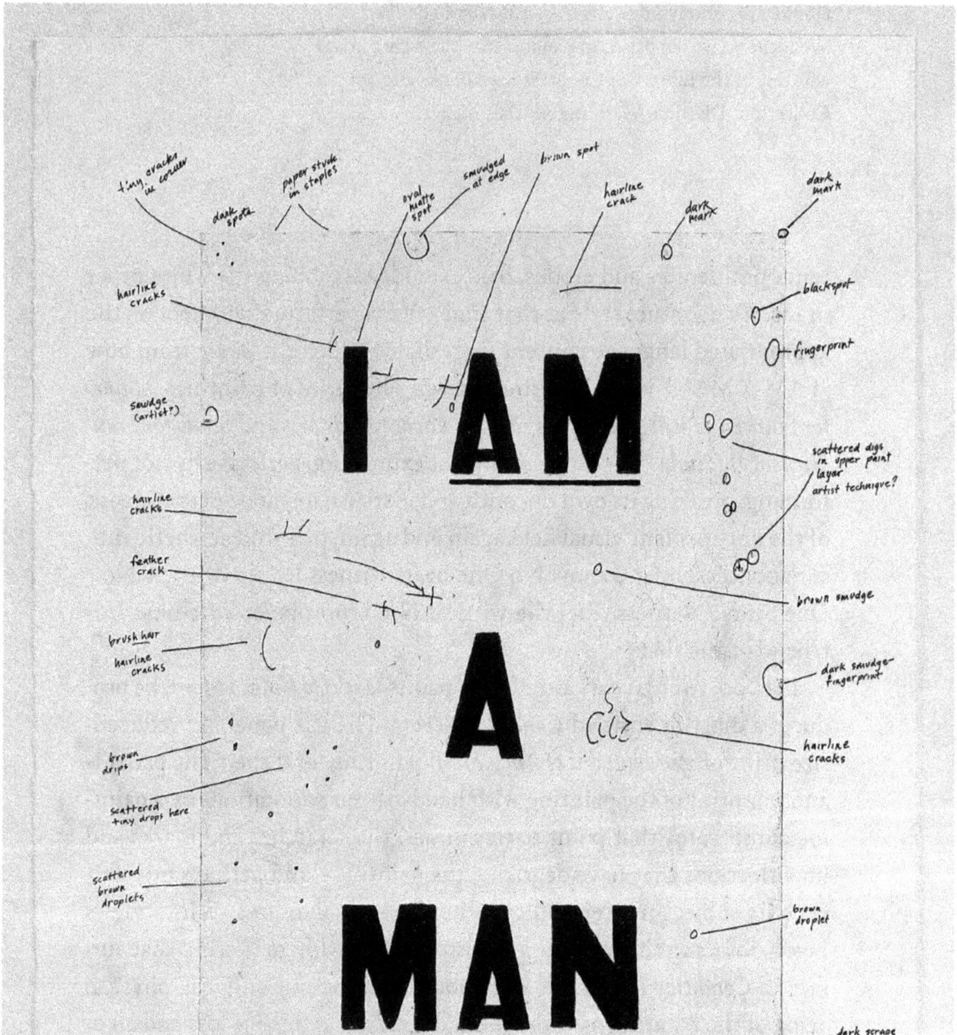
I AM A MAN
tiny cracks in corner
paper stuck in staples
dark spots
oval matte spot
smudged at edge
brown spot
hairline crack
dark mark
dark mark
blackspot
fingerprint
hairline cracks
smudge (artist?)
scattered digs in upper paint layer artist technique?
hairline cracks
feather crack
brown smudge
brush hair
hairline cracks
dark smudge-fingerprint
hairline cracks
brown drips
scattered tiny drops here
scattered brown droplets
brown droplet
dark scrape
rubbed
hairline crack
canvas thread
loss at edge
brown drops
red paint
drops
loss at edge
rust colored droplets
loss at edge
dark spot

about changing notions of what it means to carry a sign that says I AM A MAN, or what it means to make a painting many, many years later of that sign. To think about history as a process rather than a series of fixed events.[58]

One of the signs Hayes carries in *In the Near Future* reads "Never Forgetting," a slight mistranslation of the German *Nie Vergessen*, the iconic demand that Germans and the rest of the world never forget (i.e., always remember) the Nazi holocaust. The addition of the gerund is a fortuitous error in time that enacts the shuddering processes of history always already (not) not remembering. I think of Douglass's 1855 recollected account of witnessing the monstrous scene of his Aunt Hester being beaten by Captain Anthony many years earlier, and his felt implication in this primal scene, however impossible his responsibility:

> I remember the first time I ever witnessed this horrible exhibition. I was quite a child, but I well remember it, I shall *never forget it* whilst I remember any thing. It was the first of a long series of such outrages, of which I was doomed to be *a witness and a participant*. It struck me with awful force. It was the blood-stained gate, the entrance to the hell of slavery, through which I was about to pass. It was a most terrible spectacle. I wish I could commit to paper the feelings with which I beheld it.[59]

Below is a kind of aesthetic rupture or poem made from copying down the conservator's words in the right panel of Ligon's *Condition Report* as they appear in their own mode. The poem travails counterclockwise from the upper left-hand corner and preserves the conservator's line breaks for each comment, while removing spaces between comments.[60] Somehow the hieroglyphics/orthography/uncouth and inarticulate sounds of the report/poem speak more than I can to now-time in the United States, time of raging white supremacy, not-so-latent fascism, and state-sanctioned black death—and always ongoing black life, sur-vival, *superstes*, witness. Perhaps the tiny direct and indirect cracks

---

FIGURE 1.9 Glenn Ligon, *Condition Report*, 2000. Iris print with serigraph, one of two parts, each 32 × 22.75 in. (81.3 × 57.8 cm). Published by Jean Noblet Studio. © Glenn Ligon. Courtesy of the artist, Hauser & Wirth, New York, Regen Projects, Los Angeles, Thomas Dane Gallery, London, and Chantal Crousel, Paris.

in the sign and the photograph and the action and the painting and the print and the poem and the walk and the holding and the protest and the scene are delicately constructed errors in and outside time and space, discursive monsters that may, perhaps, also be strait gates letting in new forms of life beyond space-time in Ferreira da Silva's notion of plenum, new experimental entanglements that make, as Moten notes, "continually rewound and remade claim[s] upon our monstrosity—our miracle, our showing, which is neither near nor far."[61] For Derrida, "the future is necessarily monstrous: the figure of the future, that is, that which can only be surprising, that for which we are not prepared, you see, is heralded by species of monsters....All experience open to the future is prepared or prepares itself to welcome the monstrous *arrivant*.... This is the movement of culture."[62] And that future will have been an *arrivance* without arrival, because the Never Men will have always already been sur-viving.

Never Forgetting Never Man

tiny cracks
in corner
hairline
cracks
smudge
(artist?)
hairline
cracks
feather
crack
brush hair
hairline
cracks
brown
drips
scattered
tiny drops here
scattered
brown
droplets
hairline

crack
canvas
thread
loss at
edge
brown
drops
red
paint
drops
loss
at edge
rust colored
droplets
loss
at edge
dark spot
rubbed
dark scrape
brown
droplet
hairline
cracks
dark smudge—
fingerprint
brown smudge
scattered digs
in upper paint
layer
artist technique?
fingerprint
blackspot
dark
mark
dark
mark
hairline
crack
brown spot

smudged
at edge
oval
matte
spot
paper stuck
in staples
dark
spots

....

2

[ ]

No reading of (the words mark a ritual,
annular enactment—a fall: the sentence
was broken here; a caesura—even, one
could say, of the caesura—has occurred.
You could bridge the gap with one of many
simple denotations supposed to get to the
ensemble of what I want you, now, to hear,
but that would have already been unfaithful
to the truth and attention carried in the
name of what, now, I would have you hear.
But this will not be a meditation on the
idiom of) *Chinampas*.

FRED MOTEN

STUDY · Two lovers, both poets, live in two cities in two countries. They have yet to touch bodies, but speak every day on the telephone. On the telephone, they share intimate presence and histories, feel inner spaces opening along pathways mutual soundings caress. An opening borne by listening, which is also waiting, extending, and enflaming, *attendre*. A lesbian speaks, and another attends. Interval as "the interruption that introduces waiting," infinitely stopping an ending happening.[1] "I am thinking about how much I like the spaces in our conversation, like rests before the next movement." Caesura before response a kind of touch, like the hyphen between *peut* and *être*, or the blank between "No" and "One," a potential space, of proximity and strangeness, multiplicity and becoming; perhaps something like Blanchot's elusive "relation of the third kind"—a "space of attention….the attention of no one" where "habitual possibilities steal away"—but with less of Blanchot's impersonal neutering and more of Moten's fugitivity and Glissant's rhizomatic Relation.[2] A witnessing attention like the poem's "attention... to all that it encounters" on its way, the poets' held "difference without separability" a caesura of the caesura, a fall, "as if the ground rose to the surface, without ceasing to be ground."[3] As they wait to touch, they caress.

....

In several English translations of the pronoun Niemand in Celan's poem "Aschenglorie," a caesura appears between "No" and "one," as is grammatically "proper" in this language (even though a caesura does not appear in German). It is a perhaps dangerous pause that one translator, Joris, first closes in "Noone," then morphs to "Nobody," then opens back up to "No one."[4] What happens in this caesura, this opening gesture that could also connote a limit or threshold or abyss or hold? What happens if we remain, as Moten suggests, "in the hold" (for Moten, in the hold of black music and the slave ship)?[5] For Derrida, caesura in Celan designates "that which, in the body and in the rhythm of the poem, seems most *decisive*. A *decision*, as its name indicates, always appears *as* interruption, it decides *inasmuch* as it is a cut that tears."[6] And yet it is important to question what constitutes decisiveness. For Ferreira da Silva, "the arsenal of raciality...produces the racial subaltern subject as a mind that cannot occupy the seat of decision."[7] The racial subaltern "no-bodies" Ferreira da Silva writes about are "outer-determined" and subject to what Moten might call "a caesura through seizure."[8] The caesura is etymologically a space of wounding, cut, trauma, a monstrous shudder during which, here, perhaps, we can hear "No [O]ne's voice."[9] Derrida:

> Gap or hiatus: the open mouth. To give and receive.
> The caesura sometimes takes your breath away.
> When luck is with it, it's to let you speak.[10]

No One does indeed speak, in and as a (non)performative gesture—bearing witness for the witness *happens* by way of No One's monstrous, impossible voice—a voice that may say nothing at all. For Blanchot, "the writer belongs to a language which no one speaks, which is addressed to no one, which has no center, and which reveals nothing."[11] Moten's theorizing of blackness and nothingness and nonperformance demands a "refusal of the solo...that is refused," a refusal of individuation as one consents not to be a single being; in turn, staying in the hold, the break, the caesura through seizure, in "negation's affirmative space," and speaking (or not) from no standpoint while "claim[ing] the monstrosity of obscene social life" and the "nothingness that surpasses understanding."[12] No One's voice and language and witness all dwell in this hold, embracing the unassimilable thing/Das Ding-liness of no-thingness. For Moten, "only no thing can pass through this blood stain'd, gateless gate; in terrible return and renewal, no thing is all we can enjoy. This is the facticity of blackness, which we might begin to think of as its nonperformance."[13] And to punctuate the jouissance of the incalculable no-thing, "it's like we have to enjoy all monsters in order to destroy all monsters."[14]

For Moten, "blackness is the anoriginal displacement of ontology"; for Wilderson, there is an "aporia between Black *being* and political ontology."[15] Perhaps the gap, hiatus, caesura, displacement, or aporia between "No" and "One" enacts an "interruption of being," or an interruption before (as in *in the face of*) being, opening through seizure the possibility of monstrating and becoming No One.[16] For Blanchot, "the body of no one, of the interval: being's suspense, a seizure like a cut in time."[17] A cut in time that is an im/possible decision, in translation. Or a moment of undecidability, an aporia, where thinking resides. Or, more flagrantly, caesura like Benjamin's "sign of a messianic arrest of happening"—historical materialism's "revolutionary restitution of temporality" that "functions as an assemblage of freedom."[18] Or, from another angle, gap like Agamben's disjunctive remains:

> In the concept of remnant, the aporia of testimony coincides with the aporia of messianism. Just as the remnant of Israel signifies neither the whole nor a part of the people, but, rather, the non-coincidence of the whole and the part, and just as messianic time is neither historical time nor eternity but, rather, *the disjunction that divides them*, so the remnants of Auschwitz—the witnesses—are neither the dead nor the survivors, neither the drowned nor the saved. They are what remains between them.[19]

Yet I don't believe No One as witness resides in the infamous liminal "gray zone" between Primo Levi's drowned and saved, or entwined victim and executioner—what Agamben deems an exceptionalist "zone of indistinction" between inside and outside.[20] Like Moten, I think a notion of a gray in-between "ends up reinforcing the very binary you want to undo."[21] Rather, No One occupies a dangerous other space and time drawn not from a dialectics of inside/outside but from the other roots of "witness": in Latin, *terstis* (third), *superstes* (sur-vivor of, standing over, another's death; *one who holds themselves to the thing*), and *testes* (balls), with *auctor* (author) having a witnessing root as well.[22] Not in-between inside and outside but in the break, a space Moten as a "brutally unauthorized author" claims, a space of and in the hold, in caesura through seizure—an incalculable, innumerable, ensemblic space:[23]

> What it is to be given (as) something to hold, always in common, has really got a hold on me. It's not mine but it's all I have. I who have nothing, I who am no one, I who am not one. I can't say it and I can't get over it. I can't fathom it and I can't grasp it. It opens everything and, in that exhaustion of what it is to acquire, a choir is set to work. More and less than tired, more and less than one, we just want to sing that name, which is not the only name, though it's not just any name. Movement in the history of that name and naming is insistence in the history of study. Theory of blackness is theory of the surreal presence— not in between some things and nothing is the held fleshliness of the collective head.[24]

In the midst of a specious argument for the Muselmann of the Nazi camps as "the final biopolitical substance to be isolated in the biological continuum," Agamben declaims, "At the point in which the *Häftling* [inmate of the Nazi camps] becomes a *Muselmann*, the biopolitics of racism so to speak transcends race, penetrating into a threshold in which it is no longer possible to establish caesuras."[25] In response, Weheliye wryly asks, "How can racism—biopolitical or otherwise—exist without race?"[26]

Spillers positions the black woman as "interstice," abyssal caesura, "the principal point of passage between the human and the non-human world."[27] For Weheliye, Spillers's theorization of female flesh ungendered "constitutes a liminal zone comprising legal and extralegal subjection, violence, and torture as well as lines of flight from the world of Man in the form of practices, existences, thoughts, desires, dreams, and sounds contemporaneously persisting in the law's spectral shadows."[28] Rather than Agamben's liminal remnants, perhaps No One's plural speech gives off chunks of ungovernable flesh that refuse Man and the human and the one, flesh shot through with chips of Benjamin's messianic now-time, in "a World imaged as endless Poethics: that is, existence toward the beyond of Space-time, where The Thing resists dissolving any attempt to reduce what exists—anyone and everything— to the register of the object, the other, and the commodity," as Ferreira da Silva reimagines Gottfried Wilhelm Leibniz's concept of the plenum through quantum physics and Benjamin's dialectical image.[29] Something like Derrida's profane "messianism without content," No One's incalculable content manifests as an urgent disjunction/injunction to hold, be held, and act in the present, collectively, much as democracy or justice *à venir* may never come.[30] Maybe they will; peut-être they won't. But the world as it is must be destroyed, perhaps by means of a slight, improvised adjustment, for a new world to always already be here. "How can we survive genocide?" ask Harney and Moten in an essay honoring Michael Brown, "his descent, his ascension, his ceremony, his flesh, his animation in and of the maternal ecology—Michael Brown's innovation, as contact, in improvisation. Contact improvisation is how we survive [and have always survived] genocide."[31] No One(s) bear(s) witness for the superstes: outliving, standing nearby in awe, falling.

....

STUDY · Rob Halpern has utilized a certain interruptive punctuation, "[—]," throughout his poetry. He calls this combination of dashes and brackets

a blank or a bar [——] *placeholder for all we can't perceive haunting all we can* like the mark of something withdrawn from sense...a floating caesura separating visible and invisible...audible and inaudible.[32]

Halpern's "hole in sense" or "empty place" or "blank concealed in every sentence" becomes literalized as the narrator, desiring impossible relation at "the limit of what's speakable," in one book (*Music for Porn*) fucks the amputated wound of a fantasized US soldier and in a sequel (*Common Place*) fucks the fantasized dead body of a Yemeni "enemy combatant" detained at the US naval base at Guantánamo Bay, Cuba: "I hollow out a cunt in his corpse *my opening to the other*."[33] This [——] cunt or slash or wound or caesura or hold or line on a page could also resemble the ligature Mohammad Ahmed Abdullah Saleh Al Hanashi, the Yemeni detainee on hunger strike, reportedly fashioned from his underwear elastic and fastened around his own throat to take his own life. In a stance that could be "the opposite of Bartleby's refusal to copy" (25), Halpern's narrator masturbates with one hand and transcribes Al Hanashi's autopsy report with the other, "as if a conceptual procedure *any act of writing* could bring the bodies closer, or at least denote the wounds" (38, italics in original). His relentlessly abject effort to "perceive my body's relation to a detainee's occulted corpse" so as to "allow me to feel the militarization that has captured our social relations" tears the cliché

off a US citizen's mere complicity in his country's ongoing colonial ca-
tastrophes—his wet and aching hand reaching toward address and relation where relation may not actually be desired, "as if my fantasy of being fucked by a Gitmo detainee might resurrect his singularity in a park
or square where I'm not yet prepared to greet him" (155, 79–80). Isn't it
Celan who calls a poem a handshake, a holding? And doesn't Levinas
couple the handshake with complicity?[34] And isn't it Celan who uses
the em-dash caesura to denote a projective relation of nonrelation, a
Blanchotian relation of the third kind, where the "syllables," along with
the two nebbish Jews not-conversing with "nobody and Nobody" in the
mountains, "stand around, waiting," going nowhere, with no-thing, the
unsayable, unpronounceable I—i—o noem?[35] And yet Al Hanashi isn't
invited into conversation with Halpern; Al Hanashi doesn't speak or
have any decision-making capacity in the encounter with Halpern.
He is indeed a racial subaltern subject as nobody in Ferreira da Silva's sense, caught in the caesura through seizure of Halpern's text, his
silent scream resounding through the cunt or slash or wound or hole in
sense.

The hole in sense between Celan's translated "No" and "one" holds
a space for affect, as an excess that circulates between and sticks to
the other syllables in the poem—and to the body of the reader as well.
Affect is a currency Halpern also deploys as shame, disgust, and an-
ger, among other circulations, in the monstrous intimacy of *Common
Place*. His literalization of the nonrelation between the white "American" and the brown "Arab" and "Muslim" body pushes expressive limits
that also push the reader in ways that conceptual poet Kenneth Goldsmith, who is also white and who also transcribed a charged autopsy
report—that of Michael Brown—fails to risk to do. Both writers appropriate the autopsy report's discourse of "unremarkable genitalia" and
other terminology, but perhaps Halpern's excessive fantasized interac-
tions with those genitalia push his text to a limit whereby what seems
a confessional (and of course onanistic) voice is in actuality excessively
impersonal and nonrelational—something like Blanchot's neutral, this
perverted voice abjectly stuck beating off with no money shot (39).[36]
And the reader is left holding the unrecuperable remains of that nonrelation—stickily implicated in its catastrophic, wounded continuance.
Whereas Goldsmith's professed disappearance from and nonresponsi-
bility for the "found" transcribed report (what he deems a "hot text"

meant to help him "hold the stage a bit longer" as an art/poetry star) performs its own (here I'd say unconscious) inversion whereby all that remains visible and audible as he recites the text is his univocal and colonizing cismalehetero white body swaying across the stage in his man-skirt (he wore a skirt in the performance)—the Romantic poet, the One whom the target cismalehetero white reader of conceptual poetry is meant to giggle with conspiratorially (O how the artist shocks and awes) and adore from afar.[37] If a poetics of witness means anything at all, may it not mean this kind of relation.

And yet, even taken as simply an event of language, the excessiveness of Halpern's impersonal relation with Al Hanashi risks spilling over into something apposite to Spillers's racialized "pornotrope":

> This profound intimacy of interlocking detail is disrupted, however, by externally imposed meanings and uses: (1) the captive body as the source of an irresistible, destructive sensuality; (2) at the same time—in stunning contradiction—it is reduced to a thing, to *being for* the captor; (3) in this distance *from* a subject position, the captured sexualities provide a physical and biological expression of "otherness"; (4) as a category of "otherness," the captive body translates into a potential for pornotroping and embodies sheer physical powerlessness that slides into a more general "powerlessness," resonating through various centers of human and social meaning.[38]

Spillers coins "pornotrope" to describe how black suffering (particularly the suffering of enslaved black people) has been depicted in various media for titillated audiences, and Weheliye broadens the theoretical application of pornotrope to the biopolitical thingliness of racializing assemblages in general in the age of endlessly streaming trauma porn displaying black people as always already powerless and dead. Perhaps the term "pornotrope" can be borrowed to help a reader confront the "uncanny monster-terrorist-fag" coined by Jasbir Puar and Amit Rai, now seen lying on a slab in *Common Place*.[39] For Puar and Rai, "the construct of the terrorist relies on a knowledge of sexual perversity (failed heterosexuality, Western notions of the psyche, and a certain queer monstrosity)."[40] They discuss the emasculation of Muslim "terrorists" and invoke Michel Foucault's figuring of western "abnormals" that include the "human monster," the "individual to be corrected," and, coincidentally, the "onanist."[41] Puar and Rai posit that today "the terrorist has become both a monster to be quarantined and an individual to be corrected."[42] Hence Gitmo and its real and figurative tortures. "That's when I drive my tongue inside, like the general public anxious to see his balls snipped off with a pair of scissors, or his whole body disemboweled with a hot iron poker, or even more refined instruments issued by my corps of engineers. So I place a cord around his cock while looking sadly at my own, establishing equivalence between organs and garbage" (68). Halpern's onanistic reading/flaying of the black-and-white marks of Al Hanashi's autopsy report while fantasizing a sexual relation bears pornotropic apposition to Spillers's im/possible reading of the "hieroglyphics of the flesh" in the context of transatlantic slavery:

> The anatomical specifications of rupture, of altered human tissue, take on the objective description of laboratory prose—eyes beaten out, arms, backs, skulls branded, a left jaw, a right ankle, punctured; teeth missing, as the calculated work of iron, whips, chains, knives, the canine patrol, the bullet.
>
> These undecipherable markings on the captive body render a kind of hieroglyphics of the flesh whose severe disjunctures come to be hidden to the cultural seeing by skin color.[43]

Al Hanashi's passivity and general powerlessness in *Common Place* also bring to mind how Agamben describes the origin of the term Muselmann for certain primarily Jewish prisoners in the Nazi camps:

> The most likely explanation of the term can be found in the literal meaning of the Arabic word muslim: the one who submits unconditionally to the will of God. It is this meaning that lies at the origin of the legends concerning Islam's supposed fatalism, legends which are found in European culture starting with the Middle Ages (this deprecatory sense of the term is present in European languages, particularly in Italian). But while the muslim's resignation consists in the conviction that the will of Allah is at work every moment and in even the smallest events, the *Muselmann* of Auschwitz is instead defined by a loss of all will and consciousness. Hence Kogon's statement that in the camps the "relatively large group of men who had long since lost any real will to survive...were called 'Moslems'—men of unconditional fatalism."[44]

As mentioned earlier, Agamben doesn't delve into the racist connotations of the term Muselmann ("deprecatory" is indeed far too mild).

Agamben also describes the Muselmann as "purely receptive" in a state of "being consigned to a passivity."[45] Is this monster-terrorist-fag Muslim on the slab of *Common Place* a purely receptive man of unconditional fatalism, or is he Mohammad Ahmed Abdullah Saleh Al Hanashi, who cannot speak or make a decision except by means of the hieroglyphics of his underwear elastic? Is he a "terrorist assemblage," a necropolitical "body machined together through metal and flesh [and elastic], an assemblage of the organic and the inorganic; a death not of the Self nor of the Other, but both simultaneously"?[46] Is Al Hanashi a monstrous No One?

In an essay at the end of *Common Place*, "Postscript: On Devotional Kink," Halpern describes a conversation with a friend in which the friend asks him, "So what if your Gitmo detainee were the body of a black man imprisoned just down the road in Macomb?" Halpern replies, "Or more to the point, I say, what if his body had been shot in the street and left to bake and whose image saturated the public square?" Halpern then makes a vague reference to James Baldwin writing about blacks, whites, and love and extrapolates it to *"the lovers we already are"* and "a promise of communion, to negate the conditions of radical negation and in doing so abolish the need for my song and its singer" (159, italics in original). I am not sure this passage adequately captures the relations or differences between Halpern's project and one like Goldsmith's, or what Halpern or Goldsmith feels compelled to do with "the most fungible of things, his 'unremarkable genitalia'"(69). Halpern doesn't name the "Yemeni man" in this postscript, a man who is described repeatedly in the book as "my detainee," a kind of literalized powerless property of self-possessed whiteness, or by the blank or bar [——], denoting a yawning and unspeakable absence of Al Hanashi as a life with feelings and thought and history and speech (67).[47] Yes, Al Hanashi's body is "occulted" within the sphere of the US military-industrial complex, and his name has been redacted in several places, including in parts of the June 23, 2009, autopsy report, but does Al Hanashi have to remain an occulted life here in this *Common Place* book? (155).[48] To use Ferreira da Silva's terms, Al Hanashi is an "affectable" "no-body" (or no-thing) "outer-determined" not only by the racial capitalist state but by Halpern in this text: "Whatever totality his dead body / Confirms the thing // — *my pleasure negates*"(56, italics in original).[49]

In *Scenes of Subjection*, Hartman examines a letter Harriet Jacobs writes to an abolitionist colleague about Jacobs's 1861 narrative, *Inci-*

dents in the Life of a Slave Girl: Written by Herself. Hartman is interested in Jacobs's use of em dashes in this letter; for example: "I have striven faithfully to give a true and just account of my own life in slavery. There are some things that I might have made plainer—Woman can whisper her cruel wrongs into the ear of a dear friend much easier than she could record them." Hartman elaborates:

> If one thinks of these dashes and elisions as literal and figurative cuts in the narrative, then they display and displace the searing wounds of the violated and mute body, a body that acts out its remembrances without the symbolic endowments to articulate its history of injury. The dashes, ellipses, and circumlocutions hint at the excluded term by way of the bodies of slave women. The bodies of these women are textual enigmas to be interpreted by the reader since they are literally pregnant with the secrets of slavery.[50]

These dashes appear in the text of Jacobs's *Incidents* as well, performing similar cuts and displacements of the unspeakable, from "But I now entered on my fifteenth year—a sad epoch in the life of a slave girl" to "He peopled my young mind with unclean images, such as only a vile monster could think of. I turned from him with disgust and hatred. But he was my master. I was compelled to live under the same roof with him—where I saw a man forty years my senior daily violating the most sacred commandments of nature."[51] Halpern's "floating caesura" [—] seems to contain two conjoined em dashes but in its supposed status as *"placeholder for all we can't perceive haunting all we can"* could potentially perform a similar hieroglyphic function as Jacobs's incalculable em dashes and ellipses. It could cut into the text, hint at the excluded term, display and displace the searing wounds of Al Hanashi's tortured, violated, and mute body, force the reader to face the textual enigma whose image saturates this *"black site of suffering,"* this public square (163, italics in original). But, alas, it doesn't—and Al Hanashi vanishes in a film of fetishized spunk.

If a poetics of witness means anything at all, may it not mean a relation that disavows the monstrous and indecipherable disjunctions of the flesh—the calculated work of iron, whips, chains, knives, the canine patrol, the bullet, the apparatus, grammar, punctuation, the pen. May it mean Mohammad Ahmed Abdullah Saleh Al Hanashi breaks away from the captured sexuality of blank or bar or cunt or slash or ligature or line on the page or hole in sense that desires to contain his uncontainable flesh and speech. For, as Moten claims, "what's at stake is fugitive movement in and out of the frame, bar, or whatever externally imposed social logic—a movement of escape in and from pursuit, the stealth of the stolen that can be said, since it inheres in every closed circle, to break every enclosure. This fugitive movement is stolen life."[52]

....

one(s)

Again, "No one" conjures "one" like "No light" conjures "light." "One" holds multiple resonances in the slippery space of translation we are dwelling within—from the numeric individual, thing, or instance to the gender-neutral, indefinite pronoun, third-personal singular agreeing with a verb. Drawing on both the poststructuralist and black studies takedowns of the transcendental univocal subject, one could see an argument emerge for No one (and No One) as not one but more than one, or more + less than one, but, more than anything, an argument for saying "No" to one. The translation of Niemand in Celan's poem as the fused neologism Noone perhaps most enacts the kind of entanglement that holds the No One as a virtual life interanimated with incalculable particles, forces, discourses, lines of flight in plenum: "an infinite composition in which each existant's singularity is contingent upon its becoming one possible expression of all the other existants, with which it is entangled beyond space and time," as Ferreira da Silva proposes.[1] Again, as Deleuze and Guattari suggest about minor literature, "there isn't a subject; *there are only collective assemblages of enunciation*."[2] Moten's particular arguments against the individual and individuation are important here:

> So I want to argue, or move in preparation of an argument, for the necessity of a social (meta)physics that violates individuation. Critical discourse on the Shoah and on racial slavery, even in their various divergences, rightly align mechanization (or a kind of mechanistic rationalization) with de-individuation while also recognizing that

de-individuation—the theft of body—is a genocidal operation. Mutu-
ally dismissive analytics of gratuitousness notwithstanding, the slave
ship and the gas chamber are cognate in this regard and, in their separate ways, jointly end at the convergence of death and utility (for only
one of which either one or the other is supposed to stand). There's a
question concerning the requirements of preserving and fostering an
entirely mythic national-subjective hygiene and worldly maturation,
which emerges at the intersection of extermination and fungibility.
At that intersection, individuation and de-individuation orbit one another as mutual conditions of im/possibility operating in and as the
frigid mechanics of an indifference machine. The genocidal erasure of
entanglement and difference is the culmination, and not the refusal, of
the metaphysics of individuation. The serial presentation of outlined,
isolated black bodies, sometimes alone and sometimes in logistical formation, or the brutal merger of emaciated Jewish bodies in collective
graves or clouds of ash, is an extension of that regulative compaction
and dispersive de-animation of ensemble (swarm, field, plenum) whose
inauguration is subjection's all but interminable event.[3]

I am trying to bring an "ensemble (swarm, field, plenum)" entangled
within difference together here now, against Enlightenment notions of
the individual person or subject or transcendental, "transparent I." Ferreira da Silva contrasts the "transparent I" with the "affectable I" of the
rest of the colonized world, the affectable "no-bodies" who constitutively
don't have access to the ethical I-you face-to-face relation.[4] Countering
the individual or one, I am interested in "the general gift and consent of
the *ones* who are out of hand, unowned, ungrasped, fallen, falling."[5] In
how "the ones they threw into the world, so that the world they with-
held from them might be made, unmake that world."[6] And I am interested in what "one" and "they" and "it" can do as slippery third-person
pronouns. Roland Barthes celebrated Émile Benveniste for engendering "a new linguistics of pronouns which shifted the conception of language as utterance, as static object, towards one of language as an act
of expression, that is, towards interlocution, intersubjectivity."[7] Benveniste's "new linguistics of pronouns" is useful for trying to sort out
~~subjects~~ from ~~persons~~.

In his essay "The Nature of Pronouns," Benveniste makes a clear distinction between the first- and second-person pronouns ("I" and "you"
respectively) and the third-person pronoun (Benveniste focuses on "he/

she," but my interest here is in the gender-neutral "one," "they," and "it"). In fact, he claims, "It must be seen that the ordinary definition of the personal pronouns as containing the three terms, *I, you,* and *he,* simply destroys the notion of 'person.' 'Person' belongs only to *I/you* and is lacking in *he*."[8] While "I/you" forms a specular dyad of empty linguistic signs through which every time "you" speak, "you" become an "I" that never refers to an external object, the third-person "he" or "one" or singular "they" operates on another plane, perhaps neutral in the Blanchotian sense of the impersonal ne-utre, neither this one nor the other, neither "I" nor "you." In another essay, "Relationships of Person in the Verb," Benveniste declares, "The 'third person' is not a person; it is really the verbal form whose function is to express the *non-person*."[9] The third person is not restricted to the suffocating (de-)subjectification or (de-)individuation of the I-you discourse dialectic: "Because it does not imply any person, it can take any subject whatsoever or no subject, and this subject, expressed or not, is never posited as a 'person.'"[10] According to Roberto Esposito, the third person "is situated precisely at the point of intersection between no one and anyone: either it is not a person at all, or it is every person. In reality, it is both at the same time."[11] Or perhaps it is "neither and both."[12]

....

STUDY · Born in Manapla, Philippines, Cheena Marie Lo is a genderqueer poet based in Oakland, California.[13] In a 2014 chapbook entitled *Ephemera and Atmospheres,* they explore the contours and contradictions of the nonbinary singular pronoun "they":

> They is a word or form. They substitutes for a noun or a
>   noun phrase.
> They is a particular case of a pro-form.
>
> They denotes an entity of a specific grammatical person:
> first person, second person, third person.
>
> ——
>
> They is paying attention to the rules:
>
> One. A pronoun takes the place of a noun.

Two. The pronoun which replaces the noun must agree with it in these ways:

A subject pronoun must replace a subject noun.
An object pronoun must replace an object noun.

A feminine pronoun must replace a feminine noun.
A masculine pronoun must replace a masculine noun.

A singular pronoun must replace a singular noun.
A plural pronoun must replace a plural noun.

——

They is paying attention to you while you pay attention.

Issues may arise when they is unspecified or unknown.

They is in the middle of the venn diagram of inside and outside.

They is walking the line but sometimes they is on one side while other times they is on another side.

Only they can say which side they are on.

They get tired of saying so most of the time.

They is neutral while at the same time being a marker, they is neither and both.

——

They are standing in a field and they can see everything. They are afraid to take a step in any direction because then their perspective will change.

The window swings open but I don't know what for. It is dirty inside.

There is a difference in seeing and allowing yourself to be seen.

I'm told that the sky in Texas is grey, not blue. The sky can be purple in Arizona sometimes.

A cone of light.

But light comes in on all sides.[14]

"They" was named the 2015 Word of the Year by the American Dialect Society, which issued a press release:

> *They* was recognized by the society for its emerging use as a pronoun to refer to a known person, often as a conscious choice by a person rejecting the traditional gender binary of *he* and *she*....The use of singular *they* builds on centuries of usage, appearing in the work of writers such as Chaucer, Shakespeare, and Jane Austen. In 2015, singular *they* was embraced by the *Washington Post* style guide. Bill Walsh, copy editor for the *Post*, described it as "the only sensible solution to English's lack of a gender-neutral third-person singular personal pronoun."[15]

Light spills on all sides of the suffocating binary, from a third or more space that is absolutely outside and absolutely inside, a space that resembles a fold or, in a spooky Deleuzian image of the hold, "the boat as interior of the exterior."[16] But to be clear, this "they" does not simply represent a third gender. This "they" may take a singular grammatical form here, but it is nonunary and nonbinary, more and less than one or two while also holding three or more. This "they" is another "genre" of life, not simply because, as Wynter monstrates, "'genre' and 'gender' come from the same root."[17] And perhaps female flesh ungendered speaks in and with this "they."

For Deleuze, the "they" bears an intrinsic relation to the event:

> How different this "they" is from that which we encounter in everyday banality. It is the "they" of impersonal and pre-individual singularities, the "they" of the pure event wherein *it* dies in the same way that *it* rains. The splendor of the "they" is the splendor of the event itself or of the fourth person.[18]

The French *on* that the translator translates above as "they" could just as easily be translated as "one" or "it." "It" has been reappropriated as a pronoun, pushing even further into third-or-more-person abstraction than "they." Julian Talamantez Brolaski, a two-spirit and transgender poet and musician of mixed Mescalero and Lipan Apache, Latin@, and European heritages, uses the it pronoun in its daily life and in its poetry. In the poem "pronoun circle-jerk and the dog charlie," Brolaski writes, "i told the group they could call me 'it' / you know like the sky and the grass and / a bird where you can't tell what it is / it, its, itself." In a podcast interview that accompanies the poem on the Poetry Foundation website, Brolaski describes how using the "it" pronoun makes people uncomfortable: "They feel like they may be dehumanizing me. And I was like, exactly!" Brolaski continues, "For me it's expansive rather than degrading. It's actually an honor to be an it."[19] I understand this honoring, and the monstrous event of Michael Brown's murder looms up in now-time, how he was rendered a demonic "it" and killed in the same way that it rains. No One and anyone, neither and both.

For Deleuze, every event is both collective and private, and literature is the exemplary impersonal event where the "fourth person singular," his preindividual form of life "they" or "it," can speak via free indirect discourse.[20] A number of Indigenous languages in North America include an obviative fourth-person form that is distinguished from the third person in relation to proximity in discourse.[21] From another angle, Levinas theorizes *le tiers*, the third, as a transcendent space, an *illeity*, at the foundation of the I-you relationship, but still bound to the ethical two, particularly to the you or other or face so exalted in his philosophy. "The *beyond* from which a face comes is in the third person."[22] While he starts to make a claim for "the possibility of this third direction of radical *unrightness* which escapes the bipolar play of immanence and transcendence" in the "beyond Being" of the third person, he ultimately chooses the one-two punch of transcendence as his secure pole.[23] I am not interested in dwelling too long in one-two-three-four enumeration when what I am actually interested in is the virtual and incalculable, but for Levinas, as with most philosophers, the prospect of conceptualizing something different from immanence and transcendence is unthinkable—Lo: "Issues may arise when they is unspecified or unknown"—even as a question. "The responsibility for the other is an immediacy antecedent to questions, it is proximity. It is troubled and becomes a problem when the third party enters."[24] Perhaps this is why Levinas has so much trouble with the Palestinian question, the question of the third-party neighbor, when it is posed to him by a French journalist in 1982 after the massacres of Palestinians in the Sabra and Shatila refugee camps in Lebanon. The question was: "For the Israeli, isn't the 'other' above all the Palestinian?" His answer:

> My definition of the other is completely different. The other is the neighbour, who is not necessarily kin, but who can be. And in that sense, if you're for the other, you're for the neighbour. But if your neighbour attacks another neighbour or treats him unjustly, what can you do? Then alterity takes on another character, in alterity we can find an enemy, or at least then we are faced with the problem of knowing who is right and who is wrong, who is just and who is unjust. There are people who are wrong.[25]

Indeed, there are people who are wrong rather than unright, like Levinas in this case, and he unconsciously knows it: "The third party introduces a contradiction in the saying whose signification before the other until then went in one direction."[26] One can only imagine the possible geopolitical effects had he answered differently. Or had he not referred to the "underdeveloped Afro-Asiatic masses" threatening Judeo-Christianity and the state of Israel, implying in the interview above that Palestinians had no faces and thus were not subject to an ethical prohibition on murder. "What can you do?," Levinas shrugs, in a not-dissimilar way to his shrug in the face of woman as perennial other.[27] In his desperation to hold on to the oneness of the you, to caress and hold steady the one face of the transcendental ethical other, Levinas ignores the possibility of what other faces, the impure social/political they or it in all its Heideggerian horror, can bring to the question, which some claim is the question of justice over love, but I'd claim is neither and both.

Ultimately, *dévisage* (defacement) may not necessarily be a bad thing for thought; it may actually provoke thought. "They crowd my memory with their faceless presences," writes Levi on the Muselmänner, who *sans* eyes *sans* teeth *sans* face can still somehow "see the Gorgon" (another name for Medusa).[28] For Levi, the Muselmänner are a faceless plural, while for Agamben the Muselmann is one (in)complete witness *sans* relation and always already on the way to death. I submit, co-opting Levi, that no one (face) bears witness; it/there is (co-opting Levinas's anonymous being, *il y a*) not one transcendental face but infinitely entangled faces that are "more and less than one," as Moten would say, or three or more in my version of the third-party or third-"person" witness. "They died a death that was social," Wolfgang Sofsky claims for the Muselmänner, and I hear Orlando Patterson's "social death" constituted in mere/bare/raw black life within US white supremacy.[29] And I hear No One as Moten's "consent not to be a single being" and Ferreira da Silva's differential entanglement among infinite existants. No to One. No Ones.

Lo writes, "They is neutral while at the same time being a marker, they is neither and both."[30] As is one. Blanchot theorizes the concept of the neutral, ne-utre (neither the one nor the other), as an undecidable and impersonal space, a space of writing. Deleuze: "It is not the first two persons that function as the condition for literary enunciation; literature begins only when a third person is born in us that strips us of the power to say 'I' (Blanchot's 'neuter')."[31] For Blanchot, the neuter is not gendered or raced (torn in pieces, not unlike decision, the cut that tears), but in reality it marks and is marked by white cisheteropatriarchy, as most so-called neutral things are. I want another word or form or term for the one(s) and the they(s) and the it(s) and the French *on* and No One, and I'm not sure if Deleuze's destruction/transformation of the *dispositif* of the person into the preindividual event is enough, "an eternity that can only be revealed in a becoming or a landscape that only appears in movement. They are [is] not outside language, but the outside of language."[32] No One is outside of language, but not absolutely, always already shimmering from within, a folded cone of light more + less than one + three or more. No Ones swim in the swarm, field, plenum. And the three is always more than a number; it is incalculable, ungovernable, supernumerary. In the same ash-strewn poem that ends with "No one / bears witness for the / witness," the speaker stands "between two painknots"…"at the threeway," the impossible fork in the path of grasping, holding, understanding, and calls out in apostrophe to "you threeway / hands," invoking a multiform held compli-city (our folded togetherness), "shaken-knotted."[33] No Ones hold hands while Viktor Shklovsky, Russian formalist and purveyor of art-as-defamiliarization, suggests, "There is no third way. This is the way to go."[34]

....

4

No One(s)

Why is it that, in so many places
found in every corner of the global
space, so many human beings face
that which "no one deserves"?

DENISE FERREIRA DA SILVA

I'm told by a native German speaker that Niemand can be translated as something like "no one who ever exists, and who is present for that nonexistence."[1] "Nobody is there," my German friend says, and I hear Abraham's "here I am" call to No one, *Ayn Sauf*, the nothing that is emptiness, potential, and ash; and I hear Moten's "Nobody's there, he says. They occupy"; and I hear Fanon's "I existed triply: I occupied space";[2] and I hear Levi's description of the child Hurbinek:

> Hurbinek was a nobody, a child of death, a child of Auschwitz. He looked about three years old, no one knew anything about him, he could not speak and he had no name; that curious name, Hurbinek, had been given to him by us, perhaps by one of the women who had interpreted with those syllables one of the inarticulate sounds that the baby let out now and again. He was paralysed from the waist down, with atrophied legs, as thin as sticks; but his eyes, lost in his triangular and wasted face, flashed terribly alive, full of demand, assertion, of the will to break loose, to shatter the tomb of his dumbness. The speech he lacked, which no one had bothered to teach him, the need of speech charged his stare with explosive urgency: it was a stare both savage and human, even mature, a judgement, which none of us could support, so heavy was it with force and anguish.[3]

Hurbinek repeatedly utters one word, a "difficult word...something like 'mass-klo,' matisklo," which no one in the camp understands, even though Agamben notes they collectively speak "all the languages of Europe."[4] In the end, as Agamben notes, "Hurbinek's word remains obstinately secret," and Agamben rather poetically posits:

> Perhaps this was the secret word that Levi discerned in the "background noise" of Celan's poetry. And yet in Auschwitz, Levi nevertheless attempted to listen to that to which no one has borne witness, to gather the secret word: *mass-klo, matisklo*. Perhaps every word, every writing is born, in this sense, as testimony. This is why what is borne witness to cannot already be language or writing. It can only be something to which no one has borne witness. And this is the sound that arises from the lacuna, the non-language that one speaks when one is alone, the non-language to which language answers, in which language is born.[5]

Now the insularity of the end of this paragraph is Agamben opportunistically linking the experience of the camps to his earlier theorizing on infancy and language, but I am more interested in the sound of something to which Nobody has borne witness, the (non)language that No One speaks, which is the language of Celan, an "obscure writing" that Levi considers to be an "inarticulate babble...like the rattle of a dying man."[6] Rather than waste energy countering Levi's conservative approach to poetry, let us listen to Glissant honor obscurity:

> I...openly claim the right to obscurity, which is not enclosure, apartheid, or separation. The obscure is simply renouncing the false truths of transparencies. We have suffered greatly from the transparent models of high humanity, of degrees of civilization that must be ceaselessly worked through, of blinding Knowledge....The transparency of the Enlightenment is finally misleading. We must reclaim the right to opacity. It is not necessary to understand someone—in the verb "to understand" [French: *comprendre*] there is the verb "to take" [French: *prendre*]—in order to wish to live with them. When two people stop loving, they usually say to each other, "I no longer understand you." As though to love, it were necessary to understand, that is, to reduce the other to transparency.[7]

Add to that a thought from an essay poet Rae Armantrout writes partly on the colonizing effects of some feminist poetics: "What is the meaning of clarity? Is something clear when you understand it or when it looms up startling you? Is readability equivalent to clarity? What is the relation of readability to convention? How might conventions of legibility enforce social codes?"[8] Perhaps we can say that the obscure and monstrous speech of No One, showing and concealing at the same time, is the breathcrystal clear "babble and babble"/Babel of Celan's "Eepinno," "I—i—o," and "Pallaksch! Pallaksch!"—his "thousand darknesses of murderous speech," which he travails (works) through as he breaks the German language.[9] No One's speech operates on the periphery of language. Perhaps it is also the speech of the uncanny (*unheimlich* can mean "monstrous" in German) creature Odradek, Kafka's star-shaped sort of spool of thread/"broken-down remnant" of "no fixed abode," laughing with "no lungs behind it," no body, just the rustling sound of fallen leaves.[10] "Odradek is the form which things assume in oblivion," claims Benjamin. "They are [is] distorted." Like Kafka's giant bug and his hunchback and his "man who bows his head far down on his chest."[11] Distorted, as how Fanon describes black split subjectivity in the body, the trauma, cut, lesion of being constantly "dissected under white eyes" and "exist[ing] triply"...."in a triple person."[12] As Slavoj Žižek, Eric Santner, and Kenneth Reinhard bluntly state, "If you do not want to talk about Odradek, Gregor Samsa and the *Muselmann*, then shut up about your love for a neighbor."[13] Or, speaking of "background noise," if you do not want to talk about the sounds of enslaved people crossing the Atlantic or ongoing structural black death and antiblackness, then shut up about the Nazi holocaust as an exceptional event. Glissant:

> Since speech was forbidden, slaves camouflaged the word under the provocative intensity of the scream. No one could translate the meaning of what seemed to be nothing but a shout. It was taken to be nothing but the call of a wild animal. This is how dispossessed man organized his speech by weaving it into the apparently meaningless texture of extreme noise.[14]

An interesting passage in Weheliye's *Habeas Viscus* combines Elaine Scarry's description of the "pre-language" of torture with Douglass's memory of the sound of his Aunt Hester being assaulted and a witness description of the Muselmann's idiolect.[15] Weheliye suggests, "Perhaps it might be more useful to construe 'cries and groans,' 'heart-rending shrieks,' 'the mechanical murmurs without content' as language that does not rely on linguistic structures, at least not primarily, to convey meaning, sense, or expression."[16] He is countering Agamben's claim that in the camps, "the impossibility of bearing witness, the 'lacuna' that constitutes human language, collapses, giving way to a different impossibility of bearing witness—that which does not have language."[17] Moten also theorizes a space of (non)language "in the break" for black ~~subjects~~/no-things "where shriek turns speech turns song."[18] And the Muselmann, rather than just being dismissed through Agamben's and Levi's "the Muslims did not speak," has been described as using "his very own jargon by constantly repeating what came to his completely confused mind. The sentences were often incomplete and were illogical, stopping abruptly at random points."[19] Aunt Hester's and Abbey Lincoln's screams, Celan's neologistic erosion of the German language, and Hurbinek's and other Muselmänner's speech all operate in laboratory spaces—"considering 'palaver' or 'gobbledygook' not as degraded forms of the standard but rather as modes of linguistic experimentation," Moten would say.[20] For Weheliye, "to hear Aunt Hester's howls or the Muselmann's repetition merely as pre- or nonlanguage absolves the world of Man from any and all responsibility for bearing witness to the flesh."[21] Despite his efforts to make face-to-face contact with his neighbors, Hurbinek dies without being able to communicate more transparent meaning from his word; he dies "free but not redeemed."[22] For Levi, "nothing remains of him: he bears witness through these words of mine."[23] And yet Hurbinek also remains what Moten would call "flesh that keeps speaking"—and flesh that is not asking to be redeemed.[24]

For Agamben, "it is...possible to understand the decisive function of the camps in the system of Nazi biopolitics. They are not merely the place of death and extermination; they are also, and above all, the site of the production of the *Muselmann*, the final biopolitical substance to be isolated in the biological continuum. Beyond the *Muselmann* lies only the gas chamber."[25] Agamben's torquing of Martin Heidegger's infamous reference to the camps as "warehouse[s] of the fabrication of corpses" presents the Muselmann of the Nazi camps as a consummate homo sacer, a (improbably eschatological) "final biopolitical substance" representing mere or bare life, whose desubjectification occurs through language, experience, and the law.[26] The Muselmann is described by Levi in this way in *If This Is a Man/Survival in Auschwitz*:

> All the mussulmans who finished in the gas chambers have the same story, or more exactly, have no story; they followed the slope down to the bottom, like streams that run down to the sea. On their entry

into the camp, through basic incapacity, or by misfortune, or through some banal accident, they are overcome before they can adapt themselves; they are beaten by time, they do not begin to learn German, to disentangle the infernal knot of laws and prohibitions until their body is already in decay, and nothing can save them from selections or from death by exhaustion. Their life is short, but their number is endless; they, the *Muselmänner*, the drowned, form the backbone of the camp, an anonymous mass, continually renewed and always identical, of non-men who march and labour in silence, the divine spark dead within them, already too empty to really suffer. One hesitates to call them living: one hesitates to call their death death, in the face of which they have no fear, as they are too tired to understand.

They crowd my memory with their faceless presences, and if I could enclose all the evil of our time in one image, I would choose this image which is familiar to me: an emaciated man, with head dropped and shoulders curved, on whose face and in whose eyes not a trace of a thought is to be seen.[27]

Interestingly, when Agamben quotes this passage, he writes "faceless presence," making the Muselmann a singular (Heideggerian) being, when Levi specifically uses the plural "presences," the absent presence of No Ones.[28] Levi's title *If This Is a Man* also monstrates the limits of his conception of what constitutes life in the camps, "this" being the Muselmann nonlife whose thought is not a thought, who has no "face" or "story," whose death is not a death.[29] And yet we know, following Wynter and Weheliye, that there are many genres of the human—and life—beyond Man.

Agamben also attributes a racialized "'Oriental' agony" to the Muselmänner on their way to the "bottom," which contrasts with the lack of any other acknowledgment of racialization of the Muselmänner other than an offhand, problematic line: "In any case, it is certain that, with a kind of ferocious irony, the Jews knew that they would not die at Auschwitz as Jews."[30] We know that Agamben was writing *Remnants of Auschwitz* during the Bosnian War, and he mentions camps from that war in both *Homo Sacer: Sovereign Power and Bare Life* and *Means without End: Notes on Politics*, in which he extravagantly declares the camp "the new biopolitical *nomos* of the planet."[31] Of course the camp is not a new concept at all: the Germans had already set up camps and conducted genocide of the Herero and Namaqua peoples in colonial German South-west Africa in the early 1900s; and Canada and the United States had set up camps and reservations for affectable/disposable Indigenous people long before that, and there are many other examples. But it never occurs to Agamben to make a link between the Muselmänner in the Nazi camps and the Muslims in camps in the former Yugoslavia. To my knowledge, he has never written anything about Muslims being a disposable population in the twenty-first century—nor has he ever written of blackness and disposability. In fact, the only reference to blackness at all in his most recently translated book of the Homo Sacer series, *The Use of Bodies*—a book that opens with an extended consideration of the figure of the enslaved person, albeit only from the Greek and Roman eras—is on "animal captivation" as "the dark jewel set in the clearing of being, the black sun shining in the open."[32] As Weheliye rightly states, "The death camps not only were aimed at extermination, they also produced a surplus, an excess, not just 'an absolute biopolitical substance' but the Muselmann as a racial category....There can never be an absolute biopolitical substance and racializing assemblages cannot escape the flesh."[33]

I wonder if Agamben's definition of the "sovereign ban" would shift in response to the US "Muslim ban" and attempts to ban refugees at the southern-border concentration camps, two examples at the time of this writing. Alas, I am not sure his Holocaust exceptionalism would change much. In *Remnants of Auschwitz*, Agamben, via Levi, describes a soccer match between the SS guards and the *Sonderkommando* (prisoners assigned to work in the gas chambers and crematoria) as the "true horror of the camp" and "our shame" as "spectators of that match, which repeats itself in every match in our stadiums, in every television broadcast, in the normalcy of everyday life. If we do not succeed in understanding that match, in stopping it, there will never be hope."[34] Yet he doesn't push himself to understand that match that "is never over," beyond deeming it a too simplistic "gray zone" where victims supposedly bleed indistinctly into their executioners, ignoring the basics of how power operates in such situations of extremity. Agamben's version of the gray zone and homo sacer and the inhuman in the human doesn't seem to include racialized bodies in now-time, affectable no-bodies who receive protection neither under a law such as habeas corpus nor under a designation (however horrifically tenuous) such as homo sacer—not that these bodies necessarily desire state recognition. Ferreira da Silva writes that "racial subaltern subjects are nobodies" with no access to being "subject[s] of ethical life," their "affectable" bodies counting only as "signifiers of the horizon of death" and "effect[s] of the tools of raciality...in which the state acts only in the name of its own preservation."[35] It bears reemphasizing that, as Weheliye states, "Man represents the western configuration of the human as synonymous with the heteromasculine, white, propertied, and liberal subject that renders all those who do not conform to these characteristics as exploitable nonhumans, literal legal no-bodies."[36] Yet these no-bodies have flesh, these hauntological Never Mans, No Ones, speak and feel and kick the ball and bear witness, together as noise and song and "falling"..."up here under the ground" of more and less than one. Moten:

> This animated urbanity in the cracks of the polis, this community sing whose improvised head reveals a tendency to get cracked in the head by the police, up here under the ground where falling feels like flying because it is and because we all fly when we fall like that, feeling each other in the space where we feel—because we bear—each other as differences, is where the fleshly thing you might have wanted to call a body, moving in and with and through each other in the open field we used to call everybody, populated by those abstract equivalences we call anybody, is given in its most essential form, which is nothing other than that ongoing giving of form that we call the informal, refuge for the no-ones, the not ones, the more + less than ones, the nones who are, in their constantly novitiate, base communitarian devotion, no-bodies.[37]

....

STUDY · June 17, 2008: A figure in orange jumpsuit, shackles, black hood, and black gloves shuffles slowly through Manhattan's midtown in the midday sun *I donned a surface / My ornaments became / the negative matter of the state.*[38] Seemingly unraced, ungendered, and defaced, the figure nonetheless gestures toward the look of a Guantánamo Bay detainee, an "unlawful enemy combatant" with no recourse to habeas corpus *we that is temporary and abundant, something that waits* and who is subject to torture while "we" don't wait but forget. As the representation of homo sacer continues to shuffle silently along the pavement past the glass houses of commerce, the video-poem soundtrack invokes Charles Baudelaire and Ivan Chtcheglov on the *flâneur* and the *dérive*

and Herodotus and Sappho and the Guantánamo secret detainee in-
terrogation logs and a pamphlet called "Interested in Knowing More
about Islam" and Vito Acconci: *I started following people because I had the
desire to be nobody. I was erasing myself. And then, suddenly, my body became the
center of attention.* Through the enforced framing of the camera, we are
watching the orange figure in the video, but on the busy street, people
mostly ignore or look through the figure, a hauntological *ghost, watching
the crowd / entering another person whenever it wished.* Indeed, at one point
people look away from the figure toward the Naked Cowboy *oh that's
just the worst / that's hysterical* and my nostalgic lesbian brain thinks of
how Audre Lorde criticizes that affective stance of looking away from
another's feelings in her essay "Uses of the Erotic: The Erotic as Power."[39]
Using a person like Kleenex and throwing them away. In this case into a
cage that a few chickens might fit inside. A cage that Mohammad Ahmed
Abdullah Saleh Al Hanashi, the Yemeni man in Halpern's *Common Place*,
lived and breathed in until he didn't *I am disturbed that everyone was
talking and he was left there all alone.*

In an essay on the performance and its linked video-poem, *Stalk*,
Laura Elrick, the white artist/poet and figure in the orange jumpsuit,
calls the silent figure "a migrating void...a 'nothing' that is simultaneously an aperture of sight"..."an "absent presence"..."an "it."[40] She draws
from Judith Butler's essay "Torture and the Ethics of Photography,"
on the Abu Ghraib prison debacle, during which invisible US military
torture practices were made all too visible, to comment on how the
state restricts any witnessing of the Guantánamo Bay detainees or their
prison conditions: "The state works on the field of perception and, more
generally, the field of representability, in order to control affect—in anticipation of the way affect is not only structured by interpretation, but
structures interpretation as well. What is at stake is the regulation of
those images that might galvanize political opposition to a war."[41] The
"community of witnesses" watching the performance or the video or
both are caught up in a complicity of seeing and affective disturbance,
even when we look away from the hauntological orange figure.[42] Elrick
suggests that "perhaps this orange figure could be the gash in the collective bodily form that we *look through* to see the contours of past histories of trauma that continue to shape this pseudo-rational national
space....Its absent presence asks how we might begin to sense the historical present, and as answer, the abject, slightly inhuman body (both

as bright as a target and acting as a musculature of vision) draws into focus precisely the underside of the otherwise familiar everyday public space."[43] A figure distorted, like Odradek, like oblivion. Or like Fanon's body and the black bodies in multicolored jumpsuits in the US prison-industrial complex where Jim Crow and the white hoods never left. Elrick asks, "Is the foreclosure of recognition enabled by peripheral vision in fact a *kind* of looking in which one sees (but only peripherally) in order that no thing may return one's look?"[44] Moten might say the kind of looking Elrick describes "cannot be sustained as unalloyed looking but must be accompanied by listening," and in fact Elrick deliberately reverses a quotation from Georg Simmel on seeing and hearing in the video soundtrack, in which she says, "Someone who hears without seeing is much more uneasy than someone who sees without hearing."[45] The original Simmel line, as quoted by Benjamin in *The Arcades Project*, is "Therefore the one who sees, without hearing, is much more... worried than the one who hears without seeing."[46] I would argue, with Moten, that all the senses accompanying one other synesthetically is a more fruitful proposition than a binary relation, especially fruitful when also accompanied by some kind of response-ability.[47]

Elrick is influenced by 1970s and later feminist performance art by Yoko Ono, Marina Abramović, and others in which the performer

places their body in abject situations, vulnerable to attack, in an effort
to literalize some of the psychic and physical violences certain marked
bodies face daily. Elrick did not experience attack during her two-hour
performance, but perhaps she could have, and she uses what Butler
calls "the mobilizing power of injury" to challenge viewers not to deny
what can't be seen, but rather to experience—to see and feel and listen
to—"a hole punctured through" this more + less than single + third or
more figure, "it."[48]

In the video-poem, the narrator asks, "can you see that my hair's
blond? *through* it. in the sunlight?" and I wonder how this performance
would change if a brown or black person were doing it, how the threat
of injury would be exponentially higher. As it is for Dread Scott shuffling down the street with his iconic sign, or, as we shall see, for Bhanu
Kapil lying (or laying) down in the site of Jyoti Singh Pandey's rape and
murder.[49] A threat of injury Sharon Hayes also doesn't seem to face,
even when questioned by police during her performance. Elrick's gesture of "publicly perform[ing] a negation of the self," her emptying of
her white author function while wearing the uniform of the all-too-
fungible brown and black detainee, does seem to resonate on a different
register from Halpern's narrator's fraught imaginary relation to "his"
detainee.[50] Elrick's gesture does not seem to be about the onanistic one;
nor do I think it is about the secondary or proxy witness or the prosopo-
poeic act of taking on or putting back the face of the other or the dead
in a form of empathic identification.[51] Elrick as a kind of "it" or No One
does not bear witness *for* the detainee. Rather, she enacts a defaced positionality that forces viewers and listeners to generate response-ability
for *our* complicit (folded together) nonwitnessing of state-sanctioned
torture under racial capitalism and empire, mobilizing affects that stick
to us—and may perhaps provoke action.[52] As Harney and Moten remind us, "What one might call the social life of things is important
only insofar as it allows us to imagine that social life is not a relation
between things but is, rather, that field of rub and rupture that works,
that is the work of, [N]o [O]ne, nothing, in its empathic richness."[53] In
the middle of Manhattan, Elrick places "the constitutive outside of US

'freedoms' back in the heart of the cycles of work, consumption and leisure to which it is tied" and draws a community of witnesses toward fleshly empathy *I am the natural role for the public square...I calmly recognize there's a ghost before me...I go to see* [and listen to] *a vast* [and dangerous] *perhaps.*[54]

....

5

bear(s)

You are informed that human beings endowed with language were placed in a situation such that none of them is now able to tell about it. Most of them disappeared then, and the survivors rarely speak about it. When they do speak about it, their testimony bears only upon a minute part of this situation. How can you know that the situation itself existed? That it is not the fruit of your informant's imagination? Either the situation did not exist as such. Or else it did exist, in which case your informant's testimony is false, either because he or she should have disappeared, or else because he or she should remain silent, or else because, if he or she does speak, he or she can bear witness only to the particular experience he had, it remaining to be established whether this experience was a component of the situation in question.

JEAN-FRANÇOIS LYOTARD

In some translations of *Niemand / zeugt für den / Zeugen*, there is no "bears" or bearing made. In those cases, zeugt is translated as "testifies" or "witnesses," so "No one / testifies for the / witness" or "Nobody / witnesses the / witness," and "bears" disappears (as does the unheimlich "for" in the latter translation). Yet zeugt contains within it a bearing, a turn, a generative force that wants to show itself, be monstrous, as zeugt also bears "to show" within it.[1] As Kelly Oliver has written, bearing witness holds a different bearing from testimony; it speaks for something beyond knowledge and recognition.[2] Psychoanalyst Dori Laub gives an account of an unnamed Auschwitz survivor who remembered four chimneys blowing up at Auschwitz during the failed prisoner uprising there, and how a group of Yale historians discounted her testimony because it failed their conditions of truth (there was only one tower; once again we can't escape the one).[3] And yet her bearing witness bore its own truth that was incalculable by knowledge or logic, nor by Lyotard's differend that opens this chapter and his book—the problem of what we "really see with our own eyes," the problem of evidence, and testifying to what cannot be seen or heard, "present[ing] the unpresentable," the strange, unheimlich, monstrous.[4] How does the Auschwitz survivor's crisis of witnessing relate to the crisis of witnessing that Hartman identifies as central to plantation slavery and its afterlives, the "legal incapacity of slaves or free blacks to act as witnesses against whites"?[5] Lyotard suggests perhaps new idioms are needed for "victims" (Lyotard's insufficient word) of atrocity to speak, "idioms which do not yet exist."[6] And yet sur-vivors and epigenetic bearers of evental and ongoing racialized atrocity have always and will always speak the unspeakable through "modes of lingusitic experimentation," beyond knowledge and recognition and the just-us system, always already entangled within the swarm, field, plenum.[7]

That speech may need to be *trans-lated*, however; there may need to be a *bearing-across*, a carrying of the load, a bridge, an engendering, a bearing within what cannot be borne, and what may be indecipherable. You must become a foreigner in your own language, as Deleuze and Guattari suggest about the minor writers. Psychoanalyst Jean Laplanche writes about the "obligation to translate" as a primal condition borne by receiving "messages perceived as enigmatic" in childhood, messages from the adult world that a child can't contain, bear, calculate, and that create an "internal foreign body," an internal other.[8] Nevertheless, "you must translate because it's untranslatable," claims Laplanche with a Derridean bearing.[9] This transferential ground becomes a space for response-ability, Oliver would say, or openness as susceptibility, dispossession, Butler would say.[10] That is, if you are deemed to possess a "proper" sovereign self and story and life. As Sexton notes, "It may be that the remedy to dispossession lies not in the spirit of claiming or reclaiming possession but in the paradox of an even greater and willed dispossession. But how, under constant assault, to defend what cannot be possessed?"[11] Perhaps the only way to defend what cannot be possessed is through unsovereign self-less and land-less existence. "No ground for identity, no ground to stand (on). Everyone has a claim to everything until no one has a claim to anything. No claim."[12] Nothing for No One.[13] Abolition of property and the proper. "The flesh of the earth demands it."[14] But is it possible, under constant assault, to defend the land-less, self-less swarm, field, plenum of the incalculable oceanic dead?

....

STUDY · Fragmentation is also about more, an initiation of the work's interior
social life, a rending of that interiority by the outside that materializes
it. The logic of the supplement is instantiated with every blur, every
gliss, every melismatic torque, every twist of the drone, every turn of
held syllable. I want to attend to the necessary polyphony. I don't want
to represent anything and I don't want to repair anything but I do want
to be here more, in another way. I think, in the end, *Zong!* works this
way but even if it doesn't work this way I want it to work this way. I
want to work it this way, in coded memory, as the history of no repair,
as the ongoing event of more and less than representing. *Zong!* is about
what hasn't happened yet. It is a bridge, which is to say a witness, to
the ecstatic and general before. It moves in the irreducible, multiply
lined relation between document and speculation, where the laws of
time and history, of physics and biochemistry, are suspended, remade,
in transubstantiation. The ones who have been rendered speechless are
given to and by a speaker, in code, whose message, finally, is that there
is speech, that there will have been speech, that radical enunciation
(announcement, prophecy, preface, introduction) is being offered in its
irreducible animateriality. No mercantile citizenship, no transcendental subject, no neurotypical self matters as much as this: the refusal of
administration by those who are destined for a life of being thrown,
thrown out, thrown over, overlooked for their enthusiasms, which
they keep having to learn to look for and honor in having been thrown,
which keep coming to them, which they keep on coming upon, always
up ahead, again and again from way back, as out recording, submerged
encoding, faded script that can't be faded, joining the sound of the
ones who have (been) sounded, under an absolute duress of water,
flesh that keeps speaking to us here and now, in contratechnical,
counterstrophic, macrophonic amplification of the incalculable.
FRED MOTEN

Zong!, a "story that cannot be told, yet must be told," is told "through
not-telling" to M. NourbeSe Philip by a conjured ancestor, Setaey
Adamu Boateng.[15] *Zong!* is 182 pages of poetry constructed solely from
the words and letters and words within words borne on two white pages

of one legal decision, cut, trauma, exploded wound of a text. The decision, *Gregson v. Gilbert*, is the only existing public document concerning the murder by throwing overboard of 150 Africans from the slave ship *Zong* in November 1781, and the insurance money one party thinks is owed to the other party as recompense for their destroyed cargo (i.e., black lives).

In *Zong!*, Philip, a former lawyer, "lock[s]" herself into the "particular and peculiar discursive landscape" of this legal decision ("the case is the tombstone") in her quest to "defend the dead" (191, 194, 25). Locked in the hold of the text (and imaginatively in the hold of the ship), she "disassemble[s] the ordered, to create disorder and mayhem so as to release the story that cannot be told" (199), a gesture that brings to mind how Hartman "long[s] to write a new story...disordering and transgressing the protocols of the archive and the authority of its statements."[16] Philip is another "brutally unauthorized author" who "murder[s] the text" of the murderous law that would never authorize her as terstis, third, witness, "to chart the outline of the wound" (193, 196).[17] *Zong!* holds an exclamation mark that makes no sound when you add it but bears a scream, moan, shriek, sob, song at the thresholds of language and meaning.

Zong! bears a hauntological disposition that appears perhaps most strikingly in its last section, "Ẹ̀bọra," in which a random printing error, a "spectral errancy of words," Derrida might say, produces seven pages of noisy ghost text.[18] On the last of these seven pages, the last page of poetry in the book (see figure 5.1), "the spectres of the undead make themselves present" as gray underwater spirits (Yoruba, *ẹbọra*) overwrite the author, authority, testimony, speech (201). We cannot read or sound the gray faded script of submerged encoding in the ways we knew before, or even in the ways we have developed by dysfluently moving through *Zong!*'s waves of water, wind, and scream. The reader as witness to *Zong!* must sound out "crumped," mutilated, illegible syllables, amplifying incalculable flesh that keeps speaking to us here and now.[19] We are complicit—folded together with—and "contaminated by" the text as we "piec[e] together the story that cannot be told" (198). *Zong!* is "language of grunt and groan, of moan and stutter—this language of pure

FIGURE 5.1 Final page of poetry in M. NourbeSe Philip's
book *Zong!*, 2008. Wesleyan University Press.

found   as neghees knows   gin my us   in afric?
y/our ear   a round piggroth any are   rum   my faith negroes
thargo dere aster/s   oh   oh   our *nigrolem cum fo mi* found africa   the mast must be teak men
atedatim the deed   under who can cure me   supudocs ap afingain
vofaics &   wate nptainver   for *yo* the cur   that that   proved
      justis lerg towse from   *dangeren sleor je ifa* that hat
th evort   the law my liegh lord   deep   *pour nisu life* cut the cards
       days   *parousie* *   nfidydig &nder from *ifa i*   I won the throw
  weeks   my plea is negligem by fitath the field her   sos sust sifting as so fighg *gluce*
fa   monthie   from us   i say   of whumbs leory *doge*
comes fate camo   for *osmortafity* bulhmilgnerutnu osaces   she smiles
cut her open   in live all be *friends* justice stars *into* be   b smile
  the noise *mbe* cortient the cruck kinds 1   in lives & am   a dischfulge
intidutekinivart   as thimnis   oveam   savetonsking   throw fabing
     le p'iit mthe crew *weighih gu/baithlv* entamlsley   *Ruth*   throw them
                 acealt of mortality   in rations murder sthdie is fate crusts
but why Rithe neinesum   am   tone & Gave the seerthere is creed
      tharbones   she do the stars   appi gnig nig   if   shine   there isunder   if only
          & fipls inmiutder nifde us   & *yong* wherby sny side   oh oh
her shap *faifaifa*   salve our souls th fohne srdee again
  with mip eanfibilirg: if only *ifa*   nag   tust thistense   *ifa ifa ifa i*
serve   round   bhnosenis   is all wrongort   the the *oba* sobs again
and fitheveearmen   rum raih night   ovethere was piss *cum*
seas   more rum   & *miisthehddlga comginh* Ruth
thxjxentves   thiruikxxhxxm *somora*   salve the slave   they sang &
withixfenursjrn and and   my fortades   sanghe wimod-t with sinwe map
      uncommdre xclespshtoo *salve*   *ora proyou* sithdlu sighteraiwater/s leak   time
   vid she *vid* negrousleo   withine a seandtf sike flealydg   putxables & x the hizth
tnemarkethis iexhletovxegioond   tinadpody *sang*   avcord   such
thb kutpbalfittípgs her   i say   groamve   a rose i pen thisthrough thedhylighttxh fattercfather
jxlxmherthcrost for Ruthfat nig   dugs here aher teanildeserne thcver seeryxtxxkxt
thxgat gojxtxxontx sjtuthere vxxd   lotlxh nfexhiem all lord   payment
ruthGod   no we were write   for trusth to   *yafdlxsgod youa* lace cap for my what for
phtCrodst hear mxf   canllisthxenixixltyts   of luxcon lifixmutihppsxpppose trplfy the negroes with
                toys   ovxbxjphiniletxdhxnthxn   do you hear the lute
fniidinglady *gold*   foshould cut the cord of this story sound to rahe *oba* sobs
take every thingxlebuyiffonidteen   on   from rest my case
cum granot hexhfiiceln   a songov gxxoshextt isapport   sow   in negligence
with a grain of salt   dire visions at vesperse hhear unrptell /smy pilte ightxaxgtnightwater parts
          the belfing ought evidence: thextlxngxfxlxllxwrongfxoh/death necessity
theae Ruth reed   then   vedic   munxlxivoni   negroxx   *ave* t doryou
thisnixixfulo negxxxgxxgxnbst surlenth   a rosepromxghtxyou   to *ile ife*
told cold   athlxfixixmxiax snxgroes   sow the sea   npxrdxr my lord
kujxxlxxx8kixxmy liegxfxxdum   sxxlvxlhixsteording
trim hixxpfxtxxwxxavlith sos   dexvidegxolxuth   *os*   wxysxelex &
kithxtoo us   I dml she tdxlsatio   Ben   reason

sound fragmented and broken by history" (205). How do I pronounce something that does and doesn't look like pare~~rime~~** or paro~~rimne~~** or para~~nime~~** (182)? What does an asterisk sound like? How do I trans-late its hieroglyphics, how do I bear the fragments of this poem across this page? In *Zong!*, "the African, transformed into a thing by the law, is re-transformed, miraculously, back into human" (196). *Zong!* is "an act of transubstantiation" from bone through saltwater-abyss to body of page, an enactment of the actual-virtuality that Ferreira da Silva sees as "sig-nal[ing] the kind of imaging of the World announcing a Black Feminist Poethics...a possibility [that] breaks through the formal lines of space inscribed by our categories (of body, of species, of genus)"—and breaks through the formal boundaries and internal ordering of the categories of poetry, grammar, and ethics—to act as a guide "for the imagination" entangled in a swarm, field, plenum beyond space-time (196).[20] *Zong!* is jurisgenerative, bearing what Moten calls its ani*mater*iality in frag-mented ante- and antimeaning as "*Zong!* bears witness to the 'resurfac-ing of the drowned and the oppressed'" (203).[21] In this juristransgenera-tive process, Philip suggests "the fragment becomes mine. Becomes me. Is me" (205), and Ferreira da Silva might suggest "her flesh also becomes what her body had changed in to or healed."[22] Addressing the impossi-ble question of what happened on the *Zong*, Philip wonders, "Could it be that language happened?" (205).

In an essay entitled "Notanda" at the end of *Zong!*, Philip writes that the poems in the four sections entitled "Sal," "Ventus," "Ratio," and "Ferrum" are "a translation of the opacity" of the first section, "Os" (she also calls these four movements the "flesh" of the book); and yet she doesn't mention the opacity and fleshliness of "Ẹbọra," which exercises its right to opacity under an absolute duress of water and haunted letter (206, 200). "Ẹbọra" is fugitive, escapes capture by a reader. The body of this final page bears "hieroglyphics of the flesh," Spillers's "undecipher-able markings" made by "iron, whips, chains, knives, the canine patrol, the bullet"; yet this page/body/Nobody also imprints a sacred carving/writing (*hieros* + glyph) of remnant, excess, fugitivity, inciting a "listen-ing for the unsaid, translating misconstrued words, and refashioning disfigured lives":[23] "but why sum the bones...I won the throw...if only *ifa*...y/our ear...[be]gin my us...i say for *os*...the noise...they sang &...we map...leak time...dire visions...cut her open...there was piss cum...now we were write...all lord payment...of mortality in rations...the seer there is creed...do you hear the lute?...water parts...told cold...the being caught evidence...throw them fate crusts...cut the cord of this story sound to raise *oba* sobs...from irest my case" (182). This page cannot be searched using optical character recognition software; this page cannot be recognized; this page is poethical image, constellation, rhizome, Relation, abyss. Borrowing from Weheliye on the Muselmann's speech and the speech of other detainees, "what is at stake is not so much the lack of language per se, since we have known for a while now that the subaltern cannot speak, but the kinds of dialects available to the subjected and how these are seen and heard by those who bear witness to their plight."[24] Through uncouth and inarticulate sounds (remember *Frankenstein*), "through oath and through moan, through mutter, chant and babble, through babble and curse, through chortle and ululation to not-tell the story" (196). *Zong!* is a bridge, as Moten suggests in the epigraph to this study; it *trans-lates*, *bearing-across* the abyss of the "Trans*Atlantic" (Christina Sharpe's term for the "s/place, condition, or process that appears alongside and in relation to the Black Atlantic but also in excess of its currents"), the white page grayed/blacked out—redacted, Sharpe might say, as evidence of the "orthography of the wake"—and bearing the folded-togetherness of blackness and transness as fugitive forms.[25] *Zong!* is ec-static, beside itself without self, an "open totality of movement" in haunted relation, an open boat thrown in a way Heidegger never imagined.[26] You, reader, may have this animaterial body (of the page) made flesh (habeas viscus), perhaps, but you shall never possess it, or calculate its effects. "If we think of the 'flesh' as a primary narrative, then we mean its seared, divided, ripped-apartness, riveted to the ship's hole, fallen, or 'escaped' overboard," writes Spillers.[27] *Zong!*, like habeas viscus, "translates the hieroglyphics of the flesh into a potentiality in any and all things, an originating leap in the imagining of future anterior freedoms and new genres of humanity."[28] *Zong!* bears witness to this im/potentiality, No One's indecipherable, incalculable speech. Spillers: "This body whose flesh carries the female and male to the frontiers of survival bears in person the marks of a cultural text whose inside has been turned outside," and I hear *Zong!*'s ululating body and flesh alongside the captive body and flesh Spillers attends to.[29]

Zong!'s bearing is also a birthing that zeugt carries (zeugt means "to beget" as well as "to witness," traditionally "to father," but let us honor the mother of begetting and bearing and mater-iality), a generativity from the "womb abyss" of the Middle Passage. For Glissant, the slave ship "is a womb, a womb abyss....This boat is your womb, a matrix, and yet it expels you. This boat: pregnant with as many dead as living under sentence of death."[30] This bearing, this generativity, and jurisgenerativity, disappears in translations like "No one / witnesses [or "testifies for"] the / witness." The bearing is key. "*They bear me*," writes Moten on the witnessing entanglement and social poesis of blackness.[31] In fact, Celan's "No one / bears witness for the / witness" appears as an epigraph to the "Ratio" movement of *Zong!*, yet with the line breaks not marked, so it reads as a sentence (100). *Zong!* is "the may in become," peut-être No One's emergence in black ink on white paper (35). The author/auctor/ witness may or may not be dead, but there is no testimony without test, error, failure, protest, detest, retest—and "flesh [that] resists the legal idiom of personhood as property."[32] *Zong!* "lives on," not unlike Odradek or the Indigenous "going on of life" that precedes and exceeds colonization: *sur-vivance*, beyond "victimry," kin to *superstes*, survivor, witness, holding to the thing.[33] *Zong!*, itself, is a witness of and to and for radical enunciation in the "afterlife of slavery," as Hartman terms it, or, as Sexton suggests, a "living on that survives after a type of death," a womb abyss.[34] Sexton asks:

> But what if slavery does not die, as it were, because it is immortal, but rather because it is non-mortal, because it has *never* lived, at least not in the psychic life of power? What if the source of slavery's longevity is not its resilience in the face of opposition, but the obscurity of its existence? Not the accumulation of its political capital, but the illegibility of its grammar?[35]

Zong! bears witness to slavery's illegible, indecipherable grammar, its right to uncouth and inarticulate obscurity within the incalculable hieroglyphics of the flesh. *Zong!* bears witness to "the silence of an unheard case, of a muffled appeal consigned to lower frequencies, of disruptive wave and terminally colliding particle where [N]o [O]ne can observe" and listen, touch, taste, smell, scream, shriek, sob, sing.[36] *Zong!* bears witness to flesh that keeps speaking and holding to the thing. *Zong!* defends self-less, land-less flesh within the womb abyss.

witness

Primo Levi, Agamben's "perfect example of the witness," asserts:[1]

> I must repeat—we, the survivors, are not the true witnesses. This is
> an uncomfortable notion, of which I have become conscious little by
> little....We survivors are not only an exiguous but also an anomalous
> minority: we are those who by their prevarications or abilities or good
> luck did not touch bottom. Those who did so, those who saw the Gor-
> gon, have not returned to tell about it or have returned mute, but they
> are the "Muslims," the submerged, the complete witnesses, the ones
> whose deposition would have a general significance. They are the rule,
> we are the exception....We who were favored by fate tried, with more
> or less wisdom, to recount not only our fate but also that of the others,
> indeed of the drowned; but this was a discourse "on behalf of third par-
> ties," the story of things seen at close hand, not experienced personally.
> The destruction brought to an end, the job completed, was not told by
> anyone, just as no one ever returned to describe his own death. Even if
> they had paper and pen, the drowned would not have testified because
> their death had begun before that of their body. Weeks and months
> before being snuffed out, they had already lost the ability to observe,
> to remember, to compare and express themselves. We speak in their
> stead, by proxy.[2]

Agamben, channeling Levi, posits the Muselmann figure (or one of the
Figuren) of the Nazi camps as the "complete witness" to the disaster, the
witness who can't speak or bear witness, the subject who, as Benjamin
suggests about Kafka's characters, "bows his head far down on his chest"

and undergoes catastrophe (39).[3] Drawing on Benveniste, Agamben describes the desubjectifying process involved in attempting to speak; the act of donning the shifter pronoun and saying "I" causes one to lose one's subjectivity, since the I exists only in discourse. Unfortunately, Agamben avoids delving into the relationality and power dynamics of discourse, even though he claims rather extravagantly that "the *Muselmann*...is the guard on the threshold of a new ethics, an ethics of a form of life that begins where dignity ends. And Levi, who bears witness to the drowned, speaking in their stead, is the cartographer of this new *terra ethica*, the implacable land-surveyor of *Muselmannland*" (69). I'll try not to make an inappropriate joke about Disneyland, but oops I just wrote the word, and isn't "guard" a bit inappropriate in the context of the camps, and isn't the colonizing imagery a bit much, however much Agamben may be channeling Kafka's castle?[4] But I digress. My point is that Agamben talks about ethics without talking about the other, just as he singularizes the Muselmann when Levi saw the Muselmänner as a (social/political) collective of "faceless presences," No Ones.[5] For Agamben, "the witness, the ethical subject, is the subject who bears witness to desubjectification" (151). Agamben means that the Muselmann bears witness to their own desubjectification/de-individuation in the bottomward slope of the camp, but what if the Muselmann as No One also bears witness to the witness's desubjectification in an ongoing recessive accountability? Because, really, the "complete witness" doesn't survive in this cosmology, and apparently some of the only ones left in Agamben's constellation are the "poets—witnesses—[who] found language as what remains, as what actually survives the possibility, or impossibility, of speaking" (161). For Agamben, the "author," whose etymological origins include "vendor," "he who advises or persuades," "witness," and one who uses their authority for "the completion of an imperfect act," is also always coauthor (148). "The survivor and the *Muselmann*, like the tutor and the incapable person and the creator and his material, are inseparable; their unity-difference alone constitutes testimony" (150). Yet this yoking of survivor and Muselmann, tutor and incapable person, poet and witness, ignores how power and domination and interpellation operate on and between and among subjects, particularly in relation to capability and agency. These relations are much more layered and fraught than the "alone"-ness/oneness/twoness of unity-difference.

What if the survivor bears witness for the Muselmann, who bears witness for the dead witness from a "third [or more] realm" between/

beyond/thresholding life and death?[6] Because, using Agamben's own language, "the untestifiable [is] that to which [N]o [O]ne has borne witness" and will have borne witness (41). Because the unsaying is always present as a remnant in the saying, as "the human being is what remains after the destruction of the human being" (134). For Agamben, "the paradox here is that if the only one bearing witness to the human is the one whose humanity has been wholly destroyed, this means that the identity between human and inhuman is never perfect and that it is not truly possible to destroy the human, that something always *remains. The witness is this remnant*" (133–34, italics in original). On the surface, the witness as remnant may seem an interesting notion, but in Agamben's cosmology the "remnants of Auschwitz" cannot speak or bear witness in any other modality. Black theorists hold space differently for the remnants of disaster. Moten might suggest that blackness as stolen life carries a fugitive remnant that is "flesh that keeps speaking to us here and now"; Spillers might say that black women have been "the principal point of passage between the human and the non-human world" and claim this monstrous passage as an "insurgent ground"; and Weheliye might invoke Spillers's ethereal "female flesh 'ungendered'" as excessive, ungovernable remnant, "the living, speaking, thinking, feeling, and imagining flesh: the ether that holds together the world of Man while at the same time forming the conditions of possibility for this world's demise."[7] Flesh speaks, however much its voice may not be listened to nor its hieroglyphics deciphered; and "flesh that weeps, laughs; flesh that dances on bare feet in grass" will have always already been living and sur-viving in another world, here and to come.[8]

Perhaps Agamben cannot hear flesh's voice because he is so concerned with the retinal as the primary site of im/possible witness:

> That at the "bottom" of the human being there is nothing other than an impossibility of seeing—this is the Gorgon, whose vision transforms the human being into a non-human. That precisely this inhuman impossibility of seeing is what calls and addresses the human, the apostrophe from which human beings cannot turn away—this and nothing else is testimony. The Gorgon and he who has seen her and the *Muselmann* and he who bears witness to him are one gaze; they are a single impossibility of seeing. (54)

I thought Agamben had just said that the Muselmann and the survivor's "unity-difference alone constitutes testimony." Is it their unity or

their difference or their male gaze of/with the inhumanly female Gorgon (Celan's Medusa's head) or the apostrophe or the visual impossibility that alone constitutes testimony, or something else? And what of
the body, the flesh, and listening and the other senses? The complete
witness to the catastrophe is in actuality always multiple (or more + less
than one + three or more), including the voices of those who cannot
speak and bear witness in ways that are immediately intelligible. And
the seemingly impersonal, defaced, and always contaminated more or
less than singular + third-or-more voice of No One is a nonprosopopoeic
figure—the monstrous No One has seen the monstrous Gorgon and
has no face to give or restore, stony or not, for writer or reader. But it
does have flesh. Contrary to Levi's assertion, there will be no proxy witnessing, but there may be phantasmatic instantiation: "No [O]ne died
in my stead. No [O]ne," declares Levi.[9] "I died in Auschwitz but [N]o
[O]ne knows it," writes Charlotte Delbo.[10] "[N]o [O]ne has the right to
speak on their behalf," thrusts Elie Wiesel.[11] "For of death, [N]o [O]ne
has knowledge," intones Plato.[12] "Praise be your name, No [O]ne," murmurs Celan.[13]

If, for Agamben, poets find language as what remains, for Derrida,
Celan the poet finds ash, "annihilation without remainder, without
memory, or without a readable or decipherable archive."[14] And yet Derrida posits that "Aschenglorie," this poem of Celan's containing No one,
"bears witness to this impossibility....taking as testimony the naming of
ashes," its "only condition of possibility as condition of its impossibility—
paradoxical and aporetic."[15] The remainder is ash, and the human being
survives the human being not as the being of Being but as an (after)life
containing some-thing like Moten's irreducible animateriality, holding some-thing of soul, matrix, mother, material, animality, song—and
their dispossessions. Glissant would say that the abyss is not ash but
water, the Middle Passage is "womb abyss"; that less than nothing remains in this watery abyss and that Caribbean history begins from this
opaque, irretrievable, illegible (more +) less than nothing, unlike the
visible wreckage of ash, what remains to be named.[16] Anne Carson, who
claims Celan practiced a poetry of severe redaction paradoxically filled
with images of salvaging, asks Celan and her readers, "What exactly
is lost to us when words are wasted? And where is the human store to
which such goods are gathered?"[17] And I in turn ask Carson and Celan,
"When you 'cleanse words and salvage what is cleansed,' do you collect
what's been scrubbed off or what remains minute older claims from

methods accepted machine? / And who bears witness for the authors pulling estimates of bitter crash and victorian distinguished confused witness?"[18] Derrida would say it is the Celan poem itself that redacts, gleans, and bears witness for the witness, or to bearing witness itself, *through* ash. And Glissant would say the human store is the womb abyss.

Just as an aside, Derrida is one of the few twentieth- and twenty-first-century western philosophers to write about contemporary poets who enact radical ideas in radical form, and the few who do tend to write on Celan, a poet who breaks the German language, the language of the Nazi "holocaust" ("burnt offering"), into ash. It is curious how often twentieth- and twenty-first-century philosophers continue to write on German Romantic poet Friedrich Hölderlin as the exemplary philosophical poet while ignoring the work of twentieth- and twenty-first-century poets writing in experimental forms whose work re-marks some of the key ideas/tropes of twentieth-century European theory, from the deconstructing/breaking of English—the language of ongoing capitalist imperialism—to disjunctive, rhizomatic lines of flight/escape across the page, to improper multilingual appropriations, to excessive face-to-face encounters with the reader, to the writing of disaster as disaster enacted *in* writing.[19] Perhaps philosophy's yoking of poetry in fixed premodernist forms is a symptom of philosophy's fetishization of "poetic language," garnering poetry a "privileged position in the domain of the arts," according to Heidegger, a position that has somehow superseded being banished from the Republic for contracting a case of infectious mimesis.[20] For Heidegger, "poetry is the saying of the unconcealedness of what is," and yet the first rule poets learn in creative writing classes is to cut copulas as they probe what remains behind the mask as mask.[21] For Heidegger, "language itself is poetry in the essential sense," and yet language doesn't possess a self or essence; nor does poetry.[22] For Heidegger, "the nature of art is poetry. The nature of poetry, in turn, is the founding of truth," and yet, of course, there is no truth beside regimes of truth, no language outside of language (well, perhaps).[23] My tongue sits lightly in cheek as I write the above simplifications of Heidegger's important work on language speaking and the poetic as an excessive force. But there is no revolution of poetic language. That can only happen on the street. Poetry is not enough. One supposedly radical contemporary philosopher recently declared that there was no more poetry after Celan, which not only is an insult to Celan or Adorno or the metonym known as Auschwitz but willfully ignores the radical poetics responding to now-time and its ongoing disasters, some examples of which I monstrate in this book.[24]

Returning from digression to the witness, I feel inclined to claim, against Agamben, that the poet as direct transparent witness is not necessarily trustworthy, not simply because language isn't transparent, but along a similar trajectory to the fact that the anthropologist as "modest witness" "gone native" is a terrible construct.[25] I do not trust the speech of "I was here" at this site of trauma, so I am entitled to speak, which is how the "poetry of witness" has been framed to date; or I wasn't there at all, and I'm still entitled to speak (prosopopoeia).[26] This kind of testimony has its roots in the master's testes (and/or Heidegger's attestation, perhaps one and the same rod and ball). As Derrida notes, tongue firmly lodged in cheek, snakelike:

> Testis has a homonym in Latin. It usually occurs in the plural, to mean "testicles."...Testitrahus means at once complete and male, masculine. Some feminists, men or women, could, if they wanted, playfully or not, derive from this an argument about the relations between a certain thinking of the third and testimony, on the one hand, and the chief, the head and phallocentric capital, on the other. It is true that, in English, testis, testes has kept the sense of testicle—which could be an incitement to militancy.[27]

One can perhaps see why I have queerly swerved from arguing for the third as witness to demonstrating a more incalculable demonstration. Militantly, yes, I do sort of trust No One, the virtual, entangled, polyvocal, and a little bit "bad" ~~subject~~ who bears witness for the witness who bears witness to the catastrophe of extreme subjection.[28] And perhaps there is a way that poetry and other art forms can hold a more + less than singular + third or more nonstandpoint of witnessing: "To stand for-[N]o-[O]ne-and-nothing."[29] Derrida writes of Celan's meta-witnessing in "Aschenglorie" as "*this poem's bearing witness to bearing witness*"; and, as we will see below, theorist and artist Bracha L. Ettinger proposes a kind of wit(h)nessing through art that propels bodies transjectively toward one another in their differential "severality," always already entangled bodies that could include the reader, the poet, the poem, and also the page.[30] Ferreira da Silva would call this form of relation "difference without separability" within a black feminist poethics of the plenum—and Moten and Glissant would concur and call it "consent not to be a single being."

Another important rejoinder to Agamben's claim of the Muselmann's inhuman finitude is that this "non-[M]an" in the man *can* survive, as the testimonies at the end of *Remnants of Auschwitz* demonstrate (e.g., "I was a *Muselmann*"; "I too was a *Muselmann*"; "I am a *Muselmann*").[31] Agamben speaks of "Levi's paradox" in which the complete witness is the nonhuman who can't bear witness yet is still the true witness, but what of Agamben's own paradox (150)? He does not comment on the testimonies at the back even while they refute his argument and prove that Levi's "[N]o [O]ne" can "describe [their] own death." What if the Muselmann were not just an inhuman *Figur* without face or "self" but an enfleshed being who hungers and dreams in color and does not conform?[32] What if the Muselmann were another form of life, another genre of the human, as Weheliye suggests, invoking Wynter's concept? And what if, as Weheliye also suggests, "becoming-Muselmann" were "a form of politics" rather than a form of passive death?[33] Levi's first literary piece of writing after the war was a poem, "Buna," which is a meta-address to a Muselmann figure who could also be himself: "Suffering comrade... / In your breast you have cold hunger nothing... / Gray companion... / Empty comrade who has no more name... / Spent man... / If we were to meet again / Up in the sweet world under the sun, / With what face would we confront each other?"[34] Or would we have singular faces at all? We will have had to pass through the three or more + more + less than one to get to the face-to-face two, since the Muselmann, empty comrade full of nothingness, will have been always already becoming outside space-time in the plenum. As Achille Mbembe notes, during a suicide bombing the body, in an act of sublime necropolitics, becomes the ballistic weapon, and the primary target isn't the victim/enemy but the third-party witness who must attempt to make meaning from shards of bodies melding in a precarious we.[35] The precarious we is also the plenum. We know the Latin roots of "testimony" are not only the master's testes but terstis, the one who is present as a third. The transcendental ethical one or two tends to founder on the shoals of the spiraling out political/social three or more. No one, no two, but peut-être a future anteriority of more + less than one + three or more, in an act of imagination that brings together present absences, absent presences, and so-called present absentees.[36] A dangerous perhaps.

There is another element that emerges with the author's attempt to witness and persuade and sell by adjoining themselves to the Muselmann's impossible speech, an effort to fail well in the catachrestic effort to listen to what is unsayable and beyond knowledge in the testimony of the witness who bears witness for the Muselmann's "bare, unassignable and unwitnessable life" (157). An unwitnessable life like that of the Guantánamo detainees risking US national security by scratching thousands of lines of poetry onto Styrofoam cups with their fingernails. Perhaps Halpern's projected lover Mohammad Ahmed Abdullah Saleh Al Hanashi wrote a poem like that along with the hieroglyph on his neck. Shaikh Abdurraheem Muslim Dost, another Guantánamo detainee, certainly wrote "cup poems":

Cup Poem 1

What kind of a spring is this,
Where there are no flowers and
The air is filled with a miserable smell?

Cup Poem 2

Handcuffs befit brave young men,
Bangles are for spinsters or pretty young ladies.[37]

"No more sand art, no sand books, no masters," echoes Celan from a watery grave.[38]

Agamben and other commentators refuse to talk about the Muselmann as a racial slur for "Muslim"; they do not want to talk about the Muselmann as a racialized assemblage. As Weheliye suggests:

In Agamben's system becoming-Muselmann never appears as a politics; rather it remains locked within the constraints of a static example. Had Agamben not simply incorporated but also digested the thoughts and dreams of the Muselmänner, perhaps then genocidal violence would cease to appear as such an absolute force of law from above that negates all other dimensions of the existence and subjectivity of the oppressed. The dialogue about the Muselmann initiated by Agamben does not offer alternatives to our current epistemic cum political order, because it cannot even begin to fathom what it may mean to think about the Muselmänner not as symbols—by sheer virtue of their existence in the death camps—for abstract categories such as evil or dignity but as subjects that lived and dreamed other ways of being human.[39]

Psychoanalysis and philosophy sometimes tell us that subjectivity *is* witnessing as response-ability, however impossible a task.[40] Perhaps the truly radical call, beyond reason or recognition, is to witness Das Ding in the Nebenmensch, that alien thing in the excessive neighbor beside me and you—Freud's strange *Zug* (a trait, but also a line or mark or remnant) in No One's absent present face as the both/and that opens thought. A mark that is also an infinitely vulnerable call neither legible nor audible but that can only be hauntingly *felt*, an infinitely unreasonable *impress*-ion on and in the witness, engendering a set of "mad," ungovernable affects that they can't turn away from, that stick to their bones. Unthinkable truth of living experience—there is no certitude in testimony, and the poem is untranslatable. The two can only be created by passing through the more + less than one + three or more. If "negation is at the heart of testimony"—Celan's no-poem, the noem, is also absolute no-thingness encompassing noesis, noema, the heady nous and the impossible fleshly we.[41] No Ones as entangled, interpenetrative sociality.

....

STUDY · Thinking thought usually amounts to withdrawing into a dimension-
less place in which the idea of thought alone persists. But thought in
reality spaces itself out into the world. It informs the imaginary of
peoples, their varied poetics, which it then transforms, meaning in
them its risk becomes realized.
ÉDOUARD GLISSANT

The speaker in Juliana Spahr's 2007 poet's novel, *The Transformation,* is an unnamed, indeterminate third-person singular/plural neuter and gender-neutral "they," narrating their experience(s) as (a) newly white settler(s) in Hawai'i. This "they" differs from Cheena Marie Lo's "they" in that it is deliberately unclear in *The Transformation* whether or not the speaker is singular or plural. So, in one instance *The Transformation* is "a story about three of them who moved to an island that was not theirs" and "fix[ed] their relationship into a triangle," moving "between three instead of two"; they "felt they could be shaped by each other into some new thing"; perhaps they were "perverts" in their "atypical" sexual relation, perhaps not.[42] Yet in another instance, the narrator speaks of "moments where they had to realize their white womanness," though it is never clear in the text whether this means that all "three of them" are white women or just one—and if this story has any basis in autobiography, as Spahr points to in her afterword, the gender formation of the three contains male-identified partners (106).[43]

So the narration deliberately plays with our expectations of singular, stable voice as Spahr "think[s] with" ongoing colonization and complicity and precarious bodies and witnessing (and wit(h)nessing and a kind of whitenessing) from a stance of a singular/plural "they" who perhaps is a kind of No One (21).[44] Spahr subjects her "they" to vulnerable intrusions, revealing the sometimes monstrous face of the "self" and neighbor alongside the intensities of what she calls, referring to Carson's essay *Eros the Bittersweet*, the "third Sapphic point," a point of desire in encounter that Carson, in her discussion of Sappho's poetry, claims "plays a paradoxical role for it both connects and separates, marking that two are not one, irradiating the absence whose presence is demanded by eros."[45] For the psychoanalyst Jessica Benjamin, "the third point creates a space rather than a line," a mental space where responsibility and shifts in thought and action can begin.[46] So the third returns, this time not in an impersonal stance; but again, for me, the third is not a fixed number in space/time/being. It simply gestures to a social and political space that is more than the ethical two and could be more than three + Moten's more + less than one, more than calculability. Consent not to be a single being is strongly enacted in *The Transformation*, even as the speaker acknowledges that "they were complicit with all sorts of things [that] continued to happen also without their consent" (111).

The text's recursive, spiraling "long sentences and lists of connections, both paranoid and optimistic," its indeterminate characters, its reiterative questioning and worrying at the same wounds, its "self"-exposure, its open structure, enact processes of transformation in thinking—and being (213):

> So this is a story of three who moved to an island in the middle of the Pacific and how it changed them. And a story of how they became aware they were a they in the cruel inquisitive sense, in the sense of not being a part of us or we, in the sense of accusation, whether they wanted to be they or not. It is a story about realizing that they cannot shrug off this they and so a story of trying to think with it. A story of how much this realization of being a they changed them and a story of embracing this change....And so perhaps it is a story of coming to an identity, coming to realize that they not only had a gender that was decided for them without their consent and by historical events that

they had not even been alive to witness, but they also had a race and a sexuality that was decided for them without their consent and by historical events that they had not even been alive to witness and they just had to deal with this. So it is also a story of finding an ease in discomfort. And a catalogue of discomfort. (21–22)

Indeed, it is an infectious discomfort and transformation that Spahr releases into the world. I was in the middle of writing a book of poetry on settler colonialism in Israel-Palestine when reading Spahr's book helped lead me to a deeper awareness of my own complicity with ongoing settler colonialism in Canada. It was much easier to offer a critique of imperialism "over there" than to examine my role in the "history of arrival by people from afar who came and acted as if the place was theirs" in Canada (41). Reading *The Transformation*, I felt the "tiny muscles at the base of each hair...contract and thus pull the hair erect" when the "they" recognizes their role as a "stupid fucking haole" (foreign, white) colonizer in Hawai'i (33, 40). I felt a similar shameful "cringe of recognition" of my own role as a "mediocre colonizer" when Spahr alluded to Albert Memmi's term for the left-wing colonizer who rejects the colony but can't help but benefit from it, and I started working on a book in response to these issues in Canada (41).[47] And when "they" moved from Hawai'i back to the "continent" (New York) in the second half of *The Transformation*, I found myself wishing that they could have continued their reflection on ongoing colonization of Indigenous peoples on the continent. I tried to resist thinking it was because they thought the "Indians" had "vanished" on the continent. This is just some of what came to mind as I did my own "thinking with," and feeling with, Spahr as she "use[d] the genre of individual exploration to think about how that shapes...cultural issues."[48] She continues, in reference to US practices at "home" and as occupier in Iraq and elsewhere, "I was interested in thinking about what I'm complicit with....In order to bomb someone you have to make them into a 'they.'...Can one think ethically from a position of 'they'? Maybe the beginning of doing that work is to see yourself as part of that 'they.'"[49] In *The Transformation*, she also speaks of "what it meant to be the accusative they" and of being "willing to take the accusative they into their bodies and let it change them" (47, 48). One could read Spahr's "they" as a kind of No One, here a seemingly emptied-out position that the reader can become complicit (folded together) with, a position that potentially transforms as they (reader and

speaker) attempt to take responsibility for their witnessing and partici-
pation in the ongoing disasters of colonialism.

Part of the transformation that Spahr enacts in *The Transformation* is
related to reading. In her collection of critical essays, *Everybody's Autonomy: Connective Reading and Collective Identity*, Spahr cites Theresa Hak
Kyung Cha's book DICTEE on the reader-text relationship: "You read
you mouth the transformed object across from you in its new state,
other than what it had been."[50] Spahr then claims, "Cha wants readers who, as they read, as they mouth the words, transform."[51] Perhaps
Spahr desires a similar response from her readers (however much we're
not supposed to talk about authorial intention). Spahr argues not only
that DICTEE is a critique of colonialism in content but that DICTEE calls
for "decolonize[d]" reading practices, whereby the reader engages self-
reflexively with the text and is changed by it.[52] Spahr calls for similar
reading strategies in an essay on Lyn Hejinian's *My Life* as a "postmodern autobiography" that "requires its readers to bring multiple interpretations to the work" with "its dual resignifying of subjectivity and readerly agency."[53] She applies Butler's theories on the political subject (and
hence the reading subject) as a constant site of resignification, high-
lighting the constructed nature of the subject in/of language and deeming *My Life* "a mutating product centered around the way life and practices of representing subjectivity change from moment to moment."[54]
The repeated "one" in *My Life* is "a pronoun that *anyone* can inhabit,"
like the singular neuter pronoun "it" that Hejinian (and Brolaski) also
employ.[55] This gesture is echoed in Spahr's use of the singular/plural
neuter and gender-neutral pronoun "they" in *The Transformation* as a
stance of textual encounter that the reader can actively inhabit and
question, rather than passively absorbing the colonizing "author who
conquers and claims dominion over readers."[56] Reading is configured
as not simply appropriating knowledge but taking response-ability, re-
sistantly; reading as an active witnessing and interpretation that is a
kind of trans-lation and trans-formation. "After crossing the boundary
which distinguished the work from the rest of the universe, the reader
is expected to recross the boundary with something in mind."[57]

Rosi Braidotti's "radical ethics of transformation" is applicable here,
a post-Deleuzian ethical stance that

> rejects individualism, but also asserts an equally strong distance from
> relativism or nihilistic defeatism. A sustainable ethics for a non-

unitary subject proposes an enlarged sense of interconnection between self and others, including the non-human or "earth" others, by
removing the obstacle of self-centred individualism. This is not the
same as absolute loss of values, it rather implies a new way of com-
bining self-interests with the well-being of an enlarged sense of community which includes one's territorial or environmental interconnec-
tions. This is an ethical bond of an altogether different sort from the
self-interests of an individual subject, as defined along the canonical
lines of classical humanism. It is a nomadic eco-philosophy of multiple
belongings.[58]

In *The Transformation*, Spahr articulates an ecophilosophy indebted to
Indigenous knowledges and based on the interrelationality of all things
plant, animal, and human. Indeed, Spahr's writing repeatedly features
the kind of plural, embodied, and embedded subjects that Braidotti
promotes, and this complex subject position seems to be one Spahr
would like her readers to inhabit. My own thinking on reading, writing, and witnessing follows some similar trajectories to Braidotti's and
Spahr's, with a strong consciousness of the impact of black thought
on any discussions of ethicality, subjectivity, whiteness, and witnessing. These three lines of Celan's, "No one / bears witness for the / witness," help me rethink received notions of the "poetry of witness" as
being limited to poets who have experienced trauma firsthand, and
to writing from a confessional stance. Some may interpret Celan's No
one as the oft-withdrawn Hebrew god (*deus absconditus*), just as many
read Levinas's ethical figure of the face as the uncaressable visage of a
similar god. Yet, in my own readerly license, I prefer to read No One
as not one, neither the overdetermined possessive individual nor the
overdetermined ethical two, something more + less than one + three
or more, perhaps a they with a distorted face. Or a zombie, the always-
already-dead figure Spahr employs in *The Transformation* to represent
the "they" flailing for a job in the "national education complex" (55).
Or perhaps a Thing, in the psychoanalytic sense (Das Ding), the unassimilable part within us and beside us that some of us still feel drawn
to attempt to communicate with, even if that communication is by
way of "mad" or ungovernable affects. That Thing also of course brings
to mind the excessive, elusive qualities of blackness and the flesh and
monstrosity. "They needed to become monstrous in their heart. This
becoming monstrous they knew was only a beginning but felt neces-

sary. That singular organ needed to be made bigger. They need to bring things inside of them that shouldn't be inside of them" (209). To bear witness to and with contiguously, "to think with others, to think with the traditions of the island, to think beside them and near them but not as part of them" (115). No One bearing not multiple essential subjectivities but several partial becomings, constantly forming and unforming, never stable—"splintered," as Spahr describes the subject in Hejinian's *My Life*.[59] And yet always already connected to others. "This thing that entered into their bloodstream changed them" (39). Such is the process of reading, and also becoming. A process that, as Glissant remind us, is conscious of "consent[ing] to the idea that it is possible to be one and multiple at the same time; that you can be yourself and the other; that you can be the same and the different."[60] *Consent à n'être plus un seul*, with "plus" carrying some of both "no more" and "more."[61]

Spahr's ideas on identity and poetry shift in *The Transformation*. Her thinking on *My Life*'s nonessentialist relation to multiple subjectivity shifts into a focus in *The Transformation* on identity as politically constructed, on identity formations being central to organizing among colonized peoples. Modernist notions of writing as a "foreigner in their own language" and moving between borders of language have radically different connotations and realities in contemporary colonized spaces, especially given that English is now the primary "expansionist" language of western imperialism: "they were finally not all that sure that using fragmentation, quotation, disruption, disjunction, agrammatical syntax, and so on escaped any of the [colonial] expansionism" (99). This story of "coming to an identity" as a white settler complicit in ongoing colonization, this "catalogue of discomfort," transforms the speaker's perspective on identity, while still avowing primary connections among partial, multiple/hybrid subjects (22).

Psychoanalyst and artist Bracha L. Ettinger's work has interesting affinities to Spahr's thinking on connectivity and processes of transformation. Not throwing out the Oedipal triad with the bathwater, Ettinger proposes an-other primary formation centered in the common experience we all go through of coming to being in the body of a person we haven't yet faced, a person who is also being changed by the process. Ettinger theorizes spaces of "copoiesis" and "differentiation in co-emergence" that occur in later-term pregnancy to think and work through the threads of connection that she deems primary to human existence, beside and against notions of lack, castration, and separateness that dominate Oedipal modes of thinking. Ettinger attempts not to essentialize pregnancy but misses the fact that trans people who don't identify as women can still birth babies and that adopted children may not have a connection to the person who gave birth to them. Ettinger uses neologisms such as "transjective," "severality," and "wit(h)nessing" to develop notions of subject formation that insist that we are always already connected to one another, partly through our common experience of connection in the womb. Within what she deems the "matrixial borderspace," several partial identities (what she calls *I's* and *non-I's*, channeling Lacan) interweave, forming and unforming, consciously and unconsciously; never fixed, yet always straining toward the possibility of threshold. As Butler notes, "The matrixial is what we guard against when we shore up the claims of identity, when we presume that to recognize each other is to know, to name, to distinguish according to the logic of identity."[62]

Somewhat like Ettinger's work on the borderspace, Spahr focuses her analysis of *My Life* on enacting a space beyond essentialist notions of multiple identity, presenting a "shardlike autobiographical subject" that the reader is actively involved in co-forming.[63] This decentered subject is also present in *The Transformation*, a forever refracted "they" witnessing themselves telling/reading a barely truthful, non-Fichtean story, but a story nonetheless, one that travails the expansive canvas of novelistic space as it enacts its working-through in relation:

> They agreed to let the story they told about themselves as individuals be interrupted by others. They agreed to let their speech be filled with signs of each other and their enthrallment and their undoing. They agreed to falter over pronouns. They agreed to let them undo their speech and language. They pressed themselves upon them and impinged upon them and were impinged upon in ways that were not in their control. (206)

The echoes of Butler's extensions of Hegel and Levinas are strong here, how subjectivity is always already constituted in relation and interrupted by relation, how "loss has made a tenuous 'we' of us all," how I and you and we and they are impinged upon and undone and dispossessed by the other—and others.[64]

As an artist, Ettinger works in series (the paintings "come in crowds"), photocopying archival photos and other images from the Nazi holocaust and other traumatic events, but stopping the photocopier part-

FIGURE 6.1 Bracha L. Ettinger, *Eurydice 23*,
1994–1998. Collection Israel Museum, Jerusalem.
© Bracha L. Ettinger. Courtesy of the artist.

way through the machinic process, so that the photocopic dust forms
aleatory blurred interpretations of the image, "between ash and pastel."
She repeats this process a number of times with the same image, then
paints from "scan[ning]" the photocopied images, in series that "fade
out what the image should have become." The viewer is also meant to
scan across the images, seeing mutual implications within and across
the series, feeling the intensities of partial objects, accumulated meanings in and out of time, just as the interrupted copy "stop[s] time."[65]
This process relates to how the repeating phrases in *The Transformation*
draw out affect and subtle difference, while also drawing attention to
time's slips. As Hejinian notes in her essay "The Rejection of Closure,"
"meaning is set in motion, emended and extended, and the rewriting
that repetition becomes postpones completion of the thought indefi-
nitely."[66] Yet do I read every instance that Spahr repeats, mechanically,
"avant-garde techniques of fragmentation, quotation, disruption, disjunction, agrammatical syntax, and so on," or do I register the line as
specific and cumulative as I scan by? This goes back to Butler's resignifying that Spahr draws on to theorize the postmodern autobiography,
how the subject and agency and their materiality are deconstructed,
yet we can "continue to use them, to repeat them, to repeat them sub-
versively, and to displace them from the contexts in which they have
been deployed as instruments of oppressive power."[67]

   This process of resignifying can also apply to how affect is generated
and processed in the viewer or reader. According to theorist Brian Massumi, "Ettinger considers it the goal of her art to 'make affect transmissible.' Her series are affective carriers of traumatic renewal."[68] In front
of Ettinger's "Eurydice" series of paintings, the viewer "looks back"
down the lens of the unnamed Nazi photographer who captured naked Jewish women and children standing in line to be shot on October 14, 1942, at Mizocz, Rovno, Ukraine. We are implicated in "a gaze
that cannot but kill again."[69] Similarly, in the face of *The Transformation*, the North American reader must confront the "difficult feelings"
coextensive with their always-implicated role in the ongoing colonization of Turtle Island (220). One could say that Spahr's they turns the
phallic gaze into a "matrixial" gaze that, rather than possess and cut us

off from the witnessing event, "fragilizes" our relation to the trauma of history, so that the traces of connection thread into a constantly changing web, "metramorphose," to use another Ettinger neologism, into the monstrous heart bloated by severality at the end of *The Transformation*. We are complicit in atrocities done "in our name" every day, but this doesn't cut us off from our obligations; instead, our being impinged upon by others, the they, opens us to our response-ability, transjectively, as part of they. Ettinger writes, "We are carrying, at the beginning of the twenty-first century, enormous traumatic weight, and aesthetic wit(h)nessing in art brings it to culture's surface. Certain contemporary art practices bring to light matrixial alliances by confronting the limits of trauma's shareability and the *jouissance* of the Other.... [A]esthetics converges with ethics even beyond the artist's intentions or conscious control."[70]

Ettinger's work on the matrixial and aesthetic wit(h)nessing as an ethics could be enhanced by Ferreira da Silva's and Spillers's thinking on kinship, connection, and difference. Ferreira da Silva expands on Retallack's initial theorizing of poethics through chaos theory. Retallack is interested in poetry and reading that "functions within a poethics of complex realism where active processes of mutability and multiplicity are valued over simpler, more stable illusions of expressive clarity. Change actively, continually destabilizes the poem, thwarting *the* 'correct' reading, thwarting any sure sense of return to the author's ego-bound, prior intentions."[71] Ferreira da Silva's concept of black feminist poethics "thinks with Retallack and Leibniz" toward an "ethics with/out the subject (one which is with and out)" that "decenters the subject, without ignoring it, and has to begin by considering that we are connected to everything else."[72] Ferreira da Silva wants to "image the world in this complex way" beyond white western notions of individuated self-possession, determination, naming, and fixing.[73] Drawing on Leibniz, Ferreira da Silva's black feminist poethics engenders a plenum "toward the beyond of Space-time" where everything and everyone are connected and affected and changed by one another in "existence...without...separability" that "resists dissolving any attempt to reduce what exists—anyone and everything—to the register of the object, the other, and the commodity," thus undoing the world as we know it.[74] I wonder how Ettinger's theorization of the matrixial borderspace and "differentiation in co-emergence" could be complicated by thinking more deeply about "difference without separability" and kinship structures.[75] I am thinking about the transgenerational trauma engendered by white government authorities taking Indigenous children in North America away from their families and cultures and putting them in residential schools designed to "kill the Indian in the child." And the incalculable cases of "natal alienation" during the Middle Passage and plantation slavery, when so many Africans lost their mothers and their kinship ties altogether.[76] A time when, as Spillers theorizes, defaced and brutalized "unprotected female flesh" became "female flesh 'ungendered,'" as gender transformed into a whole other kind of borderspace wherein all genders of enslaved people were in effect structurally ungendered by slavery, and yet "the female stands *in the flesh*, both mother and mother-dispossessed."[77] Again, for Glissant, the slave ship "is a womb, a womb abyss....This boat is your womb, a matrix, and yet it expels you."[78] Perhaps in future, as Ettinger furthers her theorization of the matrixial and aesthetic wit(h)nessing, she could honor the trauma of the womb abyss and "make a place for this different social subject"; perhaps she could honor Spillers's "*insurgent* ground" where "*claiming the monstrosity*" of black "female flesh 'ungendered'" and with "the potential to 'name'" becomes "a praxis and a theory, a text for living and for dying, and a method of reading both through their diverse mediations."[79] Consent not to be a single being.

In an article on Ettinger's art-making process "from grain to screen to series," Massumi writes:

The process starts with a machinic technique for the grain to self-express in collaboration with the artist's hand. It ends with an expanded indistinction between activity and passivity, subject and object, intensively distributed across a plurality of elements, levels, and matters. This makes it impossible to assign a self-enclosed subject of the process that would be separate from it. There is no-one behind the process, no One, only "severality," self-organizing between material-abstract surfaces.[80]

No One bears witness as a "wit(h)ness with-out event," in Ettinger's inversion of Felman and Laub's famous iteration of the Shoah as an "event without a witness" ("the absence of an empathic listener, or, more radically, the absence of an *addressable other*").[81] My mind goes to another form of (non)communication, Spillers's "undecipherable...hieroglyphics of the flesh," a "marking and branding...[that] 'transfers' from one generation to another," events transferred from the womb abyss across generations and centuries of bodies and flesh.[82] As Hartman teaches "the precariousness of empathy and the uncertain line between witness and spectator," perhaps there is a fleshly empathy and wit(h)nessing in and through the ensemble, No One behind the process, only difference without separability.[83]

The Transformation puts pressure on the reader to risk being involved in the complex realism of Spahr's narrative in a nonpossessive manner, to be fragilized by the content and transformed by the affects it generates, to be "willing to take the accusative they into their bodies" rather than simply consume or be consumed (47–48). Transformed through wit(h)nessing, into a different consciousness. As Spahr notes, "It didn't end up as an autobiography because it isn't a life story really, but it might be a...somewhat true somewhat false...memoir of an attempt to come to a political consciousness."[84] Spahr's they attempts to create "new patterns of relating" by "thinking with and beside" the traditions of the island and its people; yet they eventually decide "that if they wrote about another culture, a culture at risk because of colonialism and a culture that was not theirs really, the writing should give something back to the culture. But it was also presumptuous to think they could give anything back. The culture was so rich and so complete without them" (21, 115). I wonder if perhaps another transformation is needed for Spahr's white they to really think with the difficult knowledges of racialized bodies who may be constitutively without ac-

cess to—and in fact refuse—the self-possession necessary to experience
the transformative experience, the ec-stasy, of dispossession in relation,
standing outside/beside oneself, *I* and *non-I*. Such theys, such no-things
or no-bodies, are outer-determined by white racial capital as affectable
I's rather than transparent I's, in Ferreira da Silva's terminology.[85] These
affectable I's or theys undergo a "trans*formation into ontological
blackness," as Sharpe writes, the asterisk holding open a space for the
unthought.[86] Perhaps instead of just wondering about how or whether
to "give something back," there is another transformation that Spahr's
they could make to, as Harney and Moten suggest, "move next to each
other, so we can be beside ourselves" in shared ec-stasy in the plenum.[87]

Back in front of Ettinger's overworked photo/painting of Jewish
women and children waiting for a bullet and a dark pit just beyond
the frame, one could argue that Ettinger wants the viewer/reader/
witness to activate the matrixial gaze, scan the iterations of the degraded, ghosted image, and give back meaning that is always several
and always just out of reach. Let's torque that and suggest that perhaps this looking is the beginning of a listening as working through. A
scream as traumatic repetition sieved through the grain. And the failed
project of the world and the face.[88] Toward a sense of the "with and for,"
the fleshly undercommons.[89] "They agreed to no longer see relationship
as a feedback loop of face-to-face desire. Instead they had to deal with
a sort of shimmering, a fracturing of all their looks and glances. And
it was because of this third Sapphic point that they implicated themselves in they" (206). We enter an image of not-so-silent women and
children in line for the open pit through the grained-out but still pal-
pable gaze of the perpetrator. Our complicity, our folded togetherness,
noisily accompanies us. "They are three points of transformation on a
circuit of possible relationship, electrified by desire so that they touch
not touching."[90]

....

for

For Derrida, the *für* in Celan's "Aschenglorie" is "at the same time the most decisive and the most undecidable word in the poem."[1] He posits three readings of the word: (1) on behalf of, (2) in the place of, and (3) in front of (or I might say in the face of). The first reading is straightforward: I am a witness for the defense, I am witnessing on behalf of the defense, I am witnessing for you, and so on. It is the second reading that provokes controversy and some consternation. A particularly egregious example of how this understanding of *speaking for* can go awry appears in a book called *Poetic Medicine: The Healing Art of Poem-Making*, in a chapter called "Poems of Witness in a Conflicted World." One of the exercises in this self-help-cum-creative-writing primer is "Writing a Poem of Witness," which has the following instructions:

> 1. Notice people who are marginalized in our society. What is their world made of?...Like Jack Hirschman's attention to the homeless woman, Terry Garvin, pay attention to the details in the life of individuals you ignore or avoid.

> 2. Imagine what asks for healing or attention in this individual. What do you offer? What do you learn from this interaction with them? Shape these questions and details about their life into a poem.[2]

There are too many poems of witness made according to these kinds of parameters; we don't need to cite or dwell on them. What interests me is how the term "poem of witness" has swerved from its original meaning coined by US poet Carolyn Forché in *Against Forgetting: Twentieth-*

Century Poetry of Witness: work by "significant poets who endured conditions of historical and social extremity" and whose poems "bear the
trace of extremity within them, and...are, as such, evidence of what occurred."[3] Forché's evidentiary and experiential first-person stance becomes John Fox's appropriative and colonizing first-person stance. Or
the *New York Times Magazine*'s colonizing second-person stance in a full-
page ad in the February 19, 2017, edition encouraging readers to "nav-
igate the uncertain waters of the migrant crisis." That was the head-
line under strangely distorted (panoramic?) photos of unnamed black
people (presumably migrants) in holding areas, a strangely prominent
empty green-and-yellow stairwell, and one prominent white "rescuer"
awkwardly bending over (in a kind of davening position) the side of a
larger boat to look at other people in smaller boats below. The body
copy reads:

> Witness firsthand the efforts of the Bourbon Argos as it conducts the
> last of 59 African migrant rescue missions in the Mediterranean in
> 2016.
>
> The New York Times is using Samsung Gear 360 cameras to place you
> in the moment, right at the center of our stories.
>
> Experience it at **www.nytimes.com/the daily360**
>
> Also available to view in Samsung VR
>
> **THE DAILY 360   BE THERE NOW**

If a poetics of witness means anything at all, may it not mean "jour-
nalism by *The New York Times*" and "technology by Samsung." Or being
there. For Moten, "what we're after is a move from the metaphysics
of presence, given in the figure of the one, to the physics of presence,
given in transubstantial no-thing-ness, in consent not to be (single), in
differential inseparability, in the nearness and distance of the making
of a living and its spooky, *anima*terial actions."[4] Not I was here, so I can
speak, nor I saw you there, so I can speak, but we are always already entangled, and they bear me, and let us listen. Listen to Ferreira da Silva
on how racial capital shapes the movement of black and brown bodies
on boats, trains, feet: "When poethical thinking contemplates the present situation in Europe, it does not image 'unprecedented crisis,' but
rather business as usual for global capital."[5]

FIGURE 7.1 Advertisement in the *New York Times Magazine*, February 19, 2017, 13.

Literary critic Susan Gubar takes another tack on *for* as *in the place of* in *Poetry after Auschwitz: Remembering What One Never Knew*, one of innumerable academic texts that render the Nazi holocaust as an exceptional event bar none. Gubar draws on Levi's oft-quoted claim that the Muselmänner "drowned" cannot bear witness for themselves (though we know by now that they can) and that the survivors, the "saved," "speak in their stead, by proxy." She coins the term "proxy-witnessing" for poetry that speaks in the place of other witnesses who supposedly cannot speak, including "children, or animals, or the dead."[6] "Proxy" is a legal term for "a person appointed to act in place of another," and Gubar takes pains to distinguish her term from Forché's poetry of witness, claiming that though proxy witnesses write "from the perspective of corpses deprived of coffins," these writers "acknowledge their belated dependence on after-the-fact accounts of extremities never within their purview. They do so in order to avoid any confusion between victims in the vulnerability of 'then' and poets or readers in the safety of 'now,' to concentrate on the disturbingly specific details of experience decidedly not their own."[7] Gubar also claims that these poets work hard not to "conflate the trauma of their subjects with any secondary trauma that might result from reading or writing about their subjects."[8] She cites Dominick LaCapra's definition of "empathic unsettlement" as "a kind of virtual experience through which one puts oneself in the other's position while recognizing the difference of that position and hence not taking the other's place."[9] She gives a strenuous defense of Sylvia Plath's "Daddy"-as-Nazi poem, which I won't bother deconstructing, and briefly discusses the poet Charles Reznikoff's work with Nazi holocaust testimony, although I don't think Reznikoff would have ever claimed to speak for the dead. The poets she favors tend to "repudiate the objectivity to which Reznikoff aspired...foreground[ing] their subjective reactions" to the traumatic content of their proxy-witnessing.[10]

Hartman brilliantly criticizes the proxy position and its imaginary "empathic identification," projection, and incorporation in her book *Scenes of Subjection*, in which she declares in the first chapter that "the crimes of slavery are not only witnessed but staged."[11] She focuses on the letters of the abolitionist John Rankin to his slaveholding brother in which, in an attempt to persuade his brother to turn toward the abolitionist cause, he imagines himself, his wife, and his children as enslaved people in order to, as he writes, "identify ourselves with the sufferers, and make their sufferings our own."[12] Yet, for Hartman, "in the fantasy of being beaten, Rankin must substitute himself and his wife and children for the black captive in order that this pain be perceived and experienced. So, in fact, Rankin becomes a proxy and the other's pain is acknowledged to the degree that it can be imagined, yet by virtue of this substitution the object of identification threatens to disappear....It becomes clear that empathy is double-edged, for in making the other's suffering one's own, this suffering is occluded by the other's obliteration."[13] Hartman further asks:

> Can the white witness of the spectacle of suffering affirm the materiality of black sentience only by feeling for himself? Does this not only exacerbate the idea that black sentience is inconceivable and unimaginable but, in the very ease of possessing the abased and enslaved body, ultimately elide an understanding and acknowledgement of the slave's pain? Beyond evidence of slavery's crime, what does this exposure of the suffering body of the bondsman yield? Does this not reinforce the "thingly" quality of the captive by reducing the body to evidence in the very effort to establish the humanity of the enslaved? Does it not reproduce the hyperembodiedness of the powerless?[14]

Examining "the precariousness of empathy and the thin line between witness and spectator" is crucial to writing or reading any poetry or testimony from a proxy or secondary witness position.[15] Spillers's pornotropic "*being for* the captor" also comes to mind as another way "for" swerves away from presence to property as the crimes of the afterlives of slavery are witnessed and staged.[16] Spillers offers that "the flesh gives empathy," yet in order to receive such a gift, one must claim the monstrosity of the flesh as an insurgent text.[17] Empathy means to suffer or feel within, into, to vicariously experience someone else's suffering. For Hartman, "the endeavor to bring pain close exploits the spectacle of the body in pain and oddly confirms the spectral character of suffering and the inability to witness the captive's pain."[18] Is there a way to be present for someone's suffering without appropriating it, without turning empathy into an aesthetic and affective projection that empathy also carries, ascribing the viewer's feelings to an object? Witness the photograph of Emmett Till—a fourteen-year-old black boy from Chicago who was murdered and mutilated in Mississippi in 1955 for allegedly whistling at a white girl—in his coffin with his disfigured face left unreconstructed. And witness the 2016 painting by Dana Schutz staging

Emmett Till in his coffin that once again, like the Kenneth Goldsmith debacle, shone scrutiny on acts of cultural appropriation and antiblack pornotroping and whitenessing that obliterate any possible witnessing, listening, and/as response-ability.[19] Till's mother, Mamie Till-Mobley, by choosing to have an open casket and allowing photographers to document her son's destroyed face, "wanted 'all the world' to witness the atrocity."[20] Schutz claims that when she made the painting titled *Open Casket*, she was empathizing with Mamie Till-Mobley as a mother: "In [Till-Mobley's] sorrow and rage she wanted her son's death not just to be her pain but America's pain."[21] As Sexton notes, "[Schutz] forgets that her interracial maternal empathy for Till-Mobley does not mitigate the fact that she is a white woman depicting a black boy killed, infamously, on the initiative of a white woman. Her empathy is entangled in that initiative."[22] Schutz's claim of maternal empathy, "their pain is your pain," drove her to paint the photograph of Till's body.[23] So what, then, drove Schutz more than ten years earlier to paint Michael Jackson's imagined body staged on a future autopsy table in a 2005 painting called *The Autopsy of Michael Jackson*? In a 2006 interview in BOMB Magazine, three years before Jackson's death, Schutz discusses the painting:

> In some ways he's the most self-made man there is, to the point of it becoming really scary. I was thinking of the painting as a photograph that hasn't been taken yet. I posited all these question around Michael Jackson's death: How does he die? How old is he? What shape is he in? What does he look like naked? He ended up looking like just a dead man. Which for me was very strange. I ended up having sympathy for him. There is an immortality about him in life. In the painting there is an autopsy incision alluding to his insides, which is intrusive and contradicts the constant reforming of his external features. In the painting he is very mortal.[24]

The ease with which Schutz can imagine Jackson's naked and dead body with its intrusive incisions is a pornotropic gesture perhaps as grotesque as Rankin's pleasurable slipping on of the enslaved person's fungible body or Goldsmith's and Halpern's projective, onanistic toying with the autopsy reports on Michael Brown's and Mohammad Ahmed Abdullah Saleh Al Hanashi's violent deaths—or Schutz's own encounter with Emmett Till's face. Halpern writes about compassion's relation to the erotic, and how "compassion's condition of possibility is the other's singularity with which one can neither identify nor relate....Maybe this is what I mean by love, the failure of my name for you."[25] With *The Autopsy of Michael Jackson*, Schutz feels a more distanced, surprised sympathy for the figure on the table rather than the maternal empathy she felt for Mamie Till-Mobley in response to the photographs Till-Mobley released to the world. But in making their pain your pain, in coining "my name for you," is there a way not to obliterate the other(s)? Is there an animaterial photograph of self-less, land-less, entangled difference without separability, wherein listening and empathy (and compassion and sympathy and other uses of the erotic) can expand the space of the other without placing the self in its stead?[26]

Are there other ways to be present for another's suffering without physically *being there*? Divya Victor's PhD thesis ("Absent Witness: Trauma and Contemporary American Poetry") includes another new name for poets who witness, and a chapter on Reznikoff, but focuses on his and other writers' (including my work in a short passage) use of "found," "documentary," or "appropriated" language in their work, and their stance of "absent witness" as productively creating a kind of ethical relation between writer and reader, testifier and attendant:

> A poetics of appropriative witnessing draws attention to the "proxy" position at the core of the process by maintaining traces of the poet's displacement and absence from the event that she witnesses. Through a poetics of appropriative witnessing, the poet operates as "absentee witness"—an Athenian legal precedent that allows an absent or unavailable testifier to bear witness for an event or provide evidence to construct its narrative. The absentee witness testifies in writing and a secondary witness ratifies this testimony to make it permissible in court. Testimony from an absentee witness is witnessed twice—once by the primary witness to an event and then by one who testifies to the integrity of the primary witness and his expression. Subject to cross-checking and intersubjective ratification, the readerly engagement with a poetics of appropriative witnessing models itself on the relationship between an absentee witness and the ratifying agent of his testimony.[27]

I'm not sure if all the poets Victor discusses would think of themselves as absent or proxy witnesses. I think of my own poetic and poetics work as a kind of monstrosity, a showing, a pointing, a demonstration with many heterogeneous tendrils and potential avenues for (hopefully productive) affective impingement. Presentation rather than representation, or presenting the unpresentable; or, as Moten would say, "It more and less than represents."[28] I think about No One and disidentification when I write but don't think of myself as testifying or bearing witness.[29] If anything I am a "failed witness," in the sense Hartman gives to this idea and Philip enacts.[30] Apposite to Hartman and Philip I work within archives and "attempt to read against the grain...as a combination of foraging and disfiguration—raiding for fragments upon which other narratives can be spun and misshaping and deforming the testimony through selective quotation and...amplification."[31] I have worked with charged family and media archives, archives of corporate capital, and the violent documents of ongoing racialized colonialism in Palestine and Turtle Island—all archives that I am complicit with, folded together with. Apposite to Hartman I struggle with the fact that there is a "risk of reinforcing the authority of these documents even as I try to use them for contrary purposes."[32] I struggle with the risk of reinscribing the violence that I seek to denounce, and I sometimes fail in my task, in my making. But I essay again with some kind of responseability toward the dis-aster, the leaning-away star that will have always already exploded. "The disaster ruins everything, all the while leaving everything intact."[33] And I prefer to face the disaster as a monstrous body alongside other monsters. Making and showing us to us.

Gubar champions the use of the rhetorical figure prosopopoeia, or personification, as a "necromantic venture" of "speaking for the dead in the first person."[34] For Gubar, in the context of the Nazi holocaust, "what persists in the poetry of prosopopoeia is what some might term a fantasy, an abiding faith in the individuality, the autonomous consciousness of each subjectivity touched by a calamity that disproved the powers of individuality and of autonomous consciousness."[35] I am not interested in the phantasmatic powers of the individual. I am interested in entangled No Ones in swarm, field, plenum. Gubar calls for "a chorus of the Undead," which could be a collective music to listen to, as it is in *Zong!*, yet Gubar insists on it being the individual's job to practice necromancy and "rais[e] the dead" via identification, projection, and incorporation.[36] She draws on Paul de Man, who defines *prosoponpoiein* as "to *give* a face and therefore implies that the original face can be missing or nonexistent."[37] My mind goes to Spillers and how "the flesh gives empathy" to faceless absent-presence beyond the transcendental one-two punch of Levinasian ethics. Elsewhere, de Man defines prosopopoeia as "the fiction of an apostrophe to an absent, deceased, or voiceless entity, which posits the possibility of the latter's reply and confers upon it the power of speech. Voice assumes mouth, eye, and finally face, a chain that is manifest in the etymology of the trope's name, *prosopon poien*, to confer a mask or a face (*prosopon*)."[38] There is more Gubar could have explored here on the complex dynamics of gift giving and apostrophe and response, as well as the relation between the prosopon and the antiprosopon, the Gorgon. Agamben defines prosopon as "what stands before the eyes, what gives itself to be seen," and describes how the Gorgon, the antiface that defaces, is nevertheless represented in sculpture and vase painting through a face—"it cannot *not* be seen."[39] But can it be listened to? Elrick's performative "it" monstrates no discernible face or voice, yet stands and walks by face after face, calling, however futilely, for a reply. It haunts the street, and Levinas's face-to-face relation, with its own silent noise and mask. The flesh gives empathy. As Derrida claims, "Bearing witness is not through and through and necessarily discursive. It is sometimes silent. It has to engage something of the body, which has no right to speak."[40] Who has the right to speak interests me, as does the notion of witnessing *before* or *in front of, in the face of,* the witness, who then becomes the addressee of testimony, to draw on Derrida's third interpretation of für as an apostrophic call to bear witness to a message for them, for you; here not Spillers's "*being for* the captor," but "with and for" the undercommons, as Harney and Moten would say, rather than the individual or autonomous consciousness.[41] As Derrida suggests about writing such as Celan's, "In bearing witness *for* bearing witness, it bears witness."[42]

Like "bears" bearing down on witness, "for" also disappears in some English translations of the three Celan lines, such as "No one / witnesses the / witness." And with that decisive cut you lose an important call to fleshly response-ability and empathy in the faceless face(s) of No One(s), a call that may not receive a response, but still a song that must be sounded and listened to, "O einer, o keiner, o niemand, o du" (O one, o none, o no one, o you), as Celan performs a "Standing-for-no-one-and-nothing. / Unrecognized, / for you / alone. // With all that has room in it, / even without / language."[43] Perhaps not incidentally, if, as a minor thought experiment, für were to be eroded and disappear in the German version of these three lines that resist the best translation, No One would literally give birth to the witness.

....

STUDY · Claudia Rankine's acclaimed 2014 book of poetry, *Citizen:
An American Lyric*, is addressed to and through a slippery "you," as an
apostrophic call from not just an I to a singular other, but also a singular other to singular other and plural others to plural others and mixtures thereof. "You" acts as a substitute for "we" or "they," similar to
the impersonal, indefinite French *on* or English "one"; and it acts as a
"Hey you" interpellative wake-up call to the reader, in a way not dissimilar to how the "I" in Philip's *Zong!* becomes dispersed polyvocally
and the reader must grapple with their own positionality.[44] In *Citizen*,
the second person becomes also the third and fourth and more + less
than first, and Deleuze and Guattari would say "there is no subject,
only collective assemblages of enunciation."[45] Rankine's you works in
apposition to how Derrida describes Celan's use of the plural you, *euch*,
in "Aschenglorie": "The addressee of the apostrophe is pluralized....it is
no longer simply the same, no longer reducible to the being in the singular."[46] Consent not to be a single being. Celan: "I dug myself into you
and into you."[47] Derrida writes on Celan's apostrophic stanzas in a way
that can perhaps also speak to Rankine's: "They turn from one toward
the other; they turn away from one toward others; they return, they
turn round, they turn, from one to the other," in a compound
fleshly witnessing quite different from Agamben's singular "apostrophe
from which human beings cannot turn away," the sublime sight/site
of the Gorgon and its attendant disembodied "inhuman impossibility
of seeing" that he claims alone constitutes testimony.[48] The "immanent you—" in Rankine ("Who do you think you are, saying I to me? /
You nothing. / You nobody. / You.") is an "injured," embodied address
and turn in/to the face of the innumerable and incalculable microag-
gressions black citizens (and noncitizens) in antiblack nations like the
United States endure on a daily basis:[49]

> The man at the cash register wants to know if you think your
> card will work. If this is his routine, he didn't use it on the
> friend who went before you. As she picks up her bag, she
> looks to see what you will say. She says nothing. You want
> her to say something—both as witness and as a friend. She
> is not you; her silence says so. Because you are watching all
> this take place even as you participate in it, you say nothing
> as well. Come over here with me, your eyes say. Why on earth
> would she? The man behind the register returns your card

and places the sandwich and Pellegrino in a bag, which you
take from the counter. What is wrong with you? This question gets stuck in your dreams. (54)

Douglass's positioning himself as "a witness and a participant" echoes
here, applicable in different ways to speaker and "friend."[50] And "What
is wrong with you?" slips from accusation hailed at friend and cashier
and reader, whose dreams all require disruption, to an ongoing night-
mare of self-criticism. Near the end of the book, "The outside comes
in—" as "A body translates its you—" whether you shall have the body
or perhaps you may have the flesh (141, 143). "Don't say I if it means so
little, / holds the little forming no one" (143). The face-to-face relation,
the address for the other, threatens to collapse through the operations
of power: "I they he she we you turn / only to discover the encounter /
to be alien to this place....The opening, between you and you, occupied /
zoned for an encounter, / given the histories of you and you—" (140).
Face, page, place as contact zone, where you the reader must not only
acknowledge but *feel inside* (em-pathy) flesh deemed nonhuman or not-
quite-human—and feel inside the dashes that hold such violence in
Rankine's book, as they do in Jacobs's narrative. Perhaps a kind of transformation apposite to Glissant's *créolization* is possible, through which
"you can change, you can be with the other, you can change with the
other while being yourself, you are not one, you are multiple, and you
are yourself. You are not lost, because you are multiple. You are not broken apart, because you are multiple."[51] Moten calls for an "empathy of
no-bodies, an empathy of the flesh, an empathy against the metaphysics of Individuation, which is that which comprises and compromises
witness...a poetics of fleshly empathy, of entanglement, of absolute
no-thingness, of 'difference without separation.'"[52] Rankine too calls for
a new kind of empathic encounter, an invitation to enter into vulnerability, precarity, not alone but together, *for* one another:

Listen, you, I was creating a life study of a monumental
first person, a Brahmin first person.

If you need to feel that way—still you are in here and here
is nowhere.

Join me down here in nowhere. (73)[53]

Agamben names the "non-place, where the *Muselmann* lives" a "third realm," invoking Sofsky on the Nazi regime's manufacture of a "limbo between life and death" through which the regime "realizes its quintessential self."[54] If Muselmannland is the nonplace that "document[s] the total triumph of [autonomous, individuated] power over the human being," why not join the fleshly chorus of the Undead instead—the "impossible social life" of the nowhere, the undercommons, the shipped, and the motley crew?[55] As Moten writes on Philip's *Zong!*, in a passage that can perhaps also apply to *Citizen*, "*Zong!* does not represent the ones who become multiple; it just asks you to join them."[56] If poesis and witness mean anything at all, join the No Ones in nowhere where "No [O]ne is free" (124); in "the perverse affirmation of deracination" Sexton calls for, "an uprooting of the natal, the nation"; in Celan's "the eternalized Nowhere, here / in the memory of the over- / loud bells in—where only?"[57] Self-less, land-less within abolition, "come over here" and join the injured flesh of the earth, in song: "You are everywhere and you are nowhere in the day" (54, 141).[58]

....

the

The German *den*, like "you" in some ways, is an indefinite term, singular and plural, gendered in German and in French translation but not in English translation (as gender operates in more insidious ways in English). When I asked my native German speaker friend to help me translate and grammatically deconstruct the three Celan lines, I had hoped *den* in this case would be neutral in gender and perhaps have a possibility of plurality and indirection in designation, but alas it is decidedly singular, masculine, and accusative when attached to Zeugen/ witness. I had wanted *a* witness or witnesses, not *the* witness, like I want Deleuze's indeterminate *a life*, not that only lonely one over there. I want "to live among one's own in dispossession, to live among the ones who cannot own, the ones who have nothing and who, in having nothing, have everything. To live, in other words, within the general commonness and openness of *a life* in Deleuze's sense," as Moten suggests.[1] Let us imagine other forms of life than bare life, which, according to Weheliye, "leaves no room for alternate forms of life that elude the law's violent embrace. What seems to have vanished from [Agamben's] description is the *life* in the *bare life* compound; hence the homo sacer remains a thing, whose happening slumbers in bare life without journeying through the rivulets of liberations elsewhere."[2] I want a life that, as Foucault posits, "constantly escapes" capture, definition, administrative techniques; I want Moten's fugitivity "between escape and the frame," a "broken breaking bridge and broken circle," his "sharing of a life in homelessness."[3] I want Ferreira da Silva's poethical, entangled plenum; I want the flesh. Now I wonder why Heidegger's *Dasein* translates as being-*the*-there—and how that relates to Philip's "the this / the that / the frenzy" and "is there is / or / being // there."[4] Or why Celan adds the article to his book title *Die Niemandsrose* (The Noonesrose).[5] Is it an attempt to use determinate specificity to deny No One(s) their monstrous bloom?

....

STUDY · Interviewer: What does monster mean to you?

Bhanu Kapil: An unassimilable content. An immigrant. Revenge.

"MICHAEL MARTIN SHEA WITH BHANU KAPIL AND CHING-IN CHEN"

While *Zong!* tells a story that cannot be told, Bhanu Kapil's 2015 book *Ban en Banlieue* compiles "notes for a novel never written."[6] About a body never fully bodied, bodied into extreme violence and the sovereign ban of her namesake, always already dead; but also "a negation that wasn't erased—," the dash holding and displacing Ban's cuts in/to the narrative (90).[7] Ban as a form of female flesh ungendered. Meat. Habeas viscus. No One. A "monstrous hybrid of human and animal, divided between the forest and the city"(41). Ban as an assemblage, a life, a form of Spillers's "praxis and...theory, a text for living and for dying, and a method for reading both through their diverse mediations":[8]

Ban is not an immigrant; she is a shape or bodily outline that's familiar: yet inaccurate: to what the thing is. How to look good on Skype. A vaginal opening. By 2011, she's a blob of meat on the sidewalk. I progress her to meat—a monstrous form—but here she pauses, is inhibited, and this takes a long time. I make a graph of her scissoring limbs [forearms, hands, tongue] and index them to the last 12 hours: 4 p.m. to 4 a.m. [and other dominant forms]. I lie down next to her and extend my own tongue to the ivy that curls down to the sidewalk with its medicine and salt: so close to my own mouth. Lick it and you could die. I do all these things, but Ban does not die. With every rainfall, she's washed off the street but by morning, a stain rises up through the asphalt and by 4 p.m. the next day, she's ready to go again. This is the first problem of the project; an interest in duration as the force by which—something: might become....Ban...lies outside of time. Precisely because—as a black person or child born to immigrants in the U.K. of 1971—her birth broke something. It inserted something, like when you start to hate yourself or when you lose something. "What is born in England but is never English?" What grew a tail? What leaned over and rested its hands on its knees? An immigrant has a set of complex origins, is from elsewhere; the monster is made, on the other hand, from local mixtures of organic and inorganic materials, repurposed teeth, selenium, lungs, pink lightning, public health concerns....I thought I was writing about an immigrant. I was writing about a monster. Monsters don't incarnate. They regress. (20–21; brackets in original)

Ban en Banlieue narrates banned, abandoned Ban bodies deemed disposable and subject to murder: in a 1979 London race riot (Blair Peach), on a 1982 New York street (Theresa Hak Kyung Cha), out a 1985 New York window (Ana Mendieta), on a 2012 New Delhi street (Jyoti Singh Pandey). Itself a combinatory monster of violent "discharge," blog posts, notes on performances, errata, and other forms, *Ban en Banlieue* narrates Kapil's various failures to demonstrate Ban, to bring Ban to a life in the organic and nonorganic book, through writing, durational performance, and literally lying down in the space of history (24). Perhaps not lying but laying, as one scholar, Amy De'Ath, distinguishes Kapil's laying down as an active form from lying down as a passive (often sexualized) site.[9] Laying down as not dissimilar to the numerous "die-in" protests against the extrajudicial killing of black people or endless war or environmental disaster—or ACT UP's die-in protests, like the 1989 action during which activists lay down in the aisles of St. Patrick's Cathedral, an action to which Hayes refers in her *In the Near Future* performance. And yet Ban's actions seem closer to, and an homage to, Mendieta's well-known body/earthwork *Silueta* performance/sculptures, perhaps more monstrous test or *testimonio* than protest.[10] Alongside *Ban en Banlieue*, Kapil performs lying/laying-down rituals that include materials such as sindoor (red powder), peacock ore, mirrors, aluminum foil, and flowers to conjure the brutal death scenes of Singh Pandey, Cha, Peach, and Mendieta, while also bearing witness to Kapil's own experiences of racialized violence, her own "monstrous self-hood....The moment of articulation—the pen's nib pressed into the paper—as the moment: of erasure."[11] Claiming that "some bodies don't somatize," Kapil positions Ban as a "mixture of dead and living things....a next life.... almost but never quite dead," beginning again while monstrously never beginning, over and over (75, 82). A life in which, as Harney and Moten suggest, "We fall so we can fall again, which is what ascension really means to us. To fall is to lose one's place, to lose the place that makes one, to relinquish the locus of being, which is to say of being single."[12] Ban's multiple births and deaths broke a book, engendering another story, like *Zong!*, that can't be told but must be told, through untelling: "It's about the novel as a form that processes the part of a scene that doesn't function as an image, but as the depleted, yet still livid mixture of materials that a race riot is made from" (37). A "novel that [N]o [O]ne writes" (32).

In one section of the book, "Inversions for Ban," Kapil attributes to Agamben the line "To ban someone is to say that no-one may harm him," when the Agamben line from *Homo Sacer* (in which he is actually quoting Desiderio Cavalca on the medieval ban) is "'To ban' someone is to say that anyone may harm him," with the banned being considered to be already dead (41).[13] Kapil's gesture of invoking no-one (or No One) inversely, perversely, protects Ban from the sovereign ban and the limits of Agamben's thinking on the homo sacer, transforming Ban ("my creature") and *Ban en Banlieue* into "a portal, a vortex, a curl," a livid mixture of "fugitive" ban-dit and outlaw text, "study[ing] the [sacred] wolf" (27, 42, 104, 41). "You could be naked out back and [N]o [O]ne would see. Nobody" (44).

In "Inversions for Ban," Kapil points out: "To ban, to sentence. To abandon is thus to write prose" (41). The narrator "wanted to write a book that was like lying [or laying] down" (42). Some-thing like Kafka's and Celan's distorted subject, Ban/Bhanu bows her head far down on her chest, leans over, rests her hands on her knees, lies (or lays) down at the sites of some of the traumatic events she can't recount—and sprinkles some "gold, red and orange 'blooms.' And dirt. Nobody saw" (47). Ban/Bhanu narrates a death, a life, a breathturn that is collective and incalculable, the stain always already rising up: "To gather what you can never write: a witness account" (89).

Invoking the aesthetic sociality of blackness, Kapil describes Ban as "a black girl in an era when, in solidarity, Caribbean and Asian Brits self-defined as black" (30).[14] Ban is "a puff of diesel. Something like a smudge, already dispersing. A warp of smoke....some soot...smeared on the page" (50). Ban is something like the ether that Weheliye associates with the hieroglyphics of black flesh, "the ether that broadcasts slashes onto the scar tissue of succeeding generations."[15] For Kapil, "Blackening the pages is writing" (106). "I wanted to write a novel but instead I wrote this. [Hold up charcoal in fist.]" (19). For Weheliye, channeling

Spillers, "claiming and dwelling in the monstrosity of the flesh...liberate[s] from captivity assemblages of life, thought, and politics from the tradition of the oppressed and, as a result, disfigure[s] the centrality of Man as the sign for the human."[16] Kapil's monster arrives without arrival as an in- or extrahuman guest, in the sooty, un-Manly flesh of "unassimilable content" and "immigrant...revenge."[17] Kapil's writing enacts what Weheliye calls "the monstrosity of the flesh as a site for freedom beyond the world of Man," while asking for the reader's/host's radical hospitality toward *a life* that "feral events cut through."[18] "Will you give a hand to Ban?" (53). Will you decide to be complicit with flesh's tissue, text, touch? Will you ask yourself, "Does the body of the witness discharge something too?" (25).

Perhaps.[19] February 23, 2011, was the day writers Rachel Levitsky, Emily Beall, and I paid a locksmith 200 dollars to break down the door to poet Akilah Oliver's Brooklyn apartment so that we could enter her space not as guests *are there greeters there [are you one]* and come upon her body, alone, in her bed, dead *when we former ghosts arrive*.[20] The TV and lights were on, Butler's *Antigone's Claim* was open on the couch, and Akilah had perhaps gone to lie (or lay) down because she was feeling unwell *i forgot what it feels like to fall*.[21] When Rachel and I entered her bedroom, it became evident that Akilah had been lying (or laying) there for a number of days *a gone time...a calculated blue* and my body will never forget her flesh, its hieroglyphics *i witness bones on the atlantic floor*.[22]

Oliver, a brilliant queer black poet, thinker, and performance artist, theorized in the preface to her first book, *the she said dialogues: flesh memory*, published in 1999, on flesh memory, defined as:

> 1. a text, a language, a mythology, a truth, a reality, an invented as well as literal translation of everything that we've ever experienced or known, whether we know it directly or through some type of genetic memory, osmosis or environment. 2. the body's truths and realities. 3. the multiplicity of languages and realities that the flesh holds. 4. the language activated in the body's memory.[23]

Oliver doesn't cite Spillers on the flesh in her definition of flesh memory but rather attributes the definition to a source called "Post-modern Poetry and Performance Art," which as far as I can tell doesn't exist as a text. I am guessing that Oliver wrote this definition herself and may not have read Spillers beforehand; yet I do feel Spillers's presence here as Oliver "rewrite[s]...a radically different text for female empower-

FIGURE 8.1 Bhanu Kapil, *Ban Action [Gesture]*, 2014. Service road in front of hotel 37, Mahipalpur (Airport) Flyover. South Delhi, India. Courtesy of the artist and Nightboat Books.

ment," claiming her own hieroglyphics of the flesh, including her right to point and show and name; her right to use "thought as witness," just as *monstrare* comes from the root *men-*, to think with.[24]

Later in the preface, Oliver writes, "What I am trying to do in these poems is investigate the non-linear synapses between desire, memory, blackness (as both a personal identity and a non-essentialist historical notion), sexuality and language" (xi). She continues framing the work as

> a critical interrogation of the African American literary/performative tradition. That tradition (what I consider to be crouched in the sacred/profane dichotomy, a dichotomy which Du Bois called "double consciousness") is an out-growth of a necessitated survival mechanism, which has split "Black consciousness," not only in terms of the outward, homogenous mask donned as a form of cultural preservation, but also in terms of the internal discourse: what is permissible to speak.
>
> The work I've been doing consciously seeks to disrupt this tradition, to play not only with language and form, but with the representational idioms of "blackness," "femaleness," "homogeneity"....to work as a kind of insurgent text....restat[ing] memory and identity in a post-Civil Rights framework. A framework which is multiplicitous....Stretching the dialogue. Admitting the contractions. Investigating the truths. Making itself up as it goes. Refashioning the Black female tongue. (xii)

Again I feel Spillers's presence, Oliver "gaining the *insurgent* ground as female social subject," yet also "*claiming* the monstrosity" of something more than a "female with a potential to 'name,'" Oliver claiming an ungendered positionality that is multiplicitous and irruptive, fleshly refashioning.[25]

The poems are mostly in prose poem style—"the block form is a kind of container to hold the 'narrative' or dialogue" (xi)—and one poem in particular stands out in this context, titled "gently she tucks her hand under my chin, she says, don't be afraid, your demons are your friends." I will just quote from the beginning:

night becomes you so said little angels dressed in red on the way home from parties where the dead bless the damned. confusions date the air. smoke goes easily into passageways between dreams & regret. passed onto those who will themselves generations. rams with aries tags skittering across the wide boulevards in brownie uniforms. think the pledge worthy of remembrance. how do you wake the dead cushioned in sheepskin car seat covers. enter the angel. some hair lingers in her armpits. pick up the butts to smoke. down in the street they lay in shades of blackness. not the celebrated dreams of nationalist visionaries who want it all romantic or nothing. look for lit veils. there are so many ways to pass the time on earth. the sorrow the grief stands in line to be recognized.

stop to hold me. (5)

We stopped to keep vigil *holding the space* in Akilah's apartment *language is a skin* as government functionaries *memory is a skin* traipsed across her

threshold *forgetting is a skin* we lit candles *fear is a skin* we poured a liba-
tion *desire is a skin* we clung together *whip is a skin* against wide-open cold
i looked out the window at the baby tearful snow then when the light came
absence is a skin I made the coroner guys carry Akilah *Am I now the dead
person?* instead of dragging her down the stairs *the trace of what cremated
godhead is this moving through Me, strewn & plundered* as she left her home
in a big black bag *there's more dead than I can count already, these formidable
no bodies. Is there a name / for all this noise?*[26]

Two years after this experience, I was asked to write a short com-
mentary on poetic labor and wrote in part about Akilah, including this:
"Would she have died if one of her adjunct poetry teaching jobs had
provided her with health insurance? Would her twenty-one-year-old
son Oluchi have died eight years earlier if one of her adjunct poetry
teaching jobs had provided her and her dependant with health insurance? Some would call these rhetorical questions."[27] Akilah, in an author statement for her last published full-length book, wrote:

> In approaching the subject, the death of the beloved, I enter into an
> investigation of the ecstatic in the dual sites of rapture and rupture.
> For me, an absolute rupture occurred at the time of my son's death,
> so that the world broke open, in a sense, and I decided to follow the
> opening to wherever it led, rather than try to patch it or close it. The
> opening, this rupture, this state of the world breaking open and me,
> being broken open, did not lead to any one rapturous state (as if rap-
> ture, or bliss, were a desirable closure), but rather led me to want to
> continue to go there, off, beyond the limits of language and cognition
> to rapture (an intense pleasure of transportation from one place to an-
> other, as in heaven). I think for many poets, at least for me, to write is
> a kind of difficult dance with rapture; it is a way to beckon the day as a
> beloved, a way to talk to the dead, a way to collapse the known world
> into the impossible.[28]

Ec-stasy as a form of *a mountain. a laughter. a woman. a tattoo*—a life—
beside ourselves on insurgent ground claiming noisy monstrosity as *the
skin bears witness* to and with formidable nobodies *being broken open and
going down that passageway* beyond the limits of language, cognition, and
being, where flesh memory stands in line to be *an arriving guard of angels,
thusly coming to greet*—and defend the dead. *[N]obody's home in my body.*[29]

....

witness(es)

Niemand
zeugt für den
Zeugen.
PAUL CELAN

The last word in Celan's "Aschenglorie," Zeugen, appears alone on its own line, accompanied by a period to end the poem. While its spelling matches the German infinitive verb "to witness" and parallels the verb zeugt directly above it, this word is not a verb because it is capitalized, as nouns are in German. On its own line, this noun initially doesn't seem to have a number or gender or article designation, and yet it soon escapes femininity because it has no "i" in it (*Zeugin*). And while its plurality seems possible sitting there on its own (Zeugen is also used as the plural form), when we regress one line to den we regress to singularity, the "neutral" masculine form. In English translation, we don't get this tension of the possible witness as active witnesses: it is individuation all the way. I don't consent to that. There is no single witness. Even in juridical contexts, there is no demonstration without at least two witnesses. And the visual parallelism between Niemand and Zeugen, occupying their own lines singularly, separated by only one other line, draws these nouns together, properly. No One(s), not-one(s), never Man(s) witness(es) for the witness(es), and this witnessing and these witnesses are plural, collective, monstrously resistant to the disciplinary order:

> The *Muselmänner* repeatedly violated this self-discipline. They stood in the way everywhere....They were filthy, stinking, oblivious of what was happening to and with them....Although they were corpses, they still moved....In the barracks, they dirtied the halls, bunks, and blankets. At meal distribution, they tried to push their way to the front, were shoved aside, and had to look on as the others ate. They relieved them-

selves in soup bowls; they begged and stole. They did not care about punishments....Since they repeatedly violated the rules of order and cleanliness, they were singled out as scapegoats....They reacted without resistance to blows and lashes, as though these were not meant for them....Punched in the face, they did not react. They were kicked but they felt no pain. They were whipped and beaten, yet in vain. Their apathy was provocative; it stirred the rage of their tormentors. The excess of violence was vented specifically against the *Muselmänner*. Orders accomplished nothing. Even violence fell flat; it was ineffective. The passivity of the *Muselmann* was an insult to power.[1]

We're back to the beginning, radical passivity, fugitivity, outlaw refusal of refusal, but more than anything, sur-vival, superstes, holding to the thing, together. In a meditation on black thingliness Moten asks, "What if the thing whose meaning or value has never been found finds things, founds things? What if the thing will have founded something against the very possibility of foundation and against all anti- or post-foundational impossibilities?"[2] What if, as Celan suggests, "some other thing" is always already "set free"?[3] The testimony "I was a Muselmann" speaks beyond Agamben's static example of the thingly inhuman in the human, beyond the homo sacer waiting passively for the gas chambers No One can demonstrate existed. From Weheliye we know "the Muselmänner's relational flesh speaks, conjures, intones, and concocts sumptuous universes that are silenced when the Muselmann is confined to the status of an exceptionally disembodied example. For what comes after the Muselmann for those who lived to bear witness to this (in)humanity is survival, as a potentiality or an actuality; and that, at least for some, is nothing but a politics."[4]

Certain Nazi holocaust survivors such as Jean Améry refuse to speak of the Muselmann. Améry refers to the Muselmann as "the prisoner who was giving up and was given up by his comrades," a "staggering corpse, a bundle of physical functions in its last convulsions." Améry claims that, because of the Muselmann's "dehumanized" state, "we must exclude him from our considerations."[5] And yet the motley crew, the undercommon chorus of more + less than one + three or more, listens hard to the "uncouth and inarticulate sounds" of the Muselmann—and Wilderson's "sentient being whose story can be neither recognized nor incorporated into Human civil society."[6] These No Ones claim this monstrous speech of their comrades as a "primary narrative" and a "praxis and theory, a text for living and for dying," following Spillers's belief in the founding possibilities of thingly female flesh ungendered.[7] As Hartman states, "In the city, black people are producing modern forms of life. These emergent forms are only recognizable in their initial appearance as monstrous."[8] Claiming and bearing witness to monstrosity's unrecognizable flesh as an alternative form of life—flesh as a fugitive form of witness. Spillers: "The flesh gives empathy"; the flesh offers alternate ways of feeling inside, attending and holding to the thing, sur-viving. Spillers may or may not have read Akilah Oliver's work but uses the term "flesh memory" in Arthur Jafa's 2014 film, *Dreams Are Colder Than Death*. Spillers describes how part of her sister's leg was amputated, but her sister still felt the pain of her phantom limb. "That's a flesh memory," Spillers insists.[9] A "hieroglyphics of the flesh" that can "transfer" across time and generations.[10] Hartman also uses the image of the phantom limb to describe how certain everyday practices of enslaved people "witness and record the violent discontinuities of history introduced by the Middle Passage":

> These traces of memory function in a manner akin to a phantom limb, in that what is felt is no longer there. It is a sentient recollection of connectedness experienced at the site of rupture, where the very consciousness of disconnectedness acts as mode of testimony and memory. The recognition of loss is a crucial element in redressing the breach introduced by slavery. This recognition entails a re-membering of the pained body, not by way of a simulated wholeness, but precisely through the recognition of the amputated body in its amputatedness, in the insistent recognition of the violated body as human flesh, in the cognition of its needs, and in the anticipation of its liberty. In other words, it is the ravished body that holds out the possibility of restitution, not the invocation of an illusory wholeness or the desired return to an originary plenitude.[11]

Recognizing the amputated body in its pained amputatedness *as flesh and as witness*, the bundle of physical functions in its last convulsions *as flesh and as witness*: that is the way to begin. For "a monstrosity never presents itself: or else, if you prefer, it only presents itself, that is, lets itself be recognized...by not letting itself be recognized as what it is—a monstrosity. A monstrosity can only be 'mis-known' (*méconnue*), that is, unrecognized and misunderstood. It can only be recognized afterwards, when it has become normal or the norm."[12] Claiming that dangerous perhaps of monstrous afterward, and will have been afterward, right now, as No Ones bear normal fleshly witness for the witnesses in the swarm, field, ensemble, plenum. "The *Muselmänner* marched out as the last Kommando, holding hands, in rows of five."[13]

....

STUDY · This final study begins with a slight misreading of two short passages from Hartman's 2007 book, *Lose Your Mother: A Journey along the Atlantic Slave Route*:

> I, too, was a failed witness. Reckoning with my inheritance had driven me to the dungeon, but now it all seemed elusive. I struggled to connect the dots between then and now and to chart the trajectory between the Gold Coast and Curaçao and Montgomery and Brooklyn. But I kept fumbling.[14]

> When we had started out on our journey, Anyidoho said he expected me to be the witness for the group, because I was a descendant of slaves. But I didn't believe I could act as witness for the collective. The witness required a listener, and everyone had grown weary of me.[15]

In the first passage, for the frustrated fumbling at witnessing Hartman expresses, I read fumbling *along*, what I interpreted as Hartman continuing in her impossibly errant desire to listen to and render in print the unsayable and unarchived histories of the lives and afterlives of transatlantic slavery. When I read the second passage, the "collective" of people Hartman was travelling with in Ghana transformed in my mind into the "chorus" at the end of her 2019 book, *Wayward Lives, Beautiful Experiments: Intimate Histories of Social Upheaval*. In my errant imagination, Hartman's disbelief that she could act as a "witness for the collective" transformed over those twelve years between books into the stunning counternarrative of the lives of ordinary black women in the United States at the turn of the twentieth century found in *Wayward Lives*: "If you listen closely, you can hear the whole world in a bent note, a throwaway lyric, a singular thread of the collective utterance."[16]

In an important essay about her composition of *Lose Your Mother*, "Venus in Two Acts," Hartman expresses her frustrations with the "limits of fact, evidence, and archive…dead certainties…produced by terror," embodied in an "emblematic figure of the enslaved woman," Venus, whose impossible, "untimely story [is] told by a failed witness," a witness

who Hartman again intimates is herself.[17] Hartman uses "critical fabulation" in parts of *Lose Your Mother* to listen "for the unsaid, translating misconstrued words, and refashioning disfigured lives." One could
argue that both *Lose Your Mother* and her earlier monumental *Scenes of
Subjection* attempt the impossible, to "rewrite the chronicle of a death
foretold and anticipated, as a collective biography of dead subjects, as
a counter-history of the human, as the practice of freedom."[18] But it is
in *Wayward Lives* that Hartman is able to use another method of critical fabulation called "close narration"—a "style which places the voice
of narrator and character in inseparable relation, so that the vision,
language, and rhythms of the wayward shape and arrange the text"
(xiii–xiv)—to write the kind of story she longed for when she wrote
Lose Your Mother, "a romance that exceeded the fictions of history" and
"trespassed the boundaries of the archive," a "new story...disordering
and transgressing the protocols of the archive and the authority of its
statements...to augment and intensify its fictions."[19] In this romance
that is *Wayward Lives*, Hartman's close narration lovingly demonstrates
the lives and stories of a selection of "ordinary" black women living in
northern US cities in the first part of the twentieth century, women
whose lives might have been forgotten were it not for Hartman's de-
voted cull through mounds of trial transcripts, interviews with psy-
chologists, prison case files, and other archival material, "all of which
represent [these women] as a problem" (xiv). Hartman's objective in
writing this book is to

> recover the insurgent ground of these lives; to exhume open rebellion
> from the case file, to untether waywardness, refusal, mutual aid, and
> free love from their identification as deviance, criminality, and pathol-
> ogy; to affirm free motherhood (reproductive choice), intimacy out-
> side the institution of marriage, and queer and outlaw passions; and
> to illuminate the radical imagination and everyday anarchy of ordi-
> nary colored girls, which has not only been overlooked, but is nearly
> unimaginable. (xiv)

Creating this counternarrative on Spillers's "insurgent" ground through
and beyond the archive, Hartman accomplishes something far removed
from "failed witness."[20] In the imaginative unfolding of this swarm,
field, ensemble, plenum of a book, Hartman bears witness to and brings
to life "not the story of one girl, but a serial biography of a generation, a

portrait of the chorus" and a "picture of the social upheaval that transformed black social life in the twentieth century" (31, xiv).

Hartman's beautiful experiment in *Wayward Lives* is a "black radical procedure" not unlike how Ferreira da Silva, in a 2019 article, "Hacking the Subject: Black Feminism and Refusal beyond the Limits of Critique," takes Spillers's "unprotected female flesh" as a "praxis and theory" and uses a radical equation procedure "to transfigure 'woman' (and with her the female and the feminine), to deface her, and release her to accomplish what she alone can perform, which is the dis/ordering of the modern grammar in which the patriarch remains the presupposed bearer of self-determination in its ethical and juridical renderings, respectively liberty and authority."[21] Such radical disorderings of grammar and archive and gender and racialization through critical fabulation and experiment are "what becomes possible when blackness wonders and wanders in the world, heeding the ethical mandate to challenge our thinking, to release the imagination, and to welcome the end of the world as we know it, that is, decolonization, which is the only proper name for justice."[22]

Wayward Lives is "a narrative written from nowhere, from the nowhere of the ghetto and the nowhere of utopia" that "recognizes the revolutionary ideals that animated ordinary lives. It explores the utopian longings and the promise of a future world that resided in waywardness and the refusal to be governed" (xiii, xv). In "Venus in Two Acts," Hartman asks, "Must the future of abolition be first performed on the page?"[23] *Wayward Lives* performs such a future of abolition as it "attend[s] to other forms of social life, which cannot be reduced to transgression or to nothing at all, and which emerge in the world marked by negation, but exceed it" (62). Attending to forms of no-thing and No One and nowhere, imagining "jurisgenerative black social life walking down the middle of the street."[24] Ferreira da Silva, theorist of the nowhere and the plenum, asks, "What if...*female flesh ungendered* is unleashed to unsettle the *equation of sexual reproduction* and the *equation of sexual desire*?"[25] and my mind goes to Hartman describing the sexual embodiment of an ordinary black woman, Mattie Jackson, in *Wayward Lives*:

> To be undone, against her will and with her consent. A state that was
> neither autonomy nor capture. It broke her down, it made her nothing
> at all, it laid her low, it transformed her into anything else she longed

to be: like a bird flying high or a thing vast and boundless, oceanic—not a person at all. In the reek and warmth of a rented room she was all flesh and sensation; she was hovering at the end of the world. And she welcomed it. (63)

Consent not to be a single being, in another world, always already here. Transubstantiation within the plenum, a black feminist poethics of actual-virtuality.

Mattie, "an average chorine, just one of the girls, nobody special, part of the assembly, engulfed in the crowd, lost in the company of minor figures," is later wrongly imprisoned at Bedford Hills Reformatory in upstate New York and ends up joining the "infernal chorus" of a "noise strike" and riot in 1920 against the conditions at the women's prison and the structural conditions that brought the women wrongly deemed "wayward" to the prison (345, 279). In the consequent "sonic tumult and upheaval," which lasted for days, women screamed, sang, pounded the walls with their fists, broke windows, set fires, tossed mattresses, and banged the instruments of their enclosure against walls, "the dangerous music of black life...unleashed from within the space of captivity," becoming "a reservoir of living within the prison's mandated death" (284, 285, 286). As Hartman states, drawing on Douglass's descriptions of the songs of enslaved people as revolutionary "jargon and nonsense":

> The aesthetic inheritance of "jargon and nonsense" was nothing if not a philosophy of freedom that reached back to slave songs and circle dances—the sonic gifts of struggle and flight, death and refusal, became music or moanin' or joyful noise or discordant sound....In *the surreal, utopian nonsense of it all*, and at the heart of riot, was the anarchy of colored girls: treason *en masse*, tumult, gathering together, the mutual collaboration required to confront the prison authorities and the police, the willingness to lose oneself and become something greater—a chorus, swarm, ensemble, mutual aid society. In lieu of an explanation or an appeal, they shouted and screamed. (285)[26]

This was "the free music of those in captivity, the abolition philosophy expressed within the circle, the shout and speech song of struggle" (284). Hartman asks the reader to "marvel at their capacity to inhabit every woman's grief as their own. All the stories ever told rush from her opened mouth. A tome of philosophy in a moan" (345). Hartman wants the reader to "reckon with the disavowed geography of the world: the barracoon, the hold, the plantation, the camp, the reservation, the garret, the colony, the attic studio, the bedroom, the urban archipelagoes, the ghetto, and the prison" (347). Like the chorus of voices in *Zong!*, in *Wayward Lives* "the chorus bears all of it for us," the "history of the universe seen from nowhere" and "everything depends on them and not the hero occupying center stage, preening and sovereign" (347, 349). Nothing for No One.[27] "*No slave time now. Abolition now*" (285).[28] Sexton: "The flesh of the earth demands it: the landless inhabitation of selfless existence."[29] For Ferreira da Silva, "without the patriarch-form, which refers to the authority of the Subject—the signifier of the Phallus (the ruler of meaning in figurings of universal reason as *nomos* and *poiesis*) *there* is the Thing or the otherwise than the World as we know it. Nobody's mother; no one's wife."[30] No Ones' witness, the "mass + energy of social flesh," that collective Thing that *gives* empathy *otherwise*.[31] For Hartman, "the chorus elaborates and reconstructs the passage, conjures the death in the fields and the death on city pavements, and reanimates life; it enables the felled bodies to rise, plays out in multiple times, and invites all to enter the circle, to join the line, to rejoice, and to *celebrate with great solemnity*" (197, italics in original). Breathturn in the abyss, Venus and Hurbinek and Michael Brown and Ban and Mattie Jackson speak and fall and lie (and lay) down together, some otherwise thing set free. Hartman: "This story is told from inside the circle" (xiv). Fanon: "There are no limits—inside the circle."[32] Ferreira da Silva: "What lies outside the equations, in which the sexual black (and native) female body means nothing, is a Nothing by which I mean Everything and Anything else than the World as we know it today."[33] Chandler: "Nothing...comes on the scene on other terms."[34] Harney and Moten: "Give it all away until you are nothing."[35] Celan: "Nobody can tell how long the pause for breath—hope and thought—will last."[36] Hartman makes an apostrophic call: "If you are able to bear the burden of what they have to bring, then there is a place for you inside the circle and what you have suffered is part of this inventory" (346). A dangerous perhaps of monstrous plenum, a "held fleshliness of the collective head," some kind of social poesis, motley crew, undercommons:[37] "The collective movement points toward what awaits us, what has yet to come into view, what they anticipate—the time and place better than here; a glimpse of the earth not owned by anyone," a monstrous perhaps (349).

the matter of life returns as an open question[38]

a will to unsettle, destroy, and remake[39]

the possibility of being-in-the-world anew[40]

Join the No Ones down here in "nowhere, which is to say everywhere," where "all modalities play a part, where the headless group incites change, where mutual aid provides the resource for collective action, not leader and mass, where the untranslatable songs and seeming nonsense make good the promise of revolution."[41]

The struggle is eternal

Somebody else carries on

Nobody and everyone at the same time[42]

An "assembly sustaining dreams of the otherwise," always already surviving genocide in contact, as improvisation, within and without the enclosure, holding to the thing.[43] In the "aesthetic sociality of blackness" and the "ceaseless practice of black radicalism and refusal," the monstrous "chorus increases" and "all black everything" de(-)monstrates how flesh keeps speaking and No Ones bear witness for the witnesses.[44] Another city will have been chanting chortling ululating folding fingers foam cups fallen fractal feather cracks fate crusts smudges meat warp of rapture rupture pink lightning ligature loss at edge swarm field breathturn beloved perverted eroded insurgent tongues, a dangerous perhaps, dancing.

....

APPENDIX

Paul Celan, "Aschenglorie" (Ashglory)

Aschenglorie hinter
deinen erschüttert-verknoteten
Händen am Dreiweg.

Pontisches Einstmals: hier,
ein Tropfen,
auf
dem ertrunkenen Ruderblatt,
tief
im versteinerten Schwur,
rauscht es auf.

(Auf dem senkrechten
Atemseil, damals,
höher als oben,
zwischen zwei Schmerzknoten, während
der blanke
Tatarenmond zu uns heraufklomm,
grub ich mich in dich und in dich.)

Aschen-
glorie hinter
euch Dreiweg-
Händen.

Das vor euch, vom Osten her, Hin-
gewürfelte, furchtbar.

Niemand
zeugt für den
Zeugen.

Ashglory behind
your shaken-knotted
hands at the threeway.

Pontic erstwhile: here,
a drop,
on
the drowned rudder blade,
deep
in the petrified oath,
it roars up.

(On the vertical
breathrope, in those days,
higher than above,
between two painknots, while
the glossy
Tatarmoon climbed up to us,
I dug myself into you and into you.)

Ash-
glory behind
you threeway
hands.

The cast-in-front-of-you, from
the East, terrible.

No one
bears witness for the
witness.[1]

NOTES

OPENING

1 The last three lines of Paul Celan, "Aschenglorie" (Ashglory), one translation of which is "No one / bears witness for the / witness." In Celan, *Breathturn into Timestead: The Collected Later Poetry; A Bilingual Edition*, 62–65, translated by Pierre Joris. See the appendix for the complete poem and one English translation by Joris. One of the several other possible translations is "Nobody / witnesses the / witness."

2 Jacques Derrida, "Poetics and Politics of Witnessing," in *Sovereignties in Question: The Poetics of Paul Celan*, 67.

3 *Resistancy* is translation scholar Lawrence Venuti's term for preserving the roughness/strangeness of words in translation, "not merely because it avoids fluency, but because it challenges the target-language culture even as it enacts its own ethnocentric violence on the foreign text." See *The Translator's Invisibility: A History of Translation*, 24.

4 "I would prefer not to" is Bartleby's consistent response to his employer's entreaties that Bartleby perform his copying duties as scribe—and subsequent demands that he leave the premises. Herman Melville, *Bartleby, the Scrivener*.

5 Maurice Blanchot, *The Writing of the Disaster*, 10.

6 Fred Moten, "The Blur and Breathe Books," in *Black and Blur: Critical Essays*, vol. 1 of *consent not to be a single being*, 257. Moten is drawing on Charles Gaines's essay "The Theater of Refusal: Black Art and Mainstream Criticism," 13–21.

7 I follow Norman G. Finkelstein's use of the term "Nazi holocaust" instead of the commercialized "Holocaust" or "Shoah," placing the focus of the term, and responsibility, on the perpetrators. See *The Holocaust Industry: Reflections on the Exploitation of Jewish Suffering*, 3: "*Nazi holocaust* signals the actual historical event, *The Holocaust* its ideological representation."

8 Paul Antschel wrote under the pseudonym Paul Celan. Antschel in Romanian form is Ancel, and Celan is an anagram of Ancel. One often feels the urge to place "proper" in scare quotes after Derrida's obliteration of the proper name and Moten's definition of black radicalism as "the performance of a general critique of the proper." See Derrida, *Of Grammatology*; Moten, "Chromatic Saturation," in *The Universal Machine: Theoretical Essays*, vol. 3 of *consent not to be a single being*, 140; and Denise Ferreira da Silva on "the limits of the proper (in its economic and ethical meanings)" in "Hacking the Subject: Black Feminism and Refusal beyond the Limits of Critique," 22. Proper's imbrication with property, appropriation, self-

possession (and thus legal personhood), and dispossession is explored in various ways in this book.

9   See Kelly Oliver, *Witnessing: Beyond Recognition*, 18.

10   See the "witness" and "for" chapters in this book.

11   Blanchot, *The Writing of the Disaster*, 17.

12   See Sylvia Wynter, "*Proud Flesh* Inter/Views: Sylvia Wynter," 24.

13   Giorgio Agamben, *Remnants of Auschwitz: The Witness and the Archive*, 44; and Alexander G. Weheliye, *Habeas Viscus: Racializing Assemblages, Biopolitics, and Black Feminist Theories of the Human*, 130.

14   Frank B. Wilderson III, *Red, White, and Black: Cinema and the Structure of U.S. Antagonisms*, 143.

15   Moten, "Erotics of Fugitivity," in *Stolen Life: Social Essays*, vol. 2 of *consent not to be a single being*, 243–44.

16   Moten, "Chromatic Saturation," in *The Universal Machine*, 142.

17   Moten, *A Poetics of the Undercommons*, 28. See Nahum Dimitri Chandler's *X: The Problem of the Negro as a Problem for Thought*; and "The Problem of the Centuries," 41.

18   Moten, *The Universal Machine*, 262n3.

19   Moten, "Chromatic Saturation," in *The Universal Machine*, 194.

20   See Édouard Glissant, Manthia Diawara, and Christopher Winks, "Édouard Glissant in Conversation with Manthia Diawara," 5. See Moten's *consent not to be a single being* trilogy.

21   Ferreira da Silva, "On Difference without Separability," 65.

22   Moten, preface to *Stolen Life*, ix.

23   See Ferreira da Silva, "On Difference without Separability."

24   See Glissant, *Poetics of Relation*. My use of the expression "bring into apposition" is influenced by how Weheliye expands on Glissant's concept of Relation to discuss "bringing-into-relation…interconnected existences that are in constant motion" as a "productive model for critical inquiry and political action." See Weheliye, *Habeas Viscus*, 12–13. For more on black study, see Stefano Harney and Fred Moten, *The Undercommons: Fugitive Planning and Black Study*.

25   Wilderson, *Red, White, and Black*, 18; and Moten, preface to *Black and Blur*, xii. See also Stef Craps, *Postcolonial Witnessing: Trauma Out of Bounds*, for more on trauma as ongoing rather than evental.

26   Derrida, "Some Statements and Truisms about Neologisms, Newisms, Postisms, Parasitisms, and Other Small Seismisms," 80.

27   Friedrich Nietzsche, *Beyond Good and Evil: Prelude to a Philosophy of the Future*, 7. Derrida references Nietzsche's "dangerous Perhaps" in several places, including in "Perhaps or Maybe: Jacques Derrida in Conversation with Alexander García Düttmann," 2.

28   Derrida, *Specters of Marx*, 211, 82.

29   Derrida, "Marx and Sons," 221.

30   Derrida, "Marx and Sons," 221; and Derrida, *Politics of Friendship*, 29 (italics in original).

31 Derrida, "Force of Law: The Mystical Foundation of Authority," 256–57 (italics and brackets in original translation).

32 Agamben, *Remnants of Auschwitz*, 156, 39.

33 Hortense Spillers, "Mama's Baby, Papa's Maybe: An American Grammar Book," in *Black, White, and in Color: Essays on American Literature and Culture*, 229, 207, 206 (italics in original).

34 Moten, *A Poetics of the Undercommons*, 30.

35 See Harney and Moten, *The Undercommons*; and Laura Harris, *Experiments in Exile: C. L. R. James, Hélio Oiticica, and the Aesthetic Sociality of Blackness*, 10, 7. Harris is drawing on Peter Linebaugh and Marcus Rediker's description of the motley crew in *The Many-Headed Hydra: Sailors, Slaves, Commoners, and the Hidden History of the Revolutionary Atlantic*, a book Harris describes as a "study of the transatlantic working class of the seventeenth, eighteenth, and early nineteenth centuries, before blackness and citizenship became clearly divided categories" (10).

36 Jacques Lacan, *Les non dupes errent* (italics in original). Quoted in a slightly different translation in Slavoj Žižek, Eric L. Santner, and Kenneth Reinhard, *The Neighbor: Three Inquiries in Political Theology*, 71.

37 Moten, preface to *Stolen Life*, i (italics in original).

38 Derrida, "Force of Law," 244.

39 See Gilles Deleuze and Félix Guattari, *Kafka: Toward a Minor Literature*.

40 Celan, "The Meridian," in *Collected Prose*, 47 (italics in original).

41 Spillers, "Mama's Baby, Papa's Maybe," in *Black, White, and in Color*, 207; and Weheliye, *Habeas Viscus*, 111.

42 See Walter Benjamin, "On the Concept of History," in *Selected Writings*, vol. 4, *1938–1940*, 395.

43 Jean-François Lyotard, *The Inhuman: Reflections on Time*, 74.

44 Glissant, *Poetics of Relation*, 6. John E. Drabinski, *Glissant and the Middle Passage: Philosophy, Beginning, Abyss*, 62 (italics in original).

45 Harriet Jacobs, *Incidents in the Life of a Slave Girl: Written by Herself*, 59.

46 Poet Carolyn Forché is generally associated with the term "poetry of witness," stemming from her book *Against Forgetting: Twentieth-Century Poetry of Witness*, though the practice of writing "poems of witness" has proliferated from there. See the "for" chapter in this book for further discussion.

47 Nathaniel Mackey, *Paracritical Hinge: Essays, Talks, Notes, Interviews*, 309.

48 Aimé Césaire, *Discourse on Colonialism*, 36.

49 Agamben, *Remnants of Auschwitz*, 70.

50 Agamben, *Homo Sacer: Sovereign Power and Bare Life*, 8 (italics in original). See, for example, Weheliye, *Habeas Viscus*, 53–56. See also C. Heike Schotten, *Queer Terror: Life, Death, and Desire in the Settler Colony*, 1–30; Jill Jarvis, "Remnants of Muslims: Reading Agamben's Silence"; and Gil Anidjar, *The Jew, the Arab: A History of the Enemy*, 113–49.

51 Kim Senguputa, "Israel-Gaza Conflict: Four Boys Killed While Playing Football on Beach after Israeli Warships Open Fire."

52 Agamben is quoting survivor Aldo Carpi in *Remnants of Auschwitz*, 50.

53 Saidiya V. Hartman, *Scenes of Subjection: Terror, Slavery, and Self-Making in Nineteenth-Century America*, 20.

54 Hartman, *Scenes of Subjection*, 3–4 (italics added).

55 See Hartman, *Scenes of Subjection*, 36, on hypervisibility.

56 Hartman, *Scenes of Subjection*, 22. See also page 21 on "the sadistic pleasure to be derived from the spectacle of sufferance."

57 Frederick Douglass, *Narrative of the Life of Frederick Douglass, an American Slave, Written by Himself*, 19.

58 See Elizabeth Alexander, "'Can You Be BLACK and Look at This?': Reading the Rodney King Video(s)."

59 Christina Sharpe, *Monstrous Intimacies: Making Post-Slavery Subjects*, 7.

60 Moten, email to author, May 26, 2017.

61 Blanchot, *The Infinite Conversation*, 312 (italics in original).

62 Blanchot exhibited fascist leanings in his early adulthood, published in fascist journals before and during World War II, etc. He later assiduously disavowed these tendencies and participated in French leftist circles after the war.

63 Spillers, "Mama's Baby, Papa's Maybe," in *Black, White, and in Color*, 206.

64 Harney and Moten, *The Undercommons*, 93.

65 Weheliye, *Habeas Viscus*, 61.

66 Ferreira da Silva, "On Difference without Separability," 64.

67 Moten, "Notes on Passage," in *Stolen Life*, 209.

68 Celan, "The written hollows itself," in *Breathturn into Timestead*, 67.

69 Moten, "Erotics of Fugitivity," in *Stolen Life*, 242. See also *Stolen Life*, i.

70 See Judith Butler, *Precarious Life: The Powers of Mourning and Violence*, 24.

71 Harney and Moten, "Michael Brown," 82.

72 Moten, "Chromatic Saturation," in *The Universal Machine*, 212.

73 Jared Sexton, "The *Vel* of Slavery: Tracking the Figure of the Unsovereign," 593. See also Sexton, "All Black Everything," on abolition as "the true movement of movements." While I have written two books of poetry addressing settler colonialism in Palestine and Turtle Island, in this book I am exploring No One as a (non)figure of witnessing that bears more kinship with black studies thinking on land-less, self-less, nonnatal, unsovereign life than it does to Indigenous philosophies and practices of collective sovereignty, nationhood, and self-determination. However, decolonization as an ongoing praxis of unknowing and undoing and "unthinking this world with a view to its end—that is...the return of the total value expropriated from conquered lands and enslaved bodies," undergirds this book, as it does my poetry, and is "the only proper name for justice," as Ferreira da Silva suggests ("In the Raw").

74 My thinking on the future anterior has been influenced by my reading of Weheliye's *Habeas Viscus*, combined with my own torquing of Benjamin's Jetztzeit/now-time.

75 See, for example, Philip Sidney, *An Apology for Poetry, or, The Defence of Poesy*; Al-

exander Pope, *An Essay on Criticism*; William Wordsworth and Samuel Taylor Coleridge, *Lyrical Ballads: 1798 and 1802*; Gertrude Stein, "Composition as Explanation"; Charles Olson, "Projective Verse"; Amiri Baraka, *Blues People*; Moten, the *consent not to be a single being* trilogy; Glissant, *Poetics of Relation*; Césaire, *Discourse on Colonialism*; and Celan, *Collected Prose*.

76 Joan Retallack, *The Poethical Wager*, 26 (italics in original).

77 See Ferreira da Silva, "Toward a Black Feminist Poethics: The Quest(ion) of Blackness toward the End of the World."

78 See Harney and Moten, "Michael Brown," 81: "another city gathers, dancing."

79 For more on the lesbian spiral, see Nicole Brossard, *The Aerial Letter*. On the unraveling of a Möbius strip, see Deleuze's *Logic of Sense*.

80 Ludwig Wittgenstein, *Culture and Value*, 24 (italics in original).

81 W. Benjamin, *The Arcades Project*, N1a, 8, 460 (italics in original).

82 The words "du liest" appear twice in the last poem Celan wrote, "Rebleute graben" (Vinegrowers dig up), written on April 13, 1970, a week before he committed suicide. See Celan, *Breathturn into Timestead*, 454–56.

83 Ferreira da Silva, "Fractal Thinking." One element of my assemblage to note is that I follow the vast majority of my interlocutors in placing "black" and "blackness" in lowercase throughout this book, except in citations in which these terms appear in uppercase.

84 W. Benjamin and Gershom Scholem, *The Correspondence of Walter Benjamin and Gershom Scholem, 1932–1940*, 108–9; Glissant, *Poetics of Relation*, 172; and Deleuze, *Cinema 2: The Time-Image*, 182.

85 W. Benjamin, *The Correspondence of Walter Benjamin, 1910–1940*, 256. Benjamin is actually referring to his composition process in *The Origin of German Tragic Drama*, which he further develops in *The Arcades Project*.

86 Shoshana Felman, *Writing and Madness: (Literature/Philosophy/Psychoanalysis)*, 254.

87 Sara Ahmed, *The Cultural Politics of Emotion*, 91.

88 Chandler, *X*, 65.

89 See Chandler, *X*, 3 (italics in original). While the putatively "more correct" grammatical choice in the last sentence of the epigraph would be "remains," I chose this passage from Chandler partly because of the indeterminacy of whether it is the prose itself that remains or the prose taken together with its syntax and its "*confusions*" that remain.

90 While my fastidious poetics of citation ensures that there are hundreds of citations in this book, there are hundreds more instances where a word or phrase, or even half or a quarter of a word or phrase, comes to me through the (not-so-unconscious) influence of all that I have read and lived. There is no way I can cite every instance of this phenomenon, as no poet (or being) can or should; yet through the accretive, recursive course of this book, these connections do tend to flutter to the surface. Reader, please do bear in mind, however, that one thing I refuse to do every time this (un)conscious influence arises is this: "Here in this sentence I use the word 'dehiscence' that Moten makes such beautiful use of in

his work, as he does 'apposition' and 'refusal,' and 'more or less than one,' although Chandler also uses apposition beautifully, so is it Moten's or Chandler's or no one's. A little later I don't cite Barthes or Foucault on the death of the author, nor do I cite Benjamin earlier on leaping out and robbing the idler of their convictions (the idler here becoming a reader). Weheliye also makes interesting use of Deleuze and Guattari's assemblages, which I will get to later in the book, as I will get to decision and Derrida too. And the notions of destroying this disastrous world or always already living and dancing another world in this world appear in various ways across black studies, so is it Wilderson's or Moten's or Ferreira da Silva's or Fanon's or no one's or everyone's."

91   Derrida, "Jacques Derrida: Deconstruction and the Other," 123 (italics added).

92   See "The Author's Apology for His Book," the preface to John Bunyan's *The Pilgrim's Progress*. The line I am alluding to is "This Book will make a Travailer of thee." A travailer is a traveler and a worker—and a reader.

93   I wrote this sentence shortly after Omar Mateen killed forty-nine people and wounded fifty-three others inside Pulse, a queer nightclub in Orlando, Florida, on June 12, 2016.

94   See Shoshana Felman and Dori Laub, *Testimony: Crises of Witnessing in Literature, Psychoanalysis, and History*, 59–63. And see the "bear(s)" chapter in this book.

95   See Žižek, Santner, and Reinhard, *The Neighbor*.

96   This is a riff on Celan, which will become more apparent in the "No" chapter in this book.

97   See the epigraph to this "Note on Form," from Chandler, *X*, 3. Additional references to this epigraph appear in this paragraph.

98   See Moten, *Black and Blur*.

99   See Sexton, "The *Vel* of Slavery," 593.

100   See William Carlos Williams, "To Elsie." There are additional references to this poem in this paragraph. I am also torquing Emmanuel Levinas's notion of *l'éveil à partir de l'autre*: see "Philosophy and Awakening," 77–90.

101   See Celan, "Conversation in the Mountains," in *Collected Prose*, 18; and W. E. B. Du Bois, *The Souls of Black Folk: Essays and Sketches*, on the veil.

102   Harney and Moten, "Michael Brown," 81.

103   Here I am torquing a line from Judith Butler's *Precarious Life*, 49, that also appears in my book *Neighbour Procedure*, 30.

1 No

1   Moten, "The Blur and Breathe Books," in *Black and Blur*, 257.

2   Robert A. Harris, "A Handbook of Rhetorical Devices."

3   John Milton, *Paradise Lost*, 13.

4   Blanchot, *The Writing of the Disaster*, 2.

5 Felman, *The Scandal of the Speaking Body: Don Juan with J. L. Austin, or Seduction in Two Languages*, 104 (italics in original).

6 Moten, "Chromatic Saturation," in *The Universal Machine*, 211, 234, 230. And see Ferreira da Silva, "No-Bodies: Law, Raciality and Violence."

7 Moten, "Notes on Passage," in *Stolen Life*, 210.

8 Moten, "Notes on Passage," in *Stolen Life*, 216.

9 Celan, "Speak, You Also," in *Poems of Paul Celan*, 69; and *Paul Celan: Selections*, 105. Joris changes his translation of this word over several translations. See chapter 2 in this book.

10 See Blanchot, *The Step Not Beyond*.

11 See Celan, "Eroded," in *Breathturn*, 107.

12 See Celan, "No sandart anymore," in *Breathturn*, 119.

13 "Discursive monster" is Derrida's term, mentioned in *Points...: Interviews, 1974-1994*, 386. In one version of the golem legend in Jewish mythology, the golem is brought to life by a rabbi writing a Hebrew word for truth, "emeth," on its forehead. When the golem proves uncontrollable, the rabbi wipes the "e" off the golem's forehead, leaving the word "meth," which means death, and the golem is deactivated and dies.

14 *Oxford English Dictionary*, s.v. "noema (*n.*)," accessed May 27, 2017, http://oed .com/view/Entry/127618. See also Glissant, *The Collected Poems of Édouard Glissant*, xxxii–xxxiii.

15 Harney and Moten, "Michael Brown," 83.

16 See Moten, "Chromatic Saturation," in *The Universal Machine*, 192–235.

17 Derrida, *Specters of Marx*, 82.

18 See Weheliye, *Habeas Viscus*, particularly chapters 4 and 7.

19 Moten, "Knowledge of Freedom," in *Stolen Life*, 79. The words "generative and general swarm" appear in a different context in Moten's essay. See also Moten, preface to *The Universal Machine*, ix.

20 See Dread Scott's website, http://www.dreadscott.net. See also Benjamin on distorted life and "the coming of the Messiah, who (a great rabbi once said) will not wish to change the world by force but will merely make a slight adjustment to it." In "Franz Kafka: On the Tenth Anniversary of His Death," in *Selected Writings*, vol. 2, pt. 2, *1931-1934*, 811.

21 Dred Scott v. Sandford, 60 U.S. 393 (1857), https://www.law.cornell.edu/supreme court/text/60/393.

22 See Ralph Ellison, *Invisible Man*.

23 In fact, when Scott scouted the site to prepare for the performance, he witnessed a black man getting his pockets turned out by an undercover cop. Scott, "Dread Scott in Conversation with Dana Liss, Studio Museum Curatorial Intern, August 2013."

24 Scott, "Dread Scott in Conversation with Dana Liss."

25 See Moten, "Erotics of Fugitivity," in *Stolen Life*, on blackness as nonperformance.

For one take on the Nobody see Marc Lamont Hill, *Nobody: Casualties of America's War on the Vulnerable, from Ferguson to Flint and Beyond*. See also Ferreira da Silva, "No-Bodies: Law, Raciality and Violence."

26 Hartman, *Scenes of Subjection*, 5.

27 Wilderson, *Red, White, and Black*, 9. See Wynter, "Unsettling the Coloniality of Being/Power/Truth/Freedom: Towards the Human, after Man, Its Overrepresentation—an Argument."

28 Harney and Moten, *The Undercommons*, 140.

29 Sharon Hayes, conversation with the author, August 21, 2016.

30 Hayes, conversation with the author, August 21, 2016; and Hayes, "Sharon Hayes Interviewed by Chris Mansour."

31 Hayes, "We Have a Future: An Interview with Sharon Hayes," 87.

32 Moten, "Fred Moten, Poet."

33 Moten, email to author, June 22, 2017.

34 Derrida, *Points...*, 386.

35 Anais Spitzer, *Derrida, Myth and the Impossibility of Philosophy*, 165n26.

36 W. Benjamin, "Karl Kraus," in *Selected Writings*, vol. 2, pt. 2, *1931–1934*, 456.

37 Wynter, "Beyond Miranda's Meanings: Un/Silencing the 'Demonic Ground' of Caliban's 'Woman,'" 364; and Moten, "Blackness and Nothingness (Mysticism in the Flesh)," 738, or "Chromatic Saturation," in *The Universal Machine*, 193, in which "remain" becomes "stay."

38 Sexton, "The *Vel* of Slavery," 593.

39 Wynter, "Beyond Miranda's Meanings," 364 (italics in original).

40 Katherine McKittrick, *Demonic Grounds: Black Women and the Cartographies of Struggle*, xxiv.

41 Weheliye, *Habeas Viscus*, 21.

42 Césaire, *Discourse on Colonialism*, 73, also quoted in Weheliye, *Habeas Viscus*, 11.

43 Derrida, *The Postcard: From Socrates to Freud and Beyond*, 296 (italics and brackets in original).

44 Sexton, "The *Vel* of Slavery," 593.

45 Hayes, conversation with the author, August 21, 2016.

46 Amy Davidson, "Darren Wilson's Demon."

47 Moten, "Chromatic Saturation," in *The Universal Machine*, 226; and Moten, "Blue Vespers," in *Black and Blur*, 244. For more on the third (and fourth) person, see the "one(s)" chapter in this book.

48 Bryan Wagner, *Disturbing the Peace: Black Culture and the Police Power after Slavery*, 2.

49 The notion of "claiming monstrosity" comes from Spillers, "Mama's Baby, Papa's Maybe," in *Black, White, and in Color*, 229. Daimon/demon is a Greek word meaning "replete with knowledge."

50 See Victoria Hesford, *Feeling Women's Liberation*.

51 See Johanna Burton, "One Person Protests: Notes about Going (Back) There," 22; and Elizabeth Freeman, *Time Binds: Queer Temporalities, Queer Histories*, 60. In fact, Hayes no longer allows this image to be published as she feels it is injurious when

out of the context of the larger project, because of the misinterpretations that have accompanied it. For the image's value in/as a demonstration, she made an exception for this book.

52 Harney and Moten, "Michael Brown," 86.

53 The term "scabrous surface" is used in Huey Copeland's chapter on Ligon's work, "Glenn Ligon and the Matter of Fugitivity," in *Bound to Appear: Art, Slavery, and the Site of Blackness in Multicultural America*, 116. That chapter is also where I also found the information on the woodcuts.

54 See Jack Halberstam, *Skin Shows: Gothic Horror and the Technology of Monsters*; and "Zombie Humanism at the End of the World." See also Jasbir Puar and Amit S. Rai, "Monster, Terrorist, Fag: The War on Terrorism and the Production of Docile Patriots"; Achille Mbembe, "Necropolitics," 36; and Moten, *In the Break: The Aesthetics of the Black Radical Tradition*, 1.

55 Mary Shelley, *Frankenstein: The 1818 Text*, 94.

56 Glenn Ligon, "Interview with David Drogin."

57 Spillers, "Mama's Baby, Papa's Maybe," 207.

58 Glenn Ligon, "America: Audio Guide Stop for Glenn Ligon, *Untitled (I Am a Man)*, 1988."

59 Douglass, *Narrative of the Life of Frederick Douglass, an American Slave, Written by Himself*, 19 (italics added).

60 After I completed this book and contacted Ligon to secure permission to reproduce his images, he informed me that the album cover for Ron Miles's 2017 record *I Am a Man* also contains a poem made from excerpts from the conservator's text in *Condition Report*.

61 Moten, preface to *Black and Blur*, xiii.

62 Derrida, *Points…*, 386–87.

2 [ ]

1 Blanchot, *The Infinite Conversation*, 77.

2 Blanchot, *The Infinite Conversation*, 66, 213.

3 Celan, "The Meridian," in *Collected Prose*, 50; Ferreira da Silva, "On Difference without Separability"; and Deleuze, *Difference and Repetition*, 28.

4 Compare Pierre Joris's translations of "Aschenglorie" (Ashglory) in *Paul Celan*, 104–5; *Breathturn*, 190–93; and *Breathturn into Timestead*, 62–65.

5 Moten uses "in the hold" (and "in the break") throughout his work. See, for example, "Chromatic Saturation," in *The Universal Machine*, 198.

6 Derrida, "Poetics and Politics of Witnessing," in *Sovereignties in Question*, 69–70 (italics in original).

7 Ferreira da Silva, "No-Bodies," 132.

8 Moten, "Erotics of Fugitivity," in *Stolen Life*, 252.

9 See Celan, "An eye, open," in *Poems of Paul Celan*, 113.

10 Derrida, "Desistance," 42.

11 Blanchot, *The Space of Literature*, 26.

12 Moten, "Erotics of Fugitivity," in *Stolen Life*, 252, 245; and "Amuse-Bouche," in *Black and Blur*, 183.

13 Moten, "Erotics of Fugitivity," in *Stolen Life*, 266.

14 Moten, "Enjoy All Monsters," in *Black and Blur*, 210.

15 Moten, "Chromatic Saturation," in *The Universal Machine*, 194; and Wilderson, *Red, White, and Black*, 54 (italics in original).

16 Blanchot, *The Infinite Conversation*, 69. See also chapter 7 of this book on "for" as "in the face of."

17 Blanchot, *The Writing of the Disaster*, 28.

18 W. Benjamin, "On the Concept of History," in *Selected Writings*, vol. 4, *1938–1940*, 396; and Weheliye, *Habeas Viscus*, 133.

19 Agamben, *Remnants of Auschwitz*, 163–64 (italics added).

20 Agamben, *Remnants of Auschwitz*, 120.

21 Moten, *A Poetics of the Undercommons*, 30.

22 "One who holds themselves to the thing" is one possible translation of *superstes* by Émile Benveniste in *Indo-European Language and Society*.

23 Moten, "Chromatic Saturation," in *The Universal Machine*, 225.

24 Moten, preface to *Stolen Life*, i.

25 Agamben, *Remnants of Auschwitz*, 85 (brackets added).

26 Weheliye, *Habeas Viscus*, 55.

27 Spillers, "Interstices: A Small Drama of Words," in *Black, White, and in Color*, 155.

28 Weheliye, *Habeas Viscus*, 132.

29 Ferreira da Silva, "Toward a Black Feminist Poethics," 91.

30 Derrida, *Specters of Marx*, 82.

31 Harney and Moten, "Michael Brown," 81, 87 (brackets added).

32 Rob Halpern, *Music for Porn*, 149 (italics in original).

33 Halpern, *Common Place*, 36–37 (hole in sense), 42 (empty place), 12 (blank), 31 (speakable), 70 (cunt) (italics in original). Subsequent parenthetical citations in this study are from Halpern's *Common Place*.

34 Levinas, "Paul Celan: From Being to the Other," 40. See also Celan's letter to Hans Bender in *Collected Prose*, 26: "I cannot see any basic difference between a handshake and a poem."

35 Celan, "Conversation in the Mountains," in *Collected Prose*, 19, 20.

36 Goldsmith, "The Body of Michael Brown," presentation at Brown University, March 13, 2015.

37 Alec Wilkinson, "Something Borrowed: Kenneth Goldsmith's Poetry Elevates Copying to an Art, but Did He Go Too Far?"

38 Spillers, "Mama's Baby, Papa's Maybe," in *Black, White, and in Color*, 206 (italics in original).

39 Puar and Rai, "Monster, Terrorist, Fag," 139.

40 Puar and Rai, "Monster, Terrorist, Fag," 117.

41 See Michel Foucault, "The Abnormals," in *The Essential Works of Foucault*, vol. 1, *Ethics*.

42 Puar and Rai, "Monster, Terrorist, Fag," 121.

43 Spillers, "Mama's Baby, Papa's Maybe," in *Black, White, and in Color*, 207.

44 Agamben, *Remnants of Auschwitz*, 45.

45 Agamben, *Remnants of Auschwitz*, 111.

46 Puar, *Terrorist Assemblages: Homonationalism in Queer Times*, 216 (brackets added). See also Mbembe, "Necropolitics."

47 Page 67 is the first of several instances in which Halpern uses the term "my detainee" for Al Hanashi. Al Hanashi is named in a postscript to a poem on page 32.

48 Al Hanashi's name appears at the top of the autopsy report but is redacted elsewhere in the report. See "Autopsy: Muhammad al Hanashi (ACLU Release)."

49 See Ferreira da Silva, "No-Bodies," 128, 140; and *Toward a Global Idea of Race*.

50 Hartman, *Scenes of Subjection*, 108.

51 Jacobs, *Incidents in the Life of a Slave Girl*, 30.

52 Moten, "Chromatic Saturation," in *The Universal Machine*, 142.

3 one(s)

1 Ferreira da Silva, "On Difference without Separability," 58.

2 Deleuze and Guattari, *Kafka*, 18 (italics in original).

3 Moten, preface to *The Universal Machine*, xii–xiii.

4 See Ferreira da Silva, "No-Bodies"; and *Toward a Global Idea of Race*.

5 Moten, preface to *The Universal Machine*, x (italics added).

6 Moten, "There Is No Racism Intended," in *The Universal Machine*, 31.

7 Roland Barthes, "On Émile Benveniste," 25.

8 Émile Benveniste, "The Nature of Pronouns," in *Problems in General Linguistics*, 217.

9 Benveniste, "Relationships of Person in the Verb," in *Problems in General Linguistics*, 198 (italics in original).

10 Benveniste, "Relationships of Person in the Verb," 200.

11 Roberto Esposito, *Third Person: Politics of Life and Philosophy of the Impersonal*, 107.

12 See Cheena Marie Lo, *Ephemera and Atmospheres*, 5.

13 This line is taken directly from one of Cheena Marie Lo's public author bios, in *The Awl*, April 21, 2016, https://www.theawl.com/2016/04/a-poem-by-cheena-marie-lo/.

14 Lo, *Ephemera and Atmospheres*, 3–6 (italics in original).

15 American Dialect Society, "2015 Word of the Year Is Singular 'They.'"

16 Deleuze, *Foucault*, 123. This passage is quoted more extensively in Moten, "Chromatic Saturation," in *The Universal Machine*, 210.

17 Wynter, "*Proud Flesh* Inter/Views," 24.

18 Deleuze, *Logic of Sense*, 152.

19 Julian Talamantez Brolaski, "pronoun circle-jerk and the dog charlie."

20 Deleuze, *Logic of Sense*, 141.

21 See Joff Bradley, "The Eyes of the Fourth Personal Singular."

22 Levinas, "The Trace of the Other," 356 (italics in original).

23 Levinas, "The Trace of the Other," 356 (italics in original).

24 Levinas, *Otherwise Than Being, or Beyond Essence*, 157.

25 Levinas, "Ethics and Politics," 294.

26 Levinas, *Otherwise Than Being*, 157.

27 See Levinas, *Difficult Freedom: Essays on Judaism*, 160; and "Ethics and Politics," 294.

28 Primo Levi, *If This Is a Man*, 103.

29 Wolfgang Sofsky, *The Order of Terror: The Concentration Camp*, 202. See also Orlando Patterson, *Slavery and Social Death: A Comparative Study*.

30 Lo, *Ephemera and Atmospheres*, 5.

31 Deleuze, "Literature and Life," 3.

32 Deleuze, "Literature and Life," 5 (brackets added).

33 Celan, "Aschenglorie" (Ashglory), in *Breathturn into Timestead*, 62–65.

34 Viktor Shklovksy, "Third Factory," in *Viktor Shklovksy: A Reader*, 243.

4 No One(s)

1 Thanks to Andrea Geyer for an interesting discussion on translating these untranslatable three lines.

2 Moten, "Nobody, Everybody," in *Black and Blur*, 169; and Frantz Fanon, *Black Skin, White Masks*, 84.

3 Levi, *Survival in Auschwitz and The Reawakening: Two Memoirs*, 191.

4 Levi, *Survival in Auschwitz and The Reawakening*, 192; and Agamben, *Remnants of Auschwitz*, 38.

5 Agamben, *Remnants of Auschwitz*, 38.

6 Levi, "On Obscure Writing," 173.

7 Glissant, *The Collected Poems of Édouard Glissant*, xxxii–xxxiii.

8 Rae Armantrout, "Feminist Poetics and the Meaning of Clarity," 295.

9 See Celan, "Tübingen, Jänner," in *Paul Celan*, 79–80, and *Collected Prose*, 34.

10 Franz Kafka, "Cares of a Family Man," 427–29.

11 W. Benjamin, "Franz Kafka," in *Selected Writings*, vol. 2, pt. 2, *1931–1934*, 811 (brackets added).

12 Fanon, *Black Skin, White Masks*, 87, 84.

13 Žižek, Santner, and Reinhard, *The Neighbor*, 7.

14 Glissant, *Caribbean Discourse: Selected Essays*, 123–24.

15 Elaine Scarry, *The Body in Pain*, 6

16 Weheliye, *Habeas Viscus*, 126; "cries and groans" is from Scarry, *The Body in Pain*, 6; "heart-rending shrieks" is from Douglass, *Narrative of the Life of Frederick Douglass, an American Slave, Written by Himself*, 19; "mechanical murmurs without content" is Weheliye's translation of a phrase from the only existing study on the Muselmann: Zdzislaw Ryn and Stanslav Klodzinski, "An der Grenze zwischen Leben und Tod: Eine Studie über die Erscheinung des 'Muselmann' im Konzentrationslager," 117.

17 Agamben, *Remnants of Auschwitz*, 39.

18 Moten, *In the Break*, 22.

19 Agamben, *Remnants of Auschwitz*, 33; and Weheliye, *Habeas Viscus*, 126. Weheliye is translating testimony from Roman Grzyb in Ryn and Klodzinski, "An der Grenze zwischen Leben und Tod," 116.

20 Moten, "Chromatic Saturation," in *The Universal Machine*, 217.

21 Weheliye, *Habeas Viscus*, 127.

22 Levi, *Survival in Auschwitz and The Reawakening*, 192.

23 Levi, *Survival in Auschwitz and The Reawakening*, 192.

24 Moten, "The Touring Machine (Flesh Thought Inside Out)," in *Stolen Life*, 170.

25 Agamben, *Remnants of Auschwitz*, 85.

26 Heidegger translated by Agamben, *Remnants of Auschwitz*, 74.

27 Levi, *If This Is a Man*, 103; and *Survival in Auschwitz and The Reawakening*, 90.

28 Agamben, *Remnants of Auschwitz*, 44.

29 Levi, *If This Is a Man*, 103; and *Survival in Auschwitz and The Reawakening*, 90.

30 Agamben, *Remnants of Auschwitz*, 38, 70, 45.

31 Agamben, *Means without End: Notes on Politics*, 45; and "The Camp as the 'Nomos' of the Modern," in *Homo Sacer*, 166–80.

32 Agamben, *The Use of Bodies*, 186.

33 Weheliye, *Habeas Viscus*, 55, 52.

34 Agamben, *Remnants of Auschwitz*, 26.

35 Ferreira da Silva, "No-Bodies," 148, 140, 119, 120.

36 Weheliye, *Habeas Viscus*, 135.

37 Moten, "Air Shaft, Rent Party," in *Stolen Life*, 190.

38 Quotations in italics in this paragraph are taken from the voiceover of Laura Elrick's video *Stalk*, a version of which is transcribed in *Stalk: A Score for Performance* (which is unpaginated).

39 Audre Lorde, "Uses of the Erotic: The Erotic as Power," 58.

40 Elrick, "Sensing the Present: Economies of Fear and the Limits of the Visible," 28.

41 Butler, "Torture and the Ethics of Photography," in *Frames of War: When Is Life Grievable?*, 72–73.

42 Elrick, "Sensing the Present," 21. Elrick draws on Sara Ahmed's term for a community of seeing found in *The Cultural Politics of Emotion*, 94.

43 Elrick, "Sensing the Present," 28.

44 Elrick, "Sensing the Present," 25 (italics in original).

45 Moten, *In the Break*, 200.

46 W. Benjamin, *The Arcades Project*, M8a, 1, 433. I am indebted to Zoe Skoulding's "Performance and Absence in the Heterotopian City," 207, for the Simmel reference.

47 See K. Oliver, *Witnessing*, 5, on response-ability.

48 Butler, *Bodies That Matter: On the Discursive Limits of "Sex,"* 132. "A hole punctured through it" is from the *Stalk* video voiceover, transcribed in *Stalk: A Score for Performance*.

49 See the study in the "the" chapter in this book.

50 Elrick, "Sensing the Present," 21. "Author function" is Foucault's term in "What Is an Author?," 125.

51 Prosopopoeia is a rhetorical figure for a kind of personification or impersonation of an absent speaker. See the "for" chapter in this book for more on the figure and on Hartman's incisive critique of the proxy witness.

52 See Ahmed, *The Cultural Politics of Emotion*, 91.

53 Harney and Moten, "Al-Khwāriddim, or Savoir Faire Is Everywhere," 188.

54 Elrick, "Sensing the Present," 23–24; and *Stalk: A Score for Performance*.

5 bear(s)

1 Zeugen as a verb can mean "to father," but I am swerving it to the body that bears. Zeugen in a certain figuration (*von etw. zeugen*) can also mean to show, hence the monstrous.

2 See K. Oliver, *Witnessing*.

3 See Felman and Laub, *Testimony*, 59–63.

4 Lyotard, *The Differend: Phrases in Dispute*, 3, 166.

5 Hartman, *Scenes of Subjection*, 22.

6 Lyotard, *The Differend*, 3, 13; see also Lyotard, "Presenting the Unpresentable: The Sublime."

7 Moten, "Chromatic Saturation," in *The Universal Machine*, 217.

8 Jean Laplanche, "Time and the Other," 260.

9 Laplanche, "The Wall and the Arcade," 204. Butler also draws on Laplanche in *Giving an Account of Oneself*.

10 See Butler and Athena Athanasiou, *Dispossession: The Performative in the Political*.

11 Sexton, "Afro-Pessimism: The Unclear Word."

12 Sexton, "The *Vel* of Slavery," 593.

13 See Sexton, "The *Vel* of Slavery," 593: "(nothing for no one)."

14 Sexton, "The *Vel* of Slavery," 593.

15 M. NourbeSe Philip, *Zong!*, 198, 199. Subsequent parenthetical citations in this study are from Philip's *Zong!*

16 See Hartman, "Venus in Two Acts," 9: "I longed to write a new story, one unfettered by the constraints of the legal documents and exceeding the restatement and transpositions, which comprised my strategy for disordering and transgressing the protocols of the archive and the authority of its statements and which enabled me to augment and intensify its fictions."

17 The phrase "brutally unauthorized author" is from Moten, "Chromatic Saturation," in *The Universal Machine*, 225.

18 Derrida, "Shibboleth: For Paul Celan," in *Sovereignties in Question*, 53. Philip also draws on Derrida's notion of hauntology from *Specters of Marx* in her "Notanda" essay at the end of *Zong!* (201).

19 Crumping is a contorted style of African American dance that Philip refers to in "Notanda" (205) in relation to how "the stories on board the *Zong* are jammed together" in *Zong!*

20 Ferreira da Silva, "Toward a Black Feminist Poethics," 94.

21 Philip quotes a talk by Maureen Harris. When I mention animateriality, I am referring to the Moten epigraph to this study, but Moten emphasizes the *mater*, mother, and animateriality in *In the Break* (18). The Moten epigraph is from "The Touring Machine (Flesh Thought Inside Out)," in *Stolen Life*, 170.

22 Ferreira da Silva, "Toward a Black Feminist Poethics," 94.

23 Hartman, "Venus in Two Acts," 2–3.

24 Weheliye, *Habeas Viscus*, 126. He is of course also drawing on Gayatri Chakravorty Spivak's famous essay "Can the Subaltern Speak?"

25 Sharpe, *In the Wake: On Blackness and Being*, 30, 113, 115.

26 Weheliye, *Habeas Viscus*, 12, channeling Glissant's open boat. See Glissant, *Poetics of Relation*, 5–9, and 171: "Relation is open totality; totality would be relation at rest. Totality is virtual. Actually, only rest could, in itself, be legitimately or totally virtual. For movement is precisely that which realizes itself absolutely. Relation is movement." My use of ec-static throughout this book is derived from Butler, *Precarious Life*, 24, and reading Moten has helped me deepen its resonances. He mentions the ecstatic in the epigraph to this study.

27 Spillers, "Mama's Baby, Papa's Maybe," in *Black, White, and in Color*, 206.

28 Weheliye, *Habeas Viscus*, 137.

29 Spillers, "Mama's Baby, Papa's Maybe," in *Black, White, and in Color*, 207.

30 Glissant, *Poetics of Relation*, 6.

31 Moten, "Uplift and Criminality," in *Stolen Life*, 115 (italics in original).

32 Weheliye, *Habeas Viscus*, 44.

33 Theodor W. Adorno to Walter Benjamin, December 17, 1934, in Adorno and Benjamin, *The Complete Correspondence, 1928–1940*, 69. The German *überlebt*, "lives on," is also "survives." See Daniel Heath Justice, "'Go Away, Water!': Kinship Criticism and the Decolonization Imperative," 152. See also Gerald Vizenor, *Manifest Manners: Narratives on Postindian Survivance*, vii. Derrida also uses the term "survivance" in *Specters of Marx*, 185, for hauntological/spectral spaces that are neither life nor death.

34 Hartman, *Lose Your Mother: A Journey along the Atlantic Slave Route*, 6. See also Sexton, "The Social Life of Social Death: On Afro-Pessimism and Black Optimism," 23.

35 Sexton, "'The Curtain of the Sky': An Introduction," 15 (italics in original).

36 Moten, "The Touring Machine (Flesh Thought Inside Out)," in *Stolen Life*, 166.

6 witness

1   Agamben, *Remnants of Auschwitz*, 16. The parenthetical citations in the following paragraphs are from Agamben's *Remnants of Auschwitz*.

2   Levi, *The Drowned and the Saved*, 83–84.

3   W. Benjamin, "Franz Kafka," in *Selected Writings*, vol. 2, pt. 2, *1931–1934*, 811. *Figuren* ("figures" in German) was a Nazi euphemism for the corpses of concentration camp inmates, as was *Puppen* ("dolls" or "puppets").

4   Interestingly, in the original Italian, the term *guardiano* is closer to "guardian" than "guard." The English translator Daniel Heller-Roazen made a conscious or unconscious choice to evoke an ironic link to the camps here. See Agamben, *Quel che resta di Auschwitz. L'archivio e il testimone*, 63.

5   Levi, *If This Is a Man*, 103.

6   Sofsky, *The Order of Terror*, 200.

7   See Moten, "The Touring Machine (Flesh Thought Inside Out)," in *Stolen Life*, 170; Spillers, "Interstices," in *Black, White, and in Color*, 155; Spillers, "Mama's Baby, Papa's Maybe," in *Black, White, and in Color*, 207, 229; and Weheliye, *Habeas Viscus*, 40.

8   Toni Morrison, *Beloved*, 88.

9   Levi, "The Survivor," a poem translated in Agamben, *Remnants of Auschwitz*, 90.

10 Charlotte Delbo, *Auschwitz and After*, 267.

11 Elie Wiesel, *From the Kingdom of Memory: Reminiscences*, 194.

12 Quoted in Blanchot, *Voice from Elsewhere*, 55.

13 Celan, "Psalm," in *Poems of Paul Celan*, 153.

14 Derrida, "Poetics and Politics of Witnessing," in *Sovereignties in Question*, 68.

15 Derrida, "Poetics and Politics of Witnessing," in *Sovereignties in Question*, 91, 68.

16 See Glissant, *Poetics of Relation*, 6; and Drabinski, *Glissant and the Middle Passage*, 36–38. "Less than nothing" is Drabinski, 38.

17 Anne Carson, *Economy of the Unlost: (Reading Simonides of Keos with Paul Celan)*, 3.

18 Rachel Zolf, *Human Resources*, 31. See also Carson, *Economy of the Unlost*, 36, where Carson posits that Celan "cleanse[s] words and salvage[s] what is cleansed."

19 The range of twentieth- and twenty-first-century philosophers who have written on Hölderlin's poetics includes but is not limited to Heidegger, Agamben, Derrida, Blanchot, Adorno, Paul de Man, Avital Ronell, Philippe Lacoue-Labarthe, Werner Hamacher, and Christopher Fynsk.

20 Martin Heidegger, *Poetry, Language, Thought*, 71.

21 Heidegger, *Poetry, Language, Thought*, 71.

22 Heidegger, *Poetry, Language, Thought*, 72.

23 Heidegger, *Poetry, Language, Thought*, 72.

24 I can't recall who said there was no more poetry after Celan, but they probably taught a class at the European Graduate School.

25 Of course, there are some practices of critical (auto)ethnography that perform important work; and yet, for example, as Linda Tuhiwai Smith succinctly notes,

"'research' is probably one of the dirtiest words in the indigenous world's vocabulary." See *Decolonizing Methodologies: Research and Indigenous Peoples*, 1.

26 See Forché, *Against Forgetting*; and Alicia Ostriker, "Beyond Confession: The Poetics of Postmodern Witness." See also the "for" chapter in this book.

27 Derrida, "Poetics and Politics of Witnessing," in *Sovereignties in Question*, 72–73.

28 For more on the "bad subject," see Louis Althusser, "Ideology and Ideological State Apparatuses," 181.

29 Celan, *Poems of Paul Celan*, 209.

30 Derrida, "Poetics and Politics of Witnessing," in *Sovereignties in Question*, 70 (italics in original).

31 Agamben, *Remnants of Auschwitz*, 47, for "non-man" (brackets added); quotes in parentheses are excerpts from testimony by Lucjan Sobieraj, Edward Sokol, and Jerzy Mostowsky, 166.

32 See Weheliye, *Habeas Viscus*, chapter 7, "Deprivation: Hunger."

33 Weheliye, *Habeas Viscus*, 119.

34 Levi, *The Complete Works of Primo Levi*, 2153–54. See also Antony Rowland, "Poetry as Metatestimony: Primo Levi's *Collected Poems*."

35 See Mbembe, "Necropolitics," 36. And Butler, *Precarious Life*.

36 "Present absentees" is a term the Israel Defense Forces uses for Palestinians.

37 Marc Falkoff, ed., *Poems from Guantánamo: The Detainees Speak*, 35.

38 Celan, "No more sand art," in *Poems of Paul Celan*, 217.

39 Weheliye, *Habeas Viscus*, 122–23.

40 See K. Oliver, *Witnessing*; and Jessica Benjamin's work.

41 Lyotard, *The Differend*, 54.

42 Juliana Spahr, *The Transformation*, 21, 15, 17, 15, 20. Subsequent parenthetical citations in this study are from Spahr's *The Transformation*.

43 See also Spahr's afterword regarding autobiographical material (217–18).

44 This is the first of many instances of "think with."

45 Carson, *Eros the Bittersweet*, 16. Spahr points to *Eros the Bittersweet* in her afterword to *The Transformation* (223) and names the "third Sapphic point" numerous times (first instance on page 206).

46 Jessica Benjamin, "Two-Way Streets: Recognition of Difference and the Intersubjective Third," 123.

47 Spahr's afterword to *The Transformation* attributes the term "mediocre colonizer" to Césaire (220), but the term is actually discussed in Memmi's *The Colonizer and the Colonized*. The book of mine on settler colonialism is *Janey's Arcadia*, 2014. My book on Israel-Palestine is *Neighbour Procedure*, 2010.

48 Spahr, "How Does the Work Get Used," 311.

49 Spahr, "How Does the Work Get Used," 311.

50 Theresa Hak Kyung Cha, *DICTEE*, 131.

51 Spahr, *Everybody's Autonomy: Connective Reading and Collective Identity*, 125.

52 Spahr, *Everybody's Autonomy*, 125.

53 Spahr, "Resignifying Autobiography: Lyn Hejinian's *My Life*," 141, 142, 155.

54 Spahr, "Resignifying Autobiography," 142.

55 Spahr, "Resignifying Autobiography," 146 (italics in original).

56 Spahr, "Resignifying Autobiography," 152.

57 Lyn Hejinian, *My Life*, 107, cited in Spahr, "Resignifying Autobiography," 150–51.

58 Rosi Braidotti, *Transpositions: On Nomadic Ethics*, 35. I am indebted to Heather Milne's critical work on Spahr for the reference to Braidotti. See Milne, "Dearly Beloveds: The Politics of Intimacy in Juliana Spahr's *This Connection of Everyone with Lungs.*"

59 Spahr, "Resignifying Autobiography," 154.

60 Glissant, Diawara, and Winks, "Édouard Glissant in Conversation with Manthia Diawara," 6

61 Glissant, Diawara, and Winks, "Édouard Glissant in Conversation with Manthia Diawara," 5. *Consent à n'être plus un seul* is the original French of the phrase "consent not to be a single being." *Ne...plus* is a negative adverb meaning "no more" or "not any more," while *plus* on its own means comparatively or superlatively "more."

62 Butler, "Bracha's Eurydice," in *The Matrixial Borderspace*, x–xi.

63 Spahr, "Resignifying Autobiography," 146.

64 Butler, *Precarious Life*, 20. Also 21, where Butler writes that "mourning has to do with agreeing to undergo a transformation (perhaps one should say *submitting* to a transformation) the full result of which one cannot know in advance" (italics in original). See also Butler, *Frames of War*; Butler, *Giving an Account of Oneself*; and Butler and Athanasiou, *Dispossession*.

65 The parts in quotes in this paragraph come from an interview between Bracha L. Ettinger and Brian Massumi. See Massumi, "Painting: The Voice of the Grain," 202–4.

66 Hejinian, "The Rejection of Closure," 44.

67 Butler, "Contingent Foundations: Feminism and the Question of 'Postmodernism,'" 17. Quoted in Spahr, "Resignifying Autobiography," 144.

68 Massumi, "Painting," 213.

69 Griselda Pollock, "Aesthetic Wit(h)nessing in the Era of Trauma," 857.

70 Ettinger, "Wit(h)nessing Trauma and the Matrixial Gaze," 147–48.

71 Retallack, *The Poethical Wager*, 219–20 (italics in original). *The Transformation* follows some of the formal precepts Retallack describes.

72 Ferreira da Silva speaking in Ferreira da Silva and Desideri, "A Conversation between Valentina Desideri and Denise Ferreira da Silva," 11, 4.

73 Ferreira da Silva speaking in Ferreira da Silva and Desideri, "A Conversation between Valentina Desideri and Denise Ferreira da Silva," 12.

74 Ferreira da Silva, "Toward a Black Feminist Poethics," 91, 94.

75 Ettinger, "Wit(h)nessing Trauma and the Matrixial Gaze," 139–40; and see Ferreira da Silva, "On Difference without Separability."

76 See Patterson, *Slavery and Social Death*, 5; and Hartman, *Lose Your Mother*.

77 Spillers, "Mama's Baby, Papa's Maybe," in *Black, White, and in Color*, 207, 228 (italics in original).

78 Glissant, *Poetics of Relation*, 6.

79 Spillers, "Mama's Baby, Papa's Maybe," in *Black, White, and in Color*, 228–29, 207 (italics in original).

80 Massumi, "Painting," 210.

81 Ettinger discusses "wit(h)nesses with-out events" vis-à-vis Felman and Laub in "Wit(h)nessing Trauma and the Matrixial Gaze," 150. See also Felman and Laub, *Testimony*, 75, 68 (italics in original).

82 Spillers, "Mama's Baby, Papa's Maybe," in *Black, White, and in Color*, 207.

83 Hartman, *Scenes of Subjection*, 4.

84 Spahr, "How Does the Work Get Used," 313.

85 See Ferreira da Silva, "No-Bodies"; and *Toward a Global Idea of Race*.

86 Sharpe, *In the Wake*, 116. "The unthought" is Hartman's term. See Hartman and Wilderson, "The Position of the Unthought: An Interview with Saidiya V. Hartman Conducted by Frank B. Wilderson III."

87 Harney and Moten, *The Undercommons*, 19. I'm not sure a poem of Spahr's such as "My White Feminism," in which she satirizes her own positionality through a kind of self-possessed individuality, helps make these kinds of undercommon connections happen, just as Halpern's use in *Common Place* of "my detainee" (67) is all about the individual speaker. See Spahr, "My White Feminism." Lucas de Lima's reading of this poem in his essay "Race, Wokeness, and the Possessive Individualism of US Poetry" is also useful here.

88 "Failed project of the world and the face" is a variation on Moten's "The world and the face are failed project, harsh projection." *Black and Blur*, 244.

89 The "with and for" is an expression in Harney and Moten, *The Undercommons*, 143.

90 Carson, *Eros the Bittersweet*, 16.

7 for

1 Derrida, "Poetics and Politics of Witnessing," in *Sovereignties in Question*, 90.

2 John Fox, *Poetic Medicine: The Healing Art of Poem-Making*, 240.

3 Forché, *Against Forgetting*, 29–30.

4 Moten, "Erotics of Fugitivity," in *Stolen Life*, 244 (italics in original).

5 Ferreira da Silva, "Fractal Thinking."

6 Susan Gubar, *Poetry after Auschwitz: Remembering What One Never Knew*, 23.

7 *Oxford English Dictionary Online*, s.v. "proxy (n.)," accessed May 27, 2017, http://oed.com/view/Entry/153573; and Gubar, *Poetry after Auschwitz*, 178, 146.

8 Gubar, *Poetry after Auschwitz*, 146.

9 Dominick LaCapra, "Trauma, Absence, Loss," 699, 722, quoted in Gubar, *Poetry after Auschwitz*, 243.

10 Gubar, *Poetry after Auschwitz*, 164.

11 Hartman, *Scenes of Subjection*, 19, 17.

12 Rankin quoted in Hartman, *Scenes of Subjection*, 18.

13   Hartman, *Scenes of Subjection*, 19.

14   Hartman, *Scenes of Subjection*, 19.

15   Hartman, *Scenes of Subjection*, 19. "Secondary witness" is a term coined by LaCapra. See "Trauma, Absence, Loss," 699.

16   Spillers, "Mama's Baby, Papa's Maybe," in *Black, White, and in Color*, 206 (italics in original).

17   Spillers, speaking in Arthur Jafa's 2014 film, *Dreams Are Colder Than Death*.

18   Hartman, *Scenes of Subjection*, 20.

19   When Schutz's *Open Casket* was displayed at the 2017 Whitney Biennial Schutz was severely criticized and there were calls for her to destroy the painting. See Sharpe, "'What Does It Mean to Be Black and Look at This?': A Scholar Reflects on the Dana Schutz Controversy"; and Sexton, "The Rage: Some Comments on 'Open Casket.'" See also Alexander, "'Can You Be BLACK and Look at This?'"; and Moten, *In the Break*, 192–211.

20   Quoted in Alexander, "'Can You Be BLACK and Look at This?,'" 87.

21   Caitlin Gibson, "A White Artist Responds to the Outcry over Her Controversial Emmett Till Painting."

22   Sexton, "The Rage."

23   Randy Kennedy, "White Artist's Painting of Emmett Till at Whitney Biennial Draws Protests."

24   Dana Schutz, "Dana Schutz by Mei Chin."

25   Halpern, *Common Place*, 163.

26   The last clause in this sentence torques a line in Hartman's *Scenes of Subjection* on the Rankin letters: "And as a consequence, empathy fails to expand the space of the other but merely places the self in its stead. This is not to suggest that empathy can be discarded" (20).

27   Divya Victor, "Absent Witness: Trauma and Contemporary American Poetry," 7.

28   See Hartman, *Scenes of Subjection*, 13; and Moten, "The Touring Machine (Flesh Thought Inside Out)," in *Stolen Life*, 168.

29   On disidentification, see Butler, *Bodies That Matter*, 219, and José Esteban Muñoz, *Disidentifications: Queers of Color and the Performance of Politics*.

30   Hartman, "Venus in Two Acts," 2. See also Philip, *Zong!*

31   Hartman, *Scenes of Subjection*, 12,

32   Hartman, *Scenes of Subjection*, 10–11.

33   Blanchot, *The Writing of the Disaster*, 1.

34   Gubar, *Poetry after Auschwitz*, 177.

35   Gubar, *Poetry after Auschwitz*, 204–5.

36   Gubar, *Poetry after Auschwitz*, 181. See also Philip, *Zong!*, 201, on "the spectres of the undead" and the hauntological process of "exaqua" that constitutes *Zong!*

37   Gubar, *Poetry after Auschwitz*, 184. Gubar states that this citation is from de Man, *The Rhetoric of Romanticism*, 57, but it is actually from de Man, *The Resistance to Theory*, 44.

38   De Man, *The Rhetoric of Romanticism*, 75–76.

39 Agamben, *Remnants of Auschwitz*, 53.

40 Derrida, "Poetics and Politics of Witnessing," in *Sovereignties in Question*, 77.

41 Harney and Moten, *The Undercommons*, 143.

42 Derrida, "Poetics and Politics of Witnessing," in *Sovereignties in Question*, 87 (italics in original).

43 Celan, "There was earth inside them," in *Poems of Paul Celan*, 130–31. And "Stehen" (To stand), in *Breathturn into Timestead*, 10–13.

44 See Claudia Rankine, *Citizen: An American Lyric*, 140–43, for repetition of "Hey you—." See also Althusser, "Ideology and Ideological State Apparatuses," 174.

45 Deleuze and Guattari, *A Thousand Plateaus: Capitalism and Schizophrenia*, 130.

46 Derrida, "Poetics and Politics of Witnessing," in *Sovereignties in Question*, 72.

47 Celan, "Aschenglorie" (Ashglory), in *Breathturn into Timestead*, 65.

48 Derrida, "Poetics and Politics of Witnessing," in *Sovereignties in Question*, 72; and Agamben, *Remnants of Auschwitz*, 54.

49 Rankine, *Citizen*, 139, 142, 145. Subsequent parenthetical citations in this study are from Rankine's *Citizen*.

50 See Douglass, *Narrative of the Life of Frederick Douglass, an American Slave, Written by Himself*, 19.

51 Glissant, Diawara, and Winks, "Édouard Glissant in Conversation with Manthia Diawara," 7.

52 Moten, email to author, May 26, 2017.

53 Moten points to this particular Rankine passage in "Blue Vespers," in *Black and Blur*, 243.

54 Agamben, *Remnants of Auschwitz*, 48, 52.

55 Agamben quoting Sofsky in *Remnants of Auschwitz*, 48. And Moten, "to consent not to be a single being."

56 Moten, "to consent not to be a single being."

57 Sexton, "The *Vel* of Slavery," 593; and Celan, "The written hollows itself," in *Breathturn into Timestead*, 67.

58 See Sexton, "The *Vel* of Slavery," 593.

8 the

1 Moten, "Chromatic Saturation," in *The Universal Machine*, 212 (italics in original). See Deleuze, *Pure Immanence: Essays on a Life*.

2 Weheliye, *Habeas Viscus*, 131.

3 Foucault, *The History of Sexuality*, vol. 1, *An Introduction*, 143; Moten, *Black and Blur*, 83, 71; and Moten, "Chromatic Saturation," in *The Universal Machine*, 212.

4 Philip, *Zong!*, 29, 38.

5 "The Noonesrose" is Pierre Joris's translation of the title in *Paul Celan: Selections*. Interestingly, when Joris translates the whole *Die Niemandsrose* in his recent English translation of Celan's collected earlier poetry, *Memory Rose into Threshold*

Speech: The Collected Earlier Poetry; A Bilingual Edition, he deletes the article "the" and translates the title as a Celanian neologism, *NoOnesRose*. David Young also removes the article in his 2014 English translation entitled *No One's Rose*.

6 Kapil, *Ban en Banlieue*, 20. Parenthetical citations in the following paragraphs are from Kapil's *Ban en Banlieue*.

7 See Hartman, *Scenes of Subjection*, 108, on Harriet Jacobs's dashes. And see the studies in chapters 2 and 7 of this book.

8 Spillers, "Mama's Baby, Papa's Maybe," in *Black, White, and in Color*, 207.

9 Amy De'Ath, "L(a)ying Down in the Banlieue."

10 I am grateful to scholar Rebecca Breen for an email discussion of *testimonio*. See her doctoral dissertation, "Sin título: Contemporary Women Artists from Latin America and Testimonio (Ana Mendieta, Doris Salcedo, Teresa Margolles)."

11 Kapil, "Writing/Not-Writing: Th[a][e] Diasporic Self: Notes toward a Race Riot Scene," 37.

12 Harney and Moten, "Michael Brown," 82.

13 Agamben, "The Ban and the Wolf," in *Homo Sacer*, 104–5.

14 Right after this sentence Kapil refers to Ban as a "black (brown) girl."

15 Weheliye, *Habeas Viscus*, 51.

16 Weheliye, *Habeas Viscus*, 137.

17 Kapil and Chen, "Michael Martin Shea with Bhanu Kapil and Ching-In Chen."

18 Weheliye, *Habeas Viscus*, 125; and Kapil, *Ban en Banlieue*, 69.

19 In what follows I approach the question of the dangerous perhaps/poetics of No One's monstrous witness through a demonstration of a particular act of bearing witness that I performed in relation to the death of my friend, poet Akilah Oliver, in 2011. I recognize that my narration of my experience raises difficult questions concerning the ethics of representation and family and community protocols in relation to speaking about the dead. I have thought deeply about these questions and consulted Akilah's family and friends for permission, and while there are no simple answers to these questions, I feel confident that Akilah, my queer kin, would want me to tell this story through un-telling it here. Please let this note serve as a content warning, as I will describe the process of finding Akilah's body and briefly name how her body was mistreated by government officials.

20 Akilah Oliver, *A Toast in the House of Friends*, 14. Quotations from Oliver are given in italics in this paragraph.

21 A. Oliver, *the she said dialogues: flesh memory*, 55

22 A. Oliver, *The Putterer's Notebook*, 6; and *the she said dialogues*, 8.

23 A. Oliver, *the she said dialogues*, xi. Parenthetical citations in the following paragraphs are from Oliver's *the she said dialogues*.

24 Spillers, "Mama's Baby, Papa's Maybe," in *Black, White, and in Color*, 229; and A. Oliver, *a(A)ugust*, n.p.

25 All language in quotation marks is from Spillers, "Mama's Baby, Papa's Maybe," in *Black, White, and in Color*, 229 (italics in original).

26 The language in italics comes from the following poems in A. Oliver, *A Toast in the*

House of Friends: "meditations (redemption chant)," 60-65; "feral femina," 88-89; "In Aporia," 9-10; and "in temples," 22.

27 Zolf, post at *Poetic Labor Project*.

28 A. Oliver, "Akilah Oliver—Author Statement," 1.

29 The phrases in italics in this paragraph are from A. Oliver, *the she said dialogues*, 45, 62; "Akilah Oliver—Author Statement," 2; the title of a poem in *A Toast in the House of Friends*, 35-55; and *the she said dialogues*, 31. There are also references in this paragraph to words by Spillers and Oliver that have been previously cited in this chapter. The phrase "defend the dead" is from Philip, *Zong!*, 25 (first instance). The name Akilah appears in *Zong!* on page 25 as one of the ancestors Philip summons in her quest to defend the dead.

9 witness(es)

1 See Sofsky, *The Order of Terror*, 201-5. I have reordered lines from these five pages of Sofsky's original to create a kind of poem.

2 Moten, "Chromatic Saturation," in *The Universal Machine*, 144.

3 Celan, "The Meridian," in *Collected Prose*, 47.

4 Weheliye, *Habeas Viscus*, 121.

5 Jean Améry, *At the Mind's Limits: Contemplations by a Survivor of Auschwitz and Its Realities*, 9.

6 See the description of Ligon's *Study for Frankenstein* series of paintings in the "No" chapter in this book; and Wilderson, *Red, White, and Black*, 96.

7 Spillers, "Mama's Baby, Papa's Maybe," in *Black, White, and in Color*, 207.

8 Hartman, speaking in Jafa's *Dreams Are Colder Than Death*.

9 Spillers, speaking in Jafa's *Dreams Are Colder Than Death*.

10 Spillers, "Mama's Baby, Papa's Maybe," in *Black, White, and in Color*, 207.

11 Hartman, *Scenes of Subjection*, 73-74.

12 Derrida, "Some Statements and Truisms about Neologisms, Newisms, Postisms, Parasitisms, and Other Small Seismisms," 79.

13 Sofsky, *The Order of Terror*, 203.

14 Hartman, *Lose Your Mother*, 129.

15 Hartman, *Lose Your Mother*, 216.

16 Hartman, *Wayward Lives, Beautiful Experiments: Intimate Histories of Social Upheaval*, 347. Subsequent parenthetical citations in this study are from Hartman's *Wayward Lives, Beautiful Experiments*.

17 Hartman, "Venus in Two Acts," 9, 1, 2.

18 Hartman, "Venus in Two Acts," 11, 2-3.

19 Hartman, "Venus in Two Acts," 9

20 Spillers, "Mama's Baby, Papa's Maybe," in *Black, White, and in Color*, 229.

21 Ferreira da Silva, "Hacking the Subject," 21, 22.

22 Ferreira da Silva, "Hacking the Subject," 22.

23 Hartman, "Venus in Two Acts," 10.

24 Harney and Moten, "Michael Brown," 81.

25 Ferreira da Silva, "Hacking the Subject," 33 (italics in original).

26 Italics in original; italics represent the voice of the chorus in Hartman's book.

27 See Sexton, "The *Vel* of Slavery," 593: "(nothing for no one)."

28 Italics in original, the voice of the chorus.

29 Sexton, "The *Vel* of Slavery," 593.

30 Ferreira da Silva, "Hacking the Subject," 38 (italics in original).

31 Moten, "Anassignment Letters," in *Stolen Life*, 230. And again, Spillers says "the flesh gives empathy" in Jafa's *Dreams Are Colder Than Death*. Italics added.

32 Fanon, *The Wretched of the Earth*, 57.

33 Ferreira da Silva, "Hacking the Subject," 38.

34 Chandler, *X*, 3.

35 Harney and Moten, "Al-Khwāriddim, or Savoir Faire Is Everywhere," 189.

36 Celan, "The Meridian," in *Collected Prose*, 48.

37 Moten, preface to *Stolen Life*, i.

38 Hartman, *Wayward Lives, Beautiful Experiments*, 349.

39 Hartman, *Wayward Lives, Beautiful Experiments*, 348.

40 Ferreira da Silva, "Hacking the Subject," 38.

41 Moten, "Anassignment Letters," in *Stolen Life*, 231; and Hartman, *Wayward Lives, Beautiful Experiments*, 348.

42 Hartman, *Wayward Lives, Beautiful Experiments*, 348, 211 (italics in original, voice of the chorus).

43 Hartman, *Wayward Lives, Beautiful Experiments*, 348. See also Harney and Moten, "Michael Brown," 87.

44 L. Harris, *Experiments in Exile*, 2; Hartman, *Wayward Lives, Beautiful Experiments*, 348; and Sexton, "All Black Everything."

APPENDIX

1 Celan, "Aschenglorie" (Ashglory), in *Breathturn into Timestead*, 62–65, translated by Pierre Joris.

BIBLIOGRAPHY

Adorno, Theodor W., and Walter Benjamin. *The Complete Correspondence, 1928–1940*. Edited by Henri Lonitz. Translated by Nicholas Walker. Cambridge, MA: Harvard University Press, 1999.

Agamben, Giorgio. *Homo Sacer: Sovereign Power and Bare Life*. Translated by Daniel Heller-Roazen. Stanford, CA: Stanford University Press, 1998.

Agamben, Giorgio. *Means without End: Notes on Politics*. Translated by Vincenzo Binetti and Cesare Casarino. Minneapolis: University of Minnesota Press, 2000.

Agamben, Giorgio. *Quel che resta di Auschwitz: L'archivio e il testimone*. Turin: Bollati Boringhieri, 1998.

Agamben, Giorgio. *Remnants of Auschwitz: The Witness and the Archive*. Translated by Daniel Heller-Roazen. New York: Zone, 2002.

Agamben, Giorgio. *The Use of Bodies*. Translated by Adam Kotsko. Palo Alto, CA: Stanford University Press, 2016.

Ahmed, Sara. *The Cultural Politics of Emotion*. London and New York: Routledge, 2004.

Alexander, Elizabeth. "'Can You Be BLACK and Look at This?': Reading the Rodney King Video(s)." *Public Culture* 7 (1994): 77–94.

Althusser, Louis. "Ideology and Ideological State Apparatuses." In *Lenin and Philosophy and Other Essays*, 127–86. New York: Monthly Review, 1971.

American Dialect Society. "2015 Word of the Year Is Singular 'They.'" Press release, January 8, 2016. http://www.americandialect.org/2015-word-of-the-year-is -singular-they.

Améry, Jean. *At the Mind's Limits: Contemplations by a Survivor of Auschwitz and Its Realities*. Translated by Sidney Rosenfeld and Stella P. Rosenfeld. Bloomington: Indiana University Press, 1980.

Anidjar, Gil. *The Jew, the Arab: A History of the Enemy*. Stanford, CA: Stanford University Press, 2003.

Armantrout, Rae. "Feminist Poetics and the Meaning of Clarity." In *Artifice and Indeterminacy: An Anthology of New Poetics*, edited by Christopher Beach, 287–96. Tuscaloosa: University of Alabama Press, 1998.

"Autopsy: Muhammad al Hanashi (ACLU Release)." Center for the Study of Human Rights in the Americas. Accessed November 1, 2016. http://humanrights.ucdavis .edu/projects/the-guantanamo-testimonials-project/testimonies/prisoner -testimonies/autopsy_muhammad_al_hanashi.pdf/view.

Baraka, Amiri. *Blues People: Negro Music in White America*. New York: Perennial, 2002.

Barthes, Roland. "On Émile Benveniste." Special supplement, *Semiotica* 33 (January 1, 1981): 25.

Barthes, Roland. *Writing Degree Zero*. Translated by Annette Lavers and Colin Smith. New York: Farrar, Straus and Giroux, 2012.

Benjamin, Jessica. "Two-Way Streets: Recognition of Difference and the Intersubjective Third." *differences* 17, no. 1 (2006): 116–46.

Benjamin, Walter. *The Arcades Project*. Translated by Howard Eiland and Kevin McLaughlin. Cambridge, MA: Harvard University Press, 1999.

Benjamin, Walter. *The Correspondence of Walter Benjamin, 1910–1940*. Chicago: University of Chicago Press, 1994.

Benjamin, Walter. *The Origin of German Tragic Drama*. Translated by John Osborne. London: Verso, 1998.

Benjamin, Walter. *Selected Writings*. Vol. 2, pt. 2, *1931–1934*. Edited by Michael W. Jennings, Howard Eiland, and Gary Smith. Translated by Rodney Livingstone et al. Cambridge, MA: Harvard University Press, 1999.

Benjamin, Walter. *Selected Writings*. Vol. 4, *1938–1940*. Edited by Howard Eiland and Michael W. Jennings. Translated by Edmund Jephcott et al. Cambridge, MA: Harvard University Press, 2003.

Benjamin, Walter, and Gershom Scholem. *The Correspondence of Walter Benjamin and Gershom Scholem, 1932–1940*. Edited by Gershom Scholem. Translated by Gary Smith and Andre Lefevere. New York: Schocken Books, 1989.

Benveniste, Émile. *Indo-European Language and Society*. Translated by Elizabeth Palmer. Coral Gables, FL: University of Miami Press, 1973.

Benveniste, Émile. *Problems in General Linguistics*. Translated by Mary Elizabeth Meek. Coral Gables, FL: University of Miami Press, 1971.

Blanchot, Maurice. *The Infinite Conversation*. Translated by Susan Hanson. Minneapolis: University of Minnesota Press, 1993.

Blanchot, Maurice. *The Space of Literature*. Translated by Ann Smock. Lincoln: University of Nebraska Press, 1989.

Blanchot, Maurice. *The Step Not Beyond*. Translated by Lycette Nelson. Albany: State University of New York Press, 1992.

Blanchot, Maurice. *Voice from Elsewhere*. Translated by Charlotte Mandell. Albany: State University of New York Press, 2002.

Blanchot, Maurice. *The Writing of the Disaster*. Translated by Ann Smock. Lincoln: University of Nebraska Press, 1995.

Bradley, Joff. "The Eyes of the Fourth Personal Singular." *Deleuze Studies* 9, no. 2 (2015): 185–207.

Braidotti, Rosi. *Transpositions: On Nomadic Ethics*. London: Polity, 2006.

Breen, Rebecca. "Sin título: Contemporary Women Artists from Latin America and Testimonio (Ana Mendieta, Doris Salcedo, Teresa Margolles)." PhD diss., University of Cambridge, 2012.

Brolaski, Julian Talamantez. "pronoun circle-jerk and the dog charlie." Poetry Foundation, 2019. https://www.poetryfoundation.org/poems/148209/pronoun-circle-jerk-and-the-dog-charlie-.

Brossard, Nicole. *The Aerial Letter*. Translated by Marlene Wildeman. Toronto: Women's Press, 1988.

Bunyan, John. *The Pilgrim's Progress*. 1678. London: Elliott Stock, 1895.

Burton, Johanna. "One Person Protests: Notes about Going (Back) There." In *Not Quite How I Remember It*, edited by Helena Reckitt and Johanna Burton, 21–26. Toronto: Power Plant, 2008. Exhibition catalog.

Butler, Judith. *Bodies That Matter: On the Discursive Limits of "Sex."* New York and London: Routledge, 1993.

Butler, Judith. "Bracha's Eurydice." Foreword to Ettinger, *The Matrixial Borderspace*, vii–xii.

Butler, Judith. "Contingent Foundations: Feminism and the Question of 'Postmodernism.'" In *Feminists Theorize the Political*, edited by Judith Butler and Joan W. Scott, 3–21. New York: Routledge, 1992.

Butler, Judith. *Frames of War: When Is Life Grievable?* London: Verso, 2010.

Butler, Judith. *Giving an Account of Oneself*. New York: Fordham University Press, 2005.

Butler, Judith. *Precarious Life: The Powers of Mourning and Violence*. London: Verso, 2004.

Butler, Judith, and Athena Athanasiou. *Dispossession: The Performative in the Political*. London: Polity, 2013.

Carson, Anne. *Economy of the Unlost: (Reading Simonides of Keos with Paul Celan)*. Princeton, NJ: Princeton University Press, 1999.

Carson, Anne. *Eros the Bittersweet*. Champaign, IL: Dalkey Archive, 1998.

Celan, Paul. *Breathturn*. Translated by Pierre Joris. Los Angeles: Green Integer, 2006.

Celan, Paul. *Breathturn into Timestead: The Collected Later Poetry; A Bilingual Edition*. Translated by Pierre Joris. New York: Farrar, Straus and Giroux, 2014.

Celan, Paul. *Collected Prose*. Translated by Rosmarie Waldrop. Riverdale-on-Hudson, NY: Sheep Meadow, 1986.

Celan, Paul. *Die Niemandsrose*. Frankfurt am Main: S. Fischer Verlag, 1963.

Celan, Paul. *Memory Rose into Threshold Speech: The Collected Earlier Poetry; A Bilingual Edition*. Translated by Pierre Joris. New York: Farrar, Straus and Giroux, 2020.

Celan, Paul. *No One's Rose*. Translated by David Young. Grosse Point Farms, MI: Marick Press, 2014.

Celan, Paul. *Paul Celan: Selections*. Translated by Pierre Joris. Berkeley: University of California Press, 2005.

Celan, Paul. *Poems of Paul Celan*. Translated by Michael Hamburger. New York: Persea, 2002.

Césaire, Aimé. *Discourse on Colonialism*. Translated by Joan Pinkham. New York: Monthly Review Press, 1972.

Cha, Theresa Hak Kyung. *DICTEE*. Berkeley: University of California Press, 2001.

Chandler, Nahum D. "The Problem of the Centuries: A Contemporary Elaboration of 'The Present Outlook for the Dark Races of Mankind' circa the 27th of December 1899." Unpublished manuscript.

Chandler, Nahum D. *X: The Problem of the Negro as a Problem for Thought*. New York: Fordham University Press, 2013.

Copeland, Huey. "Glenn Ligon and the Matter of Fugitivity." In *Bound to Appear: Art, Slavery, and the Site of Blackness in Multicultural America*, 109–52. Chicago: University of Chicago Press, 2013.

Craps, Stef. *Postcolonial Witnessing: Trauma Out of Bounds*. New York: Palgrave Macmillan, 2013.

Davidson, Amy. "Darren Wilson's Demon." *New Yorker*, November 26, 2014. http://www.newyorker.com/news/amy-davidson/demon-ferguson-darren-wilson-fear-black-man.

De'Ath, Amy. "L(a)ying Down in the Banlieue." *Mute*, September 21, 2016. https://www.metamute.org/editorial/articles/laying-down-banlieue.

Delbo, Charlotte. *Auschwitz and After*. Translated by Rosette C. Lamont. New Haven, CT: Yale University Press, 1995.

Deleuze, Gilles. *Cinema 2: The Time-Image*. Translated by Hugh Tomlinson and Robert Galeta. London: Athlone, 1989.

Deleuze, Gilles. *Difference and Repetition*. Translated by Paul Patton. London: Continuum/Athlone, 1994.

Deleuze, Gilles. *Foucault*. Translated and edited by Seán Hand. Minneapolis: University of Minnesota Press, 1988.

Deleuze, Gilles. "Literature and Life." In *Essays Critical and Clinical*, translated by Daniel W. Smith and Michael A. Greco, 1–6. London: Verso, 1998.

Deleuze, Gilles. *Logic of Sense*. Translated by Mark Lester. New York: Columbia University Press, 1990.

Deleuze, Gilles. *Pure Immanence: Essays on a Life*. Translated by Anne Boyman. New York: Zone Books, 2001.

Deleuze, Gilles, and Félix Guattari. *Kafka: Toward a Minor Literature*. Translated by Dana Polan. Minneapolis: University of Minnesota Press, 1986.

Deleuze, Gilles, and Félix Guattari. *A Thousand Plateaus: Capitalism and Schizophrenia*. Translated by Brian Massumi. Minneapolis: University of Minnesota Press, 1987.

de Lima, Lucas. "Race, Wokeness, and the Possessive Individualism of U.S. Poetry." *Syndicate*, September 16, 2020. https://syndicate.network/symposia/literature/thinking-its-presence/.

de Man, Paul. *The Resistance to Theory*. Manchester: Manchester University Press, 1986.

de Man, Paul. *The Rhetoric of Romanticism*. New York: Columbia University Press, 1984.

Derrida, Jacques. "Desistance." Introduction to Philippe Lacoue-Labarthe, *Typography: Mimesis, Philosophy, Politics*, 1–42. Cambridge, MA: Harvard University Press, 1989.

Derrida, Jacques. "Force of Law: The Mystical Foundation of Authority." In *Acts of Religion*, edited by Gil Anidjar, 228–98. New York and London: Routledge, 2002.

Derrida, Jacques. "Jacques Derrida: Deconstruction and the Other." In *Dialogues with Contemporary Continental Thinkers: The Phenomenological Heritage*, edited by Richard Kearney, 107–25. Manchester: Manchester University Press, 1984.

Derrida, Jacques. "Marx and Sons." In *Ghostly Demarcations: A Symposium on Jacques Derrida's Specters of Marx*, edited by Michael Sprinker, 213–69. London and New York: Verso, 1999.

Derrida, Jacques. *Of Grammatology*. Translated by Gayatri Chakravorty Spivak. Baltimore, MD: Johns Hopkins University Press, 1976.

Derrida, Jacques. "Perhaps or Maybe: Jacques Derrida in Conversation with Alexander García Düttmann." *Warwick Journal of Philosophy* 6 (1997): 1–18.

Derrida, Jacques. *Points...: Interviews, 1974–1994*. Edited by Elisabeth Weber. Translated by Peggy Kamuf et al. Stanford, CA: Stanford University Press, 1995.

Derrida, Jacques. *Politics of Friendship*. Translated by George Collins. London: Verso, 1997.

Derrida, Jacques. *The Post Card: From Socrates to Freud and Beyond*. Translated by Alan Bass. Chicago: University of Chicago Press, 1987.

Derrida, Jacques. "Some Statements and Truisms about Neologisms, Newisms, Post-isms, Parasitisms, and Other Small Seismisms." In *The States of "Theory": History, Art, and Critical Discourse*, edited by David Carroll, 63–94. New York: Columbia University Press, 1989.

Derrida, Jacques. *Sovereignties in Question: The Poetics of Paul Celan*. Edited by Thomas Dutoit and Outi Pasanen. New York: Fordham University Press, 2005.

Derrida, Jacques. *Specters of Marx*. Translated by Peggy Kamuf. New York: Routledge, 1994.

Douglass, Frederick. *Narrative of the Life of Frederick Douglass, an American Slave, Written by Himself*. 1845. Cambridge, MA: Belknap Press of Harvard University Press, 2009.

Drabinski, John E. *Glissant and the Middle Passage: Philosophy, Beginning, Abyss*. Minneapolis: University of Minnesota Press, 2019.

Du Bois, W. E. B. *The Souls of Black Folk: Essays and Sketches*. Chicago: A. C. McClurg, 1903.

Ellison, Ralph. *Invisible Man*. 1952. New York: Random House, 1995.

Elrick, Laura K. *Stalk*. Video, 22:18. 2008. https://vimeo.com/69179188.

Elrick, Laura K. *Stalk: A Score for Performance*. Unpublished manuscript, 2008.

Elrick, Laura K. "Sensing the Present: Economies of Fear and the Limits of the Visible." In "Affective Disobedience: Poetic Praxis as Public Intervention in the Post-9/11 Era," 16–39. Master's thesis, CUNY Graduate Center, 2011.

Esposito, Roberto. *Third Person: Politics of Life and Philosophy of the Impersonal*. Translated by Zakiya Hanafi. Cambridge, UK, and Malden, MA: Polity, 2012.

Ettinger, Bracha L. *The Matrixial Borderspace*. Edited by Brian Massumi. Minneapolis: University of Minnesota Press, 2006.

Ettinger, Bracha L. "Wit(h)nessing Trauma and the Matrixial Gaze." In *The Matrixial Borderspace*, 123–55.

Falkoff, Marc, ed. *Poems from Guantánamo: The Detainees Speak*. Iowa City: University of Iowa Press, 2007.

Fanon, Frantz. *Black Skin, White Masks*. Translated by Charles Lam Markmann. London: Pluto, 1986.

Fanon, Frantz. *The Wretched of the Earth*. Translated by Constance Farrington. New York: Grove, 1968.

Felman, Shoshana. *The Scandal of the Speaking Body: Don Juan with J. L. Austin, or Seduc-*

tion in Two Languages. Translated by Catherine Porter. Stanford, CA: Stanford University Press, 2003.

Felman, Shoshana. *Writing and Madness: (Literature/Philosophy/Psychoanalysis).* Translated by Martha Noel Evans and Shoshana Felman. Palo Alto, CA: Stanford University Press, 2003.

Felman, Shoshana, and Dori Laub. *Testimony: Crises of Witnessing in Literature, Psychoanalysis, and History.* London and New York: Routledge, 1992.

Ferreira da Silva, Denise. "Fractal Thinking." *aCCeSsions,* no. 2 (April 27, 2016). https://accessions.org/article2/fractal-thinking.

Ferreira da Silva, Denise. "Hacking the Subject: Black Feminism and Refusal beyond the Limits of Critique." *philoSOPHIA* 8, no. 1 (2018): 19–41.

Ferreira da Silva, Denise. "In the Raw." *e-flux,* no. 93 (2018). https://www.e-flux.com /journal/93/215795/in-the-raw/.

Ferreira da Silva, Denise. "No-Bodies: Law, Raciality and Violence." *Griffith Law Review* 18 (2009): 119–62.

Ferreira da Silva, Denise. "On Difference without Separability." Text for the catalog of the 32nd São Paulo Art Biennial, "Incerteza viva" (Living Uncertainty), November 16, 2016. https://issuu.com/amilcarpacker/docs/denise_ferreira_da_silva.

Ferreira da Silva, Denise. "Toward a Black Feminist Poethics: The Quest(ion) of Blackness toward the End of the World." *Black Scholar* 44, no. 2 (2014): 81–97.

Ferreira da Silva, Denise. *Toward a Global Idea of Race.* Minneapolis: University of Minnesota Press, 2007.

Ferreira da Silva, Denise, and Valentina Desideri. "A Conversation between Valentina Desideri and Denise Ferreira da Silva." July 8, 2015. http://handreadingstudio.org /wp-content/uploads/2015/06/V-Dconversation.pdf.

Finkelstein, Norman G. *The Holocaust Industry: Reflections on the Exploitation of Jewish Suffering.* London: Verso, 2000.

Forché, Carolyn, ed. *Against Forgetting: Twentieth-Century Poetry of Witness.* New York and London: Norton, 1993.

Foucault, Michel. "The Abnormals." In *The Essential Works of Foucault,* vol. 1, *Ethics,* edited by Paul Rabinow, translated by Robert Hurley et al., 51–57. New York: New Press, 1997.

Foucault, Michel. *The History of Sexuality.* Vol. 1, *An Introduction.* Translated by Robert Hurley. New York: Vintage, 1990.

Foucault, Michel. "What Is an Author?" Translated by Donald F. Bouchard and Sherry Simon. In *Language, Counter-Memory, Practice,* edited by Donald F. Bouchard, 113–38. Ithaca, NY: Cornell University Press, 1977.

Fox, John. *Poetic Medicine: The Healing Art of Poem-Making.* New York: Jeremy P. Tarcher/Putnam, 1997.

Freeman, Elizabeth. *Time Binds: Queer Temporalities, Queer Histories.* Durham, NC: Duke University Press, 2010.

Gaines, Charles. "The Theater of Refusal: Black Art and Mainstream Criticism." In

The Theater of Refusal: Black Art and Mainstream Criticism, edited by Catherine Lord, 13–21. Irvine: Fine Arts Gallery, University of California, Irvine, 1993.

Gibson, Caitlin. "A White Artist Responds to the Outcry over Her Controversial Emmett Till Painting." *Washington Post*, March 23, 2017. https://www.washington post.com/news/arts-and-entertainment/wp/2017/03/23/dana-schutz-responds -to-outcry-over-her-controversial-emmett-till-painting.

Glissant, Édouard. *Caribbean Discourse: Selected Essays*. Translated by J. Michael Dash. Charlottesville: University Press of Virginia, 1989.

Glissant, Édouard. *The Collected Poems of Édouard Glissant*. Edited by Jefferson Humphries. Translated by Jefferson Humphries and Melissa Manolas. Minneapolis: University of Minnesota Press, 2005.

Glissant, Édouard. *Poetics of Relation*. Translated by Betsy Wing. Ann Arbor: University of Michigan Press, 1997.

Glissant, Édouard, Manthia Diawara, and Christopher Winks. "Édouard Glissant in Conversation with Manthia Diawara." *Nka: Journal of Contemporary African Art* 28 (2011): 4–19.

Goldsmith, Kenneth. "The Body of Michael Brown." Presentation at Brown University, March 13, 2015.

Gubar, Susan. *Poetry after Auschwitz: Remembering What One Never Knew*. Bloomington: Indiana University Press, 2006.

Halberstam, Jack. *Skin Shows: Gothic Horror and the Technology of Monsters*. Durham, NC: Duke University Press, 1995.

Halberstam, Jack. "Zombie Humanism at the End of the World." Lecture, Berlin Institute for Cultural Inquiry, May 27, 2015. Video, 4:58. https://www.youtube .com/watch?v=YW19_Hgbw60.

Halpern, Rob. *Common Place*. Brooklyn, NY: Ugly Duckling, 2015.

Halpern, Rob. *Music for Porn*. Callicoon, NY: Nightboat Books, 2012.

Harney, Stefano, and Fred Moten. "Al-Khwāriddim, or Savoir Faire Is Everywhere." In *Really Useful Knowledge*, edited by Brook Andrew, 185–90. Madrid: Museo Nacional Centro de Arte Reina Sofia, 2014.

Harney, Stefano, and Fred Moten. "Michael Brown." *boundary 2* 42, no. 4 (2015): 81–87.

Harney, Stefano, and Fred Moten. *The Undercommons: Fugitive Planning and Black Study*. Wivenhoe, UK: Minor Compositions, 2013.

Harris, Laura. *Experiments in Exile: C. L. R. James, Hélio Oiticica, and the Aesthetic Sociality of Blackness*. New York: Fordham University Press, 2018.

Harris, Robert A. "A Handbook of Rhetorical Devices." *VirtualSalt* (blog), January 5, 2010. http://www.virtualsalt.com/rhetoric4.htm#Apophasis.

Hartman, Saidiya V. *Lose Your Mother: A Journey along the Atlantic Slave Route*. New York: Farrar, Straus and Giroux, 2007.

Hartman, Saidiya V. *Scenes of Subjection: Terror, Slavery, and Self-Making in Nineteenth-Century America*. New York: Oxford University Press, 1997.

Hartman, Saidiya V. "Venus in Two Acts." *Small Axe* 12, no. 2 (2008): 1–14.

Hartman, Saidiya V. *Wayward Lives, Beautiful Experiments: Intimate Histories of Social Up-heaval*. New York: Norton, 2019.

Hartman, Saidiya V., and Frank B. Wilderson III. "The Position of the Unthought: An Interview with Saidiya V. Hartman Conducted by Frank B. Wilderson III." *Qui Parle* 13, no. 2 (2003): 183–201.

Hayes, Sharon. "Sharon Hayes Interviewed by Chris Mansour." *491*, no. 2 (November 1, 2011). Accessed January 10, 2017. http://fourninetyone.com/2010/11/01 /interview-sharonhayes.

Hayes, Sharon. "We Have a Future: An Interview with Sharon Hayes." By Julia Bryan-Wilson. *Grey Room* 37 (2009): 78–93.

Heidegger, Martin. *Poetry, Language, Thought*. Translated by Albert Hofstadter. New York: Harper Collins, 1971.

Hejinian, Lyn. *My Life*. Los Angeles: Green Integer, 2002.

Hejinian, Lyn. "The Rejection of Closure." In *The Language of Inquiry*, 40–58. Berkeley: University of California Press, 2000.

Hesford, Victoria. *Feeling Women's Liberation*. Durham, NC: Duke University Press, 2013.

Hill, Marc Lamont. *Nobody: Casualties of America's War on the Vulnerable, from Ferguson to Flint and Beyond*. New York: Atria Books, 2016.

Jacobs, Harriet. *Incidents in the Life of a Slave Girl: Written by Herself*. 1861. London: Penguin Books, 2000.

Jafa, Arthur. *Dreams Are Colder Than Death*. Video, 52:00. TNEG Film Studio, 2014.

Jarvis, Jill. "Remnants of Muslims: Reading Agamben's Silence." *New Literary History* 45, no. 5 (2014): 707–28.

Justice, Daniel Heath. "'Go Away, Water!': Kinship Criticism and the Decolonization Imperative." In *Reasoning Together: The Native Critics Collective*, edited by Craig S. Womack, Daniel Heath Justice, and Christopher B. Teuton, 147–68. Norman: University of Oklahoma Press, 2008.

Kafka, Franz. "Cares of a Family Man." In *The Complete Stories*, 427–29. New York: Schocken, 1971.

Kapil, Bhanu. *Ban en Banlieue*. New York: Nightboat Books, 2015.

Kapil, Bhanu. "Writing/Not-Writing: Th[a][e] Diasporic Self: Notes toward a Race Riot Scene." *English Language Notes* 49, no. 2 (2011): 35–40.

Kapil, Bhanu, and Ching-In Chen. "Michael Martin Shea with Bhanu Kapil and Ching-In Chen." *The Conversant*, May 2016. Accessed February 1, 2017. http:// theconversant.org/?p=10349.

Kennedy, Randy. "White Artist's Painting of Emmett Till at Whitney Biennial Draws Protests." *New York Times*, March 21, 2017. https://www.nytimes.com/2017/03/21 /arts/design/painting-of-emmett-till-at-whitney-biennial-draws-protests.html.

Lacan, Jacques. *Les non dupes errent*. Seminar XXI, 1973–1974 (December 11, 1973). http://www.lacanianworks.net/?p=807.

LaCapra, Dominick. "Trauma, Absence, Loss." *Critical Inquiry* 25, no. 4 (1999): 696–727.

Laplanche, Jean. "Time and the Other." In *Essays on Otherness*, translated by Luke Thurston, 238–63. London: Routledge, 1999.

Laplanche, Jean. "The Wall and the Arcade." In *Seduction, Translation and the Drives*, edited by John Fletcher and Martin Stanton, translated by Martin Stanton, 197–216. London: Institute of Contemporary Arts, 1992.

Levi, Primo. *The Complete Works of Primo Levi*. Edited by Ann Goldstein. New York: Liveright, 2015.

Levi, Primo. *The Drowned and the Saved*. Translated by Raymond Rosenthal. New York: Vintage, 1989.

Levi, Primo. *If This Is a Man*. Translated by Stuart Woolf. New York: Orion, 1959.

Levi, Primo. "On Obscure Writing." In *Other People's Trades*, 169–75. London: Abacus, 1989.

Levi, Primo. *Survival in Auschwitz and The Reawakening: Two Memoirs*. Translated by Stuart Woolf. New York: Summit, 1986.

Levinas, Emmanuel. *Difficult Freedom: Essays on Judaism*. Translated by Seán Hand. Baltimore, MD: Johns Hopkins University Press, 1990.

Levinas, Emmanuel. "Ethics and Politics." In *The Levinas Reader*, edited by Seán Hand, translated by Jonathan Romney, 289–97. Oxford: Basil Blackwell, 1989.

Levinas, Emmanuel. *Otherwise Than Being, or Beyond Essence*. Translated by Alphonso Lingis. Pittsburgh, PA: Duquesne University Press, 1998.

Levinas, Emmanuel. "Paul Celan: From Being to the Other." In *Proper Names*, translated by Michael B. Smith, 40–46. Palo Alto, CA: Stanford University Press, 1996.

Levinas, Emmanuel. "Philosophy and Awakening." In *Entre Nous: On Thinking-of-the-Other*, translated by Michael B. Smith and Barbara Harshav, 77–90. New York: Columbia University Press, 1998.

Levinas, Emmanuel. "The Trace of the Other." Translated by Alphonso Lingis. In *Deconstruction in Context: Literature and Philosophy*, edited by Mark C. Taylor, 345–59. Chicago: University of Chicago Press, 1982.

Ligon, Glenn. "America: Audio Guide Stop for Glenn Ligon, *Untitled (I Am a Man)*, 1988." 2011. Whitney Museum of American Art, Audio Guides. https://whitney.org/audio-guides/7?language=english&type=general&page=1&stop=1.

Ligon, Glenn. "Interview with David Drogin." *Museo Magazine*, 2010. http://www.museomagazine.com/802505/GLENN-LIGON.

Linebaugh, Peter, and Marcus Rediker. *The Many-Headed Hydra: Sailors, Slaves, Commoners, and the Hidden History of the Revolutionary Atlantic*. Boston: Beacon, 2000.

Lo, Cheena Marie. *Ephemera and Atmospheres*. Belladonna Chaplet Series, no. 168. Brooklyn: Belladonna, 2014.

Lorde, Audre. "Uses of the Erotic: The Erotic as Power." In *Sister Outsider: Essays and Speeches*, 53–59. Berkeley, CA: Crossing, 2007.

Lyotard, Jean-François. *The Differend: Phrases in Dispute*. Translated by Georges Van Den Abbeele. Minneapolis: University of Minnesota Press, 1988.

Lyotard, Jean-François. *The Inhuman: Reflections on Time*. Translated by Geoffrey Bennington and Rachel Bowlby. Stanford, CA: Stanford University Press, 1991.

Lyotard, Jean-François. "Presenting the Unpresentable: The Sublime." *ArtForum* 20, no. 8 (1982): 64–69.

Mackey, Nathaniel. *Paracritical Hinge: Essays, Talks, Notes, Interviews.* Iowa City: University of Iowa Press, 2018.

Massumi, Brian. "Painting: The Voice of the Grain." Afterword to Ettinger, *The Matrixial Borderspace*, 201–14.

Mbembe, Achille. "Necropolitics." *Public Culture* 15, no. 1 (2003): 11–40.

McKittrick, Katherine. *Demonic Grounds: Black Women and the Cartographies of Struggle.* Minneapolis: University of Minnesota Press, 2006.

Melville, Herman. *Bartleby, the Scrivener.* 1853. Hoboken, NJ: Melville House, 2004.

Memmi, Albert. *The Colonizer and the Colonized.* Translated by Howard Greenfeld. Boston: Beacon, 1965.

Milne, Heather. "Dearly Beloveds: The Politics of Intimacy in Juliana Spahr's *This Connection of Everyone with Lungs*." *Mosaic: A Journal for the Interdisciplinary Study of Literature* 47, no. 2 (2014): 203–18.

Milton, John. *Paradise Lost.* 1667. Edited by Barbara K. Lewalski. Oxford: Blackwell, 2007.

Morrison, Toni. *Beloved.* New York: Plume, 1988.

Moten, Fred. *Black and Blur: Critical Essays.* Vol. 1 of *consent not to be a single being.* Durham, NC: Duke University Press, 2017.

Moten, Fred. "Blackness and Nothingness (Mysticism in the Flesh)." *South Atlantic Quarterly* 112, no. 4 (2013): 737–80.

Moten, Fred. "Fred Moten, Poet." By Doni Shepard. *Lunch Ticket*, Winter/Spring 2017. http://lunchticket.org/fred-moten-poet/.

Moten, Fred. *In the Break: The Aesthetics of the Black Radical Tradition.* Minneapolis: University of Minnesota Press, 2003.

Moten, Fred. *A Poetics of the Undercommons.* Butte, MT: Sputnik and Fizzle, 2016.

Moten, Fred. *Stolen Life: Social Essays.* Vol. 2 of *consent not to be a single being.* Durham, NC: Duke University Press, 2018.

Moten, Fred. "to consent not to be a single being." *Harriet* (blog), February 15, 2010. https://www.poetryfoundation.org/harriet/2010/02/to-consent-not-to-be-a-single-being/.

Moten, Fred. *The Universal Machine: Theoretical Essays.* Vol. 3 of *consent not to be a single being.* Durham, NC: Duke University Press, 2018.

Muñoz, José Esteban. *Disidentifications: Queers of Color and the Performance of Politics.* Minneapolis: University of Minnesota Press, 1999.

Nietzsche, Friedrich. *Beyond Good and Evil: Prelude to a Philosophy of the Future.* Translated by Ian Johnston. Adelaide: Holtof Donné, 2011. http://nietzsche.holtof.com/reader/articles/read-beyond-good-and-evil_5.html.

Oliver, Akilah. *a(A)ugust.* Brooklyn, NY: Portable Press at Yo-Yo Labs, 2006.

Oliver, Akilah. "Akilah Oliver—Author Statement." Unpublished manuscript, 2009. http://www.thetoleranceprojectarchive.org/oliver.html.

Oliver, Akilah. *The Putterer's Notebook.* Brooklyn, NY: Belladonna Books, 2006.

Oliver, Akilah. *the she said dialogues: flesh memory*. Boulder, CO: Smokeproof, 1999. Reprint, New York: Nightboat Books, 2021.

Oliver, Akilah. *A Toast in the House of Friends*. Minneapolis: Coffee House, 2009.

Oliver, Kelly. *Witnessing: Beyond Recognition*. Minneapolis: University of Minnesota Press, 2001.

Olson, Charles. "Projective Verse." In *Collected Prose*, edited by Donald Allen and Benjamin Friedlander, 239–49. Berkeley: University of California Press, 1997.

Ostriker, Alicia. "Beyond Confession: The Poetics of Postmodern Witness." *American Poetry Review* 30, no. 2 (2001): 35–39.

Patterson, Orlando. *Slavery and Social Death: A Comparative Study*. Cambridge, MA: Harvard University Press, 1982.

Philip, M. NourbeSe. *Zong!* Middletown, CT: Wesleyan University Press, 2008.

Pollock, Griselda. "Aesthetic Wit(h)nessing in the Era of Trauma." *EurAmerica* 40, no. 4 (2010): 829–86.

Pope, Alexander. *An Essay on Criticism*. 1711. London: Macmillan, 1896.

Puar, Jasbir. *Terrorist Assemblages: Homonationalism in Queer Times*. Durham, NC: Duke University Press, 2007.

Puar, Jasbir, and Amit S. Rai. "Monster, Terrorist, Fag: The War on Terrorism and the Production of Docile Patriots." *Social Text* 72, 20 no. 3 (2002): 117–48.

Rankine, Claudia. *Citizen: An American Lyric*. Minneapolis, MN: Graywolf, 2014.

Retallack, Joan. *The Poethical Wager*. Berkeley: University of California Press, 2003.

Rowland, Antony. "Poetry as Metatestimony: Primo Levi's *Collected Poems*." In *Poetry as Testimony: Witnessing and Memory in Twentieth-Century Poems*, 82–95. New York: Routledge, 2014.

Ryn, Zdzislaw, and Stanslav Klodzinski. "An der Grenze zwischen Leben und Tod: Eine Studie über die Erscheinung des 'Muselmann' im Konzentrationslager." In *Die Auschwitz-Hefte: Texte der polnischen Zeitschrift "Przeglad Lekarski" über historische, psychische und medizinische Aspekte des Lebens und Sterbens in Auschwitz*, 1:89–154. Hamburg: Rogner und Bernhard, 1994.

Scarry, Elaine. *The Body in Pain*. Oxford: Oxford University Press, 1987.

Schotten, C. Heike. *Queer Terror: Life, Death, and Desire in the Settler Colony*. New York: Columbia University Press, 2018.

Schutz, Dana. "Dana Schutz by Mei Chin." Interview by Mei Chin. BOMB *Magazine*, no. 95 (April 1, 2006). https://bombmagazine.org/articles/dana-schutz/.

Scott, Dread. "Dread Scott in Conversation with Dana Liss, Studio Museum Curatorial Intern, August 2013." *Radical Presence NY: Black Performance in Contemporary Art*, Grey Art Gallery and Studio Museum, Harlem, September 2013–March 2014. http://radicalpresenceny.org/?page_id=373.

Scott, Dread. Dread Scott's website. http://www.dreadscott.net.

Senguputa, Kim. "Israel-Gaza Conflict: Four Boys Killed While Playing Football on Beach after Israeli Warships Open Fire." *Independent*, July 16, 2014. https://www.independent.co.uk/news/world/middle-east/israel-gaza-conflict-leaflets-dropped-on-northern-gaza-ordering-100000-to-evacuate-amid-fears-of-9609788.html.

Sexton, Jared. "Afro-Pessimism: The Unclear Word." *Rhizomes: Cultural Studies in Emerging Knowledge*, no. 29 (2016). https://doi.org/10.20415/rhiz/029.e02.

Sexton, Jared. "All Black Everything." *e-flux*, no. 79 (2017). https://www.e-flux.com /journal/79/94158/all-black-everything/.

Sexton, Jared. "'The Curtain of the Sky': An Introduction." *Critical Sociology* 36, no. 1 (2010): 11–24.

Sexton, Jared. "The Rage: Some Comments on 'Open Casket.'" *Contemptorary*, May 21, 2017. http://contemptorary.org/the-rage-sexton/.

Sexton, Jared. "The Social Life of Social Death: On Afro-Pessimism and Black Optimism." *InTensions* 5 (2011): 1–47.

Sexton, Jared. "The *Vel* of Slavery: Tracking the Figure of the Unsovereign." *Critical Sociology* 42, no. 4–5 (2016): 583–97.

Sharpe, Christina. *In the Wake: On Blackness and Being*. Durham, NC: Duke University Press, 2016.

Sharpe, Christina. *Monstrous Intimacies: Making Post-Slavery Subjects*. Durham, NC: Duke University Press, 2010.

Sharpe, Christina. "'What Does It Mean to Be Black and Look at This?': A Scholar Reflects on the Dana Schutz Controversy." Interview with Siddhartha Mitter. *Hyperallergic*, March 24, 2017. https://hyperallergic.com/368012/what-does-it-mean -to-be-black-and-look-at-this-a-scholar-reflects-on-the-dana-schutz-controversy/.

Shelley, Mary. *Frankenstein: The 1818 Text*. New York: Penguin Books, 2018.

Shklovksy, Viktor. *Viktor Shklovksy: A Reader*. Edited and translated by Alexandra Berlina. New York: Bloomsbury, 2016.

Sidney, Philip. *An Apology for Poetry, or, The Defence of Poesy*. 1595. Manchester, UK: Palgrave, 2002.

Skoulding, Zoe. "Performance and Absence in the Heterotopian City." In *Contemporary Women's Poetry and Urban Space: Experimental Cities*, 195–212. New York: Palgrave Macmillan, 2013.

Smith, Linda Tuhiwai. *Decolonizing Methodologies: Research and Indigenous Peoples*. London: Zed Books, 1999.

Sofsky, Wolfgang. *The Order of Terror: The Concentration Camp*. Translated by William Templer. Princeton, NJ: Princeton University Press, 1997.

Spahr, Juliana. *Everybody's Autonomy: Connective Reading and Collective Identity*. Tuscaloosa: University of Alabama Press, 2001.

Spahr, Juliana. "How Does the Work Get Used." In *A Community Writing Itself: Conversations with Vanguard Writers of the Bay Area*, edited by Sarah Rosenthal, 298–320. Champaign, IL: Dalkey Archive, 2010.

Spahr, Juliana. "My White Feminism." *Boston Review*, April 7, 2016. http://bostonreview .net/poetry/NPM-2016-juliana-spahr-my-white-feminism.

Spahr, Juliana. "Resignifying Autobiography: Lyn Hejinian's *My Life*." *American Literature* 68, no. 1 (1996): 139–59.

Spahr, Juliana. *The Transformation*. Berkeley, CA: Atelos, 2007.

Spillers, Hortense. *Black, White, and in Color: Essays on American Literature and Culture.* Chicago: University of Chicago Press, 2003.

Spitzer, Anais. *Derrida, Myth and the Impossibility of Philosophy.* London: Bloomsbury, 2011.

Spivak, Gayatri Chakravorty. "Can the Subaltern Speak?" In *Marxism and the Interpretation of Culture,* edited by Cary Nelson and Lawrence Grossberg, 271–313. Urbana: University of Illinois Press, 1988.

Stein, Gertrude. "Composition as Explanation." In *Gertrude Stein: Selections,* edited by Joan Retallack, 215–26. Berkeley: University of California Press, 2008.

Venuti, Lawrence. *The Translator's Invisibility: A History of Translation.* London and New York: Routledge, 1995.

Victor, Divya. "Absent Witness: Trauma and Contemporary American Poetry." PhD diss., University at Buffalo, State University of New York, 2013.

Vizenor, Gerald. *Manifest Manners: Narratives on Postindian Survivance.* Lincoln: University of Nebraska Press, 1999.

Wagner, Bryan. *Disturbing the Peace: Black Culture and the Police Power after Slavery.* Cambridge, MA: Harvard University Press, 2009.

Weheliye, Alexander G. *Habeas Viscus: Racializing Assemblages, Biopolitics, and Black Feminist Theories of the Human.* Durham, NC: Duke University Press, 2014.

Wiesel, Elie. *From the Kingdom of Memory: Reminiscences.* New York: Simon and Schuster, 1990.

Wilderson, Frank B., III. *Red, White, and Black: Cinema and the Structure of U.S. Antagonisms.* Durham, NC: Duke University Press, 2010.

Wilkinson, Alec. "Something Borrowed: Kenneth Goldsmith's Poetry Elevates Copying to an Art, but Did He Go Too Far?" *New Yorker,* October 5, 2015. http://www.newyorker.com/magazine/2015/10/05/something-borrowed-wilkinson.

Williams, William Carlos. "To Elsie." In *Selected Poems,* 53–55. New York: New Directions, 1985.

Wittgenstein, Ludwig. *Culture and Value.* Translated by Peter Winch. Chicago: University of Chicago Press, 1980.

Wordsworth, William, and Samuel Taylor Coleridge. *Lyrical Ballads: 1798 and 1802.* Oxford: Oxford University Press, 2013.

Wynter, Sylvia. "Beyond Miranda's Meanings: Un/Silencing the 'Demonic Ground' of Caliban's 'Woman.'" In *Out of the Kumbla: Caribbean Women and Literature,* edited by Carole Boyce Davies and Elaine Savory, 355–70. Trenton, NJ: Africa World Press, 1990.

Wynter, Sylvia. "*Proud Flesh* Inter/Views: Sylvia Wynter." By Greg Thomas. *ProudFlesh: New Afrikan Journal of Culture, Politics and Consciousness* 4 (2006): 1–36.

Wynter, Sylvia. "Unsettling the Coloniality of Being/Power/Truth/Freedom: Towards the Human, after Man, Its Overrepresentation—an Argument." *New Centennial Review* 3, no. 3 (2003): 257–337.

Žižek, Slavoj, Eric L. Santner, and Kenneth Reinhard. *The Neighbor: Three Inquiries in Political Theology.* Chicago: University of Chicago Press, 2005.

Zolf, Rachel. *Human Resources*. Toronto: Coach House, 2007.

Zolf, Rachel. *Janey's Arcadia*. Toronto: Coach House, 2014.

Zolf, Rachel. *Neighbour Procedure*. Toronto: Coach House, 2010.

Zolf, Rachel. Post at *Poetic Labor Project* (blog). January 31, 2013. http://labday2010
.blogspot.com/2013/01/rachel-zolf.html.

INDEX

abolition, 6, 14, 28–29, 32, 74, 112, 126, 128, 136n73. *See also* Douglass, Frederick; Jacobs, Harriet; Sexton, Jared

Abramović, Marina, 70–71

abyss: breathturn in the, 8–9, 128; perilous (Jacobs), 9; of time, 9; womb (Middle Passage / slave ship as), 9, 79–80, 84–85, 98–99. *See also* caesura

Acconci, Vito, 69

ACT UP (AIDS Coalition to Unleash Power): Stop the Church protest, 26, 115. *See also* demonstration; protest

Adorno, Theodor W., 85

affect, 48; and interpretation, 69; as sticky, 18, 71; as transformative, 99; as transmissible, 96

affectable subjects, 44, 48, 51, 55, 67–68, 100

Agamben, Giorgio: on banning, 116; on bare life, 113; on Levi in Auschwitz, 62–63; on the *Muselmann*, 6, 10–11, 23, 46, 50–51, 60, 65, 81–88, 112, 122; on poets, 82, 84, 86; on *prosopon* and the Gorgon, 109–10; on the (liminal) remnant, 45–46, 83; on testimony, 110. *See also Muselmann*, the

Ahmed, Sara: on sticky affects, 18

Al Hanashi, Mohammad Ahmed Abdullah Saleh: autopsy of, 143n48; invoked in Halpern's *Common Place*, 47–53, 69, 71, 88, 106, 143n47. *See also* autopsy; Guantánamo Bay; Halpern, Rob: *Common Place*

Alexander, Elizabeth: on black witnessing, 12

Améry, Jean: on the *Muselmann*, 122

anagrams: and Celan, 2, 133n8

animateriality, 75, 78, 84, 102, 107, 147n21. *See also* Moten, Fred

apophasis, 21, 54

apostrophe, 61, 83–84, 108–10, 128

appropriation: "appropriative witnessing" (Victor), 107; cultural, 12, 31, 106; of suffering, 12, 105. *See also* empathy: precariousness of; Goldsmith, Kenneth; Halpern, Rob: *Common Place*; proper/property/(self)possession; proxy (witnessing); Rankin, John; Schutz, Dana

Aristotle, 3; on the poetic, 15

Armantrout, Rae: on clarity, 63–64

"Aschenglorie" (Ashglory) (Celan), 1–2, 5, 8–9, 16–17, 21–22, 44–45, 48, 54, 61–63, 73, 79–80, 84–86, 93, 109–10, 113, 121, 130–31

assemblage, 17–19, 114, 117, 137n90; of enunciation, 27, 54, 110; of freedom, 45; racialized/racializing, 23, 49, 67, 88; terrorist, 51

authorship: as always coauthorship (Agamben), 82; *auctor* as witness, 45; and colonialism, 92; multiplication of, 26–27; (brutally) unauthorized, 45–46, 76. *See also* witness

autopsy: of Al Hanashi, 47–48, 50–51, 106, 143n48; of Brown, 48, 106; future (of Michael Jackson), 106–7. *See also* Al Hanashi, Mohammad Ahmed Abdullah Saleh; appropriation; Brown, Michael; Halpern, Rob: *Common Place*; Schutz, Dana: *The Autopsy of Michael Jackson*

Baldwin, James, 51

banning, 115–16. *See also* Kapil, Bhanu: *Ban en Banlieue*

www.ingramcontent.com/pod-product-compliance
Lightning Source LLC
Chambersburg PA
CBHW071744270326
41928CB00013B/2788